130

CONTRACEPTION *and* THE NATURAL LAW

CONTRACEPTION *and*
THE NATURAL LAW

by GERMAIN G. GRISEZ

Associate Professor of Philosophy

Georgetown University

With a Foreword by the Most Reverend
JOHN WRIGHT, D.D.
Bishop of Pittsburgh

THE BRUCE PUBLISHING COMPANY
MILWAUKEE

NIHIL OBSTAT:

JOHN E. TWOMEY, S.T.L., PH.D.
Censor librorum

IMPRIMATUR:

✠ ROMAN R. ATKIELSKI
Vicar General of Milwaukee
November 9, 1964

This book is dedicated
with the gratitude and filial affection
of their ninth child
to
WILLIAM JOSEPH GRISEZ
and
MARY CATHERINE LINDESMITH GRISEZ.
They, who did not prevent my life,
survive still, and now they see their children's
children to the fourth generation.
May they live forever!

FOREWORD

MAN is not only logical; he is also intricately psychological, as immediately becomes manifest when his most human emotional depths are touched in any debate.

Dr. Grisez is clearly a logician. This fact alone may bring down on his head the wrath of those whose approach to the problem of contraception tends to be subjective, even when their motives include sincere concern for the faith and for the objective law of God. The importance of the logical issues raised in the present book is not diminished by impatient wrath, however, nor will it be dismissed by emotion.

No thoughtful person doubts that much more than logic alone is needed to bring an ultimately adequate and persuasive answer, even though it must be logical, to human problems infinitely complicated by personal, social, and therefore psychological factors. Not less certainly, more than pharmaceutics alone is needed to solve human problems, precisely because they are psychological, when these involve values which are so intimately personal, so critically social, so bound up with dimensions temporal and eternal, physical and spiritual, moral and cultural, as are the ethical values at issue in marital relations.

And so, to bring the necessary wisdom born of human experience and the understanding born of divine grace to the complex problem of marriage morality, particularly in the face of modern hopes as well as fears, there are needed the testimonies of many arts and sciences, the contributions of many sources of knowledge and of discipline. Philosophy must speak to us in ever more relevant terms the truth concerning the mysteries of life and love, the nature of human society and of human personality. In the investigation of these the social, biological, medical, historical, and even political sciences will have important things to say; in the expression of the truths thus discovered, poetry and the other arts must add the grace of their beauty. For Christians (indeed for all mankind) these testimonies must be synthesized in a theology of marriage capable of providing doctrinal, moral, and ascetical substance to nourish the life and channel the love which the holy state of matrimony exists to serve.

But no one of these arts and sciences, nor all of them together, can prescind from the laws of nature and of nature's God, including the laws of logic and of right reason, if Christians (or, again, mankind) are to avoid moral chaos and cultural degeneracy. Hence the basic importance of the grave issues urgently underscored by Dr. Grisez in the argument he here develops with a courage that one can only find admirable in view of the impatient contempt with which concepts of natural law and moral philosophy are dismissed in a civilization largely permeated by moral subjectivism and increasingly shaped by the dictates of a mentality that Father de Lestapis describes in terms of the "contraceptive civilization." In this context, Dr. Grisez' contribution to a debate more often fogged by feeling (on every side) than illumined by reason is both welcome and salutary.

Some will consider that Dr. Grisez, the logician and philosopher rather than sociologist, concedes too much to the alarmist claims of "exploding population" pressure groups. Others will feel that he seems too little sensitive to the pleas of those who, moved also by love of the faith even if by solicitude for human love, ask that theologians assiduously develop in sound modern idiom that theocentric but truly humane theology of marriage the need for which is clear and the elements of which are far from lacking in Catholic tradition.

However, neither point is his direct concern nor proper field; to the just approach to both he makes an appropriate professional contribution from his own philosophical specialty. The flesh and blood of an organic philosophy of human love and theology of Christian marriage will the more quickly give living beauty to the dull, dry bones of logical reason if these skeletal but indispensable elements are acknowledged in the orderly life patterns of persons, families, and society.

Otherwise, efforts to solve contemporary marriage problems, above all those of sexual love, will hardly seek affirmatively and lovingly to regulate all things, conception included if need be, in accordance with God's laws of life and of love. Rather, they will be efforts which seek to run counter to these laws by repeated and increasing negations, like the initial denial at the core of deliberate contraception.

Such a mood of negation, especially if it spreads by unhealthy contagion to the avoidance of the other responsibilities of love and the risks of life generally, must profoundly affect every level of human thought, desire, and action. Our resultant culture will be characterized not by provident, generous promotion of life and of love, human and divine, but by a calculated sterility that is "anti-baby" (in the unlovely English phrase invariably used by European newspapers to describe contraceptive pills), but also, in the final outcome, anti-love. This would be truly tragic to married love, as that fecund, consoling, ennobling, and sacramental experience is cherished in the Christian thought and prayer of either the much-abused St. Augustine or the neglected Prosper of Aquitaine; of spiritual shepherds like Pius XII and John XXIII or poets like Coventry Patmore; of pastoral priests or of spouses unqualifiedly in love with one another and with God. *Quod tamen Deus avertat!*

✠ John Wright
Bishop of Pittsburgh

ACKNOWLEDGMENTS

I WISH to express my gratitude —
— to the President and Board of Directors of Georgetown University — in particular to Rev. Brian A. McGrath, S.J., Academic Vice-President — for a sabbatical during the academic year, 1963–1964, and to the Lilly Postdoctoral Fellowship Program in Religion for a grant, August 1, 1963 — September 15, 1964. This assistance enabled me to devote many months of study to fundamental problems in ethical theory; the research, quite unexpectedly, culminated in this book.

— to the following who answered specific inquiries, made available materials, gave advice, or offered encouragement: Rev. John Wippel; George Stevens, M. D.; Prof. Robert J. Kreyche; Peter J. Bartzen, M.D.; Rev. Thomas J. O'Donnell, S.J.; Rev. Francis J. Connell, C.SS.R.; Rev. Thomas E. Clarke, S.J.; Prof. Vernon Bourke; Rev. John C. Ford, S.J.; Benedict J. Duffy, M. D., and The Georgetown University Center for Population Research; Rev. Patrick Granfield, O.S.B.; Rev. Henry V. Sattler, C.SS.R.; Msgr. George A. Kelly; Rev. George F. McLean, O.M.I.

— to my colleague, Dr. Louis K. Dupré, who led me to undertake this study and stimulated me to carry it to completion.

— to the librarians of Georgetown University and The Catholic University of America.

— to my wife, Jeannette, for her encouragement and support as well as for her efficient assistance in the preparation of the manuscript.

— to Mr. William E. May, of The Bruce Publishing Co., for his interest and encouragement.

The writing of this book was completed on June 10, 1964.

I alone have determined the content of the study and written it; any defects which remain in it are to be ascribed solely to me.

CONTENTS

CONTRACEPTION *and* THE NATURAL LAW

I

INTRODUCTION

RECENTLY some Catholics have argued that in certain situations the prevention of conception might be morally right.[1] Most of these arguments have been theological. They begin by discussing the teaching of the Church and they employ philosophical analysis only secondarily.

The present study, by contrast, will be an examination of the question of the morality of contraception from an ethical viewpoint. It seems to me important for us to try a purely philosophical approach to the morality of contraception. Theology needs sound philosophy. This is so, not in the sense that faith is subordinate to reason, but in the sense that our imperfect faith is likely either to be corralled by anxiety about unessentials or to be goaded onto wrong paths by enthusiasm over the greener pastures projected in an illusory light by the latest phantasms of secular thought.[2]

These two contrasting faults appear in the field of morals, the first in the shape of an apathetic legalism with its confusion between the useful hints of precedent and the absolute requirements of moral principle, and the second in the guise of a pseudo-religious personalism with its confusion between the way in which human spiritual goods excel material goods and the

1

way in which divine goodness transcends finite goods. The second fault is more dangerous, because it is more appealing, than the first. Legalism obviously freezes man in finitude, but pseudo-spirituality pretends to liberate him into divine life while in fact it only confuses human sentiment with charity.

Of course, those Catholics who have prepared and published theological works about the morality of contraception are not grounding their proposals on pseudo-religious personalism. Nevertheless, the current popular tendency is to err in this direction, rather than in the direction of legalism.

Moreover, the inauthentic character of contemporary pseudo-spirituality is unusually well masked. Rather than being individualistic, a common mark in former times of pseudo-spirituality, it now pretends to represent the corporate spirit of Christian life itself at the very moment when that spirit is attaining a new and authentic development.

Thus, while most Catholics used to assent to the teaching of the Church concerning the immorality of contraception, even if they had difficulty in living according to it, more and more Catholics question the teaching itself and oppose to it their own experience, claiming that this experience constitutes an argument drawn from Christian life.[3] Assuming that births are to be controlled, they argue that rhythm and contraception are merely different means, and that rhythm happens to be the morally worse means. Its inadequacy is said to lie not only in its ineffectiveness, but also in its side effects — anxiety, tension, and irritability — which interfere with mutual love between husband and wife and drive the spirit of charity from the home.

These claims are more an attitude than an argument. They do not really give reasons for supposing that contraception is morally unobjectionable; rather they simply assume this and focus attention on the difficulties which can arise when rhythm is practiced. In the study which follows, we shall be concerned with arguments rather than with attitudes. Nevertheless, this attitude has certain presuppositions which may be examined here by way of introduction to our analysis.

In the first place, this attitude assumes a number of factual premises, none of which is criticized. How common is the experience which is described? No one knows, but in popular discussions the experience sometimes is purported to be practically universal. Yet I have talked with some parents of very large families who say that happy married life is to be based on a disdain for every form of birth limitation. And I have talked with many parents of moderately sized families who say that rhythm has worked very well for them.

The attitude we are considering assumes that births are to be controlled. Often one gets the impression that the urgency of this assumption derives from the fact that prudence was not invoked until an absolute breaking point already had been reached. Only after having several children in rapid succession was any investigation made into the ways of avoiding pregnancy. Then, after one botched attempt at rhythm, the couple were seized with panic. Visions of a birth a year until menopause filled their heads, and contraception seemed necessary.

If this description applies, however, the orientation underlying contraception was present from the beginning. That orientation is the view that technique can be depended upon to substitute for timely foresight and self-control.[4] Real proponents of contraception take for granted the necessity of orgasm. Only fertility, which is a rather unfortunate concomitant of sexual activity, needs to be controlled by one technique or another.

In truth, however, reasonable judgment and restraint should permeate all sexual activity. It is not enough that intelligence be invoked only to control consequences. From this point of view, rhythm and contraception can differ from one another more than merely by serving the same end in different ways.

Rhythm, it is true, can be practiced with the same intention which characterizes the practice of contraception, for both can be used to avoid pregnancy as if it were an evil in itself. But rhythm also can be used by those who continue to regard procreation as a positive human value, while contraception implies the submergence of this good by some other one. Thus the "mere" difference in means implies a certain difference in ends as well. We shall consider this point more fully in the latter part of Chapter VI.

Human reproduction never should be merely an unintended side effect of sexual activity engaged in primarily for other reasons. Reproduction should be freely undertaken from the very beginning through a reasonable desire based on intelligent motivation. If this principle is adopted together with the principle that reason must permeate sexual activity from the very beginning, a couple naturally will moderate their sexual activity according to their wisely chosen achievement of the procreative good and, always respecting this basic good, according to other real values to which intercourse or incomplete lovemaking can contribute. Thus their purpose in practicing rhythm will not be to avoid the "evil of unlimited fertility" but rather to regulate sexual activity according to the requirements of positive goods to which they are devoted.

The popular attitude we are considering, insofar as it is an argument, suggests that experience is an adequate basis for ethical judgment. In a certain sense, of course, this is true. We can understand what the essential human goods are and what actions will promote or hinder their achievement only with the help of experience. But, in another sense, it is false to suppose that experience can determine what is right and what is wrong.

Moral judgment is concerned with the ideal, with what ought to be. The deliverances of experience are concerned only with the facts, with what is. If there were no divergence between the two, there would be no place for ethics. Experience with life can show us that something is not as it should be, that something should be changed. But experience itself does not tell us what to change.

Only in the light of questionable theoretical assumptions can experience be made to testify on behalf of relaxation in its case against the traditional strict judgment on the morality of contraception. In some marriages, undoubtedly, even periodic continence is impossible, because there are deeper evils which demand attention. In these cases, the sacrifice of the procreative good implied by the practice of contraception will not improve matters at all.

Some may object that this judgment is too harsh, because the experience in question is not only that of those in bad faith, but also that of many sincere persons who are doing their best to live good Christian lives. Even so we must not accept experience as an argument. Good and sincere people make wrong judgments on many moral issues.

How can many people who are doing their best be so mistaken in their moral judgments? Partly through widely accepted but erroneous assumptions about the facts, which lead to common faults in practical reasoning and judgment. Partly through the subtle influence of common factors of human weakness, which strongly incline even good, though imperfect, people to approve a position on a complex and confused issue which their better selves could not so easily accept if they were completely clearheaded. Our consideration of the subjective morality of contraception in Chapter VIII will help to clarify these points.

Still some will claim that the important value of mutual love between husband and wife requires regular sexual expression, and that the use of rhythm inhibits this good.

This claim contains one glaring assumption which should be questioned immediately — that sexual expression is impossible without orgasm. All human love does demand some outward expression, and the love between husband and wife naturally assumes a sexual form. But sexual expression need not include orgasm in every instance. Nor need incomplete expression include so much stimulation that its incompleteness will cause serious frustration. Each couple must learn for themselves how to regulate their lovemaking when complete intercourse is not desired.[5]

This claim about mutual love also ignores another important distinction. In actual experience, sexual intercourse can be many different things. It can be a perfect expression of deep and genuine love. It can be a release of tension which, even without contraception, is little different from masturbation. It can be an exercise in mutual exploitation, not lacking elements of physical or psychological cruelty.[6]

When intercourse is the expression of deep and genuine love, it seals an experience of communication and cooperation. In the evening a husband and wife review all that they have done during the day, not merely exchanging news, but weaving what is new for each of them into the fabric of their common life. Perhaps they have worked or played side by side. Perhaps they must help each other to meet some difficulty of one of the children.

Their wholeness in mind and heart naturally leads to expressions of intimacy. If they allow it, they rise on a powerful but gentle tide to the height of bodily union and orgasm. This good experience, this great shared satisfaction, is not the product of expertise in technique. It is the bloom of a good life. It is not the outcome of a self-centered, instinctive need. It is the flowing together of generous plenty.

But sometimes a couple are fatigued, anxious, somewhat at odds with one another. They are not communicating very effectively; they do not enjoy wholeness in mind and heart. They lack generosity, or they lack goods to give to one another. One or both of them feel the strain of erotic tension, the desire for sexual release. They come together physically, but in spirit they remain outside each other.

The experience is less one of progression in unity than one of regression toward primitive irrationality, a mere abandonment of control. When they finish there is no afterglow of affection and gratitude. There may be distaste, even an overt expression of dislike, or there may be only disinterest. This couple has difficulties in their lives to which sexual activity gives no solution. Their drive toward orgasm is a need which can become tyrannical in its urgency.

The point of these descriptions is not that the first couple is good and that the second one is wicked. Nor is it that every single act of intercourse should match neatly with one of these two sketches. The descriptions are simplified types, and undoubtedly actual experiences are infinitely varied. Usually they contain aspects of both of these types, and perhaps some less normal aspects belonging to still other types of relationship.

The point of these descriptions is simply that extreme urgency does not characterize the ideal experience. The more one needs orgasm, the less likely is it that intercourse will be an ideal expression of mutual love. The more perfect a couple's relationship with one another, the easier it will be for them to limit their sexual activity to modes which they know from experience will neither lead to orgasm nor require any violent suppression of feeling.

The practice of contraception, therefore, is not likely to aid progress in mutual love. It alleviates a symptom, but it does not promote a cure. Rhythm, perhaps, aggravates the symptom rather than alleviating it. Of itself, this aggravation does not promote a cure either, and it can have other bad consequences.

However, the prohibition of contraception can compel a couple who are doing their best to set about the task of growth which otherwise they might delay beginning indefinitely, just as civil-rights demonstrations can compel good citizens to undertake the changes which really are required for social justice although ordinary sluggishness would incline them to put off undertaking these changes so long as no pressure was exerted.

Rhythm is too large a subject to be treated briefly here.[1] However, it is important to say that ignorance and wrong attitudes have given it a bad reputation. Every person should have complete and accurate information about rhythm by the time he is married. Many failures occur because women do not keep accurate records, or because they use only rules of thumb, rather than scientific methods, for interpreting the data they have. The newly married couple should prepare to practice rhythm, and even experiment with its practice, from the very beginning.

Moreover, those who imagine that a marriage contract should

be a sufficient excuse for the unlimited satisfaction of the demands of spontaneous passion are bound to take a dim view of the restraint required by rhythm. They will see in it only the snuffing out of the spontaneous blazes they imagined would be theirs, and so consider to be their right, in marriage. The calendar pad and the thermometer will be looked upon as enemies of love, just as the calorie table and the scale are viewed as enemies of normal living by a fat man who is forced to go on a strict diet.

Those who argue that experience shows contraception to be necessary seldom notice the social and economic characteristics of persons who have this experience. In general, contraception is practiced most often by upper-middle-class and upper-class couples. It is a fair assumption that among these classes, which include the most highly educated, most of the Catholics who consider contraception necessary are to be found.[8]

Sometimes articulate Catholics argue that contraception is necessary at least where there are very serious medical and economic reasons to limit conceptions. The picture of heartbreaking cases offered is dishonest, however, when the real experience and concern of those arguing is with their own quite different problems.

The pressure on the mother in this socioeconomic bracket is much discussed in the mass media. It is true perhaps that she has less help than did a woman of similar status a generation or two ago, although probably she has more help, especially considering mechanical aids, than did her own less prosperous grandmother or mother.

It is true also that the performance standards for the job of mother, wife, and homemaker have changed dramatically, and that the married woman in the upper classes today faces demands which are altogether new. Who sixty years ago had to worry about the psychological problems of preschool interpersonal adjustment? Who had to serve on a committee to do any of the million tasks suburban committees are set up to do?

There also are important economic factors deriving from the

rising standards of living and of culture. But the greatest changes, it seems to me, have originated in two factors which are seldom mentioned. One of them is the changed attitude of the contemporary woman toward her role as wife and mother. In many cases she feels that she should be free to fulfill herself, and that her fulfillment can be found only in doing something that men also do.[9]

Another of these changes is in the ideal number of children. This standard is set not so much by personal choice as by what others think. Today four children is a very common limit — the standard dining table, the automobile, the three-bedroom house are designed to accommodate a family of six or less.

Both the ideal of the role of the woman and the norm of family size are influenced — in some circles, determined — by couples who practice contraception. Moreover, all of us are so conscious of what others think of us that we hardly can respect ourselves if we do not feel that those in our circle accept our claim that we are enjoying the good life as fully as they.

Thus upper-middle-class and upper-class Catholic women live very uncomfortably in a culture where the possibilities of the "good life" are practically defined by contraception. In this situation, it is no surprise that when the "right" number of children is reached, the exclusion of another pregnancy becomes a matter of transcendent importance.

The point of this consideration is that as Catholics rise in social status the difficulty they confront in the matter of family planning is in many ways merely a particular instance of the difficulty from which Christians never can escape. That difficulty is this. We must live in the world, but the standards of the world are not a reflection of Christian ideals. Hence, we never can settle down to live in well-adjusted harmony with the world.[10]

The appeal to experience thus seems to depend upon two questionable assumptions. One is that the urgent need for orgasm belongs to a pattern of sexual activity which is centered in the expression of mutual love. The other is that some method of fertility regulation must have the same results for faithful Catholics as contraception does for those who practice it.

The first assumption ignores the fact that compulsiveness in sexual activity is a sign of a motivation quite different from mutual benevolence and affection. The second assumption ignores the fact that the absolute limit for family size established by those who practice contraception ordinarily should not be regarded as absolute — or, for that matter, even as a suitable limit — by Catholics.

The final claim of the appeal to experience is that contraception is preferable to rhythm, because the latter drives charity from the household. However, it should be obvious that the good feelings, tension-free relationships, and affability which sometimes are referred to as "charity" are not the Christian virtue of that name at all. The virtue of charity does not exclude any of these natural goods, of course, but it should not be defined in terms of them. Charity is not a feeling and it cannot be lost except by free consent to serious sin.[11]

Those who practice rhythm may well suffer frustration which might be avoided if orgasm were enjoyed more often. They will have to deal with the psychological consequences of such frustration, and such consequences include irritability. Those who feel it would be a tragedy if another pregnancy were to occur may suffer anxiety which might be avoided if other methods of conception-avoidance were used.

Yet anxiety and irritability do not preclude charity, although they are obstacles to its practice. On the one hand, one who encounters such obstacles should try to change himself in order to remove their sources, rather than merely concede control to irrational motivation in order temporarily to relieve tension. On the other hand, one who practices charity despite such obstacles is not less holy, although he certainly is less comfortable, than one who need not struggle with them.

Still it will be said, and it must be admitted, that there are people who have really unusual and difficult problems. Confessors sometimes tell of penitents to whom they wished it were possible to say that contraception could be permitted, since the indications against pregnancy were most serious and the difficulties of really prolonged abstinence also were very great.

Cases of this extreme sort, of course, do not constitute the much more common experience which we have been discussing. Yet the facts of such cases do constitute experience which should make us examine very carefully the judgment that contraception always is evil. However, the question whether there are any exceptions to this moral judgment cannot be settled by examining the hard facts of such difficult cases.

In other domains of moral law, adherence to principle leads to very great difficulty in certain cases. There are ethical theories, which we shall describe in Chapter III under the general title of "situationism," which allow exceptions in all these difficult cases. But these theories presuppose a notion of fundamental values and standards of morality which we cannot accept.

If, as we shall argue in Chapter VI, contraception is evil in a way which excludes exceptions, the approval of it even in a few cases simply would be the acceptance of moral evil as a legitimate means to some ulterior good. In such really difficult cases, then, we can say only that the end does not justify the means.

Much of the present popular enthusiasm over the notion that a change in the traditional teaching might be possible proceeds on the assumption that this one position on the morality of contraception could be jettisoned without affecting any other moral teaching. One implication of my study is that this assumption is false. The position that contraception is intrinsically immoral is related to other important positions. The discarding of this position can be accomplished only by ripping it loose from the whole fabric in which it is enmeshed. Much of the rest of this fabric should be expected to unravel if this were allowed to happen.

A clear explanation of the reason why contraception is intrinsically immoral seems to me to be the main contribution philosophy can make to the solution of our practical problems.[12] This clarification will provide a rational ground for ending the present confusion, and for refusing to consider further the suggestion that the teaching on the immorality of contraception might be subject to alteration or exceptions.

Moreover, this philosophical work is necessary because until it is clear *why* contraception is immoral, we cannot be certain *what* constitutes contraception, and so the exclusion of new methods cannot be completely clear and definite. A clear explanation of why contraception is evil also might help to eliminate the unfortunately widespread attitude that this moral position is a peculiarly inexplicable one with which Catholic tradition has been encumbered by some historical accident, and that sufficient ingenuity should be able to find some way around the obstacles presented by tradition in order that contraception might be approved after all.

Therefore, in Chapter II, we shall examine existing explanations of the intrinsic malice of contraception. By criticizing them, we shall show the need for a more accurate explanation of this point. In the third chapter, we shall consider three different theories of moral law which can provide a context for an ethical appraisal of the morality of contraception.

In Chapter IV, we shall explain and defend the central thesis of our study. It can be stated as follows: *For one who engages in sexual intercourse directly to will any positive deed by which conception is thought to be prevented, or even rendered less probable, is intrinsically and seriously immoral.*

Chapter V will consider some of the more relevant and important theoretical objections to the theory of natural law which underlies our thesis on the morality of contraception. The following chapter will concern the very intricate, but absolutely essential, distinction between conception-avoidance, conception-preventing behavior, and contraception. It is only through this analysis of Chapter VI that we shall clarify the meaning of "directly willed" and "positive" which appear in our central thesis.

Chapter VII and the Appendix deal with problems which are raised by several possible uses of drugs which have conception-preventing effects. The eighth chapter will complete our philosophical treatment of contraception by considering the conditions which modify subjective responsibility for this action without altering its intrinsic, objective moral significance.

Although I propose to deal with contraception philosophically, I address only my fellow Catholics throughout this study. In philosophy one must limit the circle of his interlocutors or he will have no way of limiting what will need to be said. Hence I do not expect to deal with points such as the existence and providence of God, the reality of man's responsibility for his human action, or the general objectivity of moral standards. Such points and others conceded by all Catholics will be taken for granted here.

A purely philosophical treatment of contraception will not give the practical guidance and the other factors which are needed to meet the practical situation suggested by the experiential argument. Nor should a philosophical treatment be expected to persuade many. Those not accustomed to subtle argument, as well as those who do not respect reason, will be little moved by what I have to say.

Against the heart reason has little power, and it is just as impotent against sentimentalism which has become confused with charity as it is against plain ill will. Even the good and firm heart, the heart of true charity, wants an adequate response to its distress in the face of evil. But the inadequacy of philosophy in the face of life is nowhere more apparent than in a matter like contraception, where the cold light of reason confronts a common and pitiable form of human pain. Reason is unable to yield an inch, yet mere reason can provide neither insight nor hope.

However, the philosopher is not responsible for reality, he is only responsible to it. Philosophy is insufficient for salvation; by mere reason man never has been able to cope with the facts of life. Only faith can provide us with the insight necessary to

understand the meaning of the sufferings of life and only hope
can provide us with the ability to persevere amid them. This
is true especially with respect to the sufferings which surround
the greatest of evils — sin and its consequences.

Moreover, what I present here will not be fully demonstrative
even to the philosopher. To provide philosophical demonstration is not merely a matter of finding two premises from which
a conclusion follows. The meaning of the premises must be
explained and they must be shown to be evident or reducible
to evident principles.[13] These requirements can be met only by
putting the argument into the context of a whole philosophy.

The argument for my central thesis in Chapter IV almost
meets the requirements for rigorous demonstration. However,
it belongs within the context of an ethical theory almost unknown by Catholic philosophers — that of Thomas Aquinas.
The notion that the conventional natural-law theory commonly
taught in Catholic manuals of ethics and moral theology is
Thomistic is, as we shall see in Chapter III, a mistake. Unfortunately, the theory cannot be unfolded sufficiently in the
compact sketch of Chapter III to reveal its full power.

The argument for my second most important point, that concerning indirect voluntariness in Chapter VI, is not a rigorous
demonstration, since I lack a general theory of indirect voluntariness. Nevertheless, I am convinced that the arguments offered there constitute a firm proof of the point in question.

Someone who argues from experience might wonder by this
time: "How many children have you, and what experience have
you had which leads you to be so coldly philosophical when
you are treating a problem which is a painful reality in the
lives of many people?"

My wife, Jeannette, and I married thirteen years ago. At that
time I was just entering studies for the degree of Doctor of
Philosophy. We now have four children, the oldest twelve and
the youngest six.

Life has not been easy during all of these years. Yet we have
survived without contraception, and we think the conviction

that we had to survive and could survive without it has been essential to doing so. Moreover, the permanent ineligibility of contraception as a solution to our problems, although sometimes it was a tempting possibility, seems to us to have obliged us to form a more perfect union than we would have achieved had we used contraceptives.

We have had enough experience to know some of the difficulties of the practice of rhythm. It is not at present an ideal system, especially when one first tries to follow it, and perhaps it never will be completely satisfactory. But we do not expect our sex life to be more perfect than our life as a whole, which still leaves much to be desired. The advantage of rhythm which makes us gratefully accept it, difficulties and all, is that it is compatible with the basic dedication we believe married life requires of us.

I have been told that an attitude such as mine toward the question of the morality of contraception reveals moral and spiritual immaturity, that it is a kind of condescension which deserves the name *pharisaism*. The preceding remarks about my own marriage might support this judgment. Freed, for the time being, of serious difficulties with sex, perhaps I am using this freedom as an occasion for sinful pride. If so, it would follow that my state is worse than that of those who practice contraception knowing it to be wrong.[14]

If there is to be an appeal to experience, how is one to answer fully except by appealing to his own experience? If one's qualification to discuss a subject is likely to be questioned, how is one to respond except by offering his credentials as well as he can? Yet perhaps the criticism does apply justly to me. I am not aware that it does, but blindness to one's sin is one of the effects of pride. If the criticism applies, God help me. If it does not, that could be only because God has helped me, not because I have been self-sufficient to achieve anything.

NOTES TO CHAPTER I

1. The bulk of the material cannot be cited. Much of it circulates by irregular methods of publication, often with ingenious devices to prevent

definite ascription to the author. Some of it is published in locally circulated periodicals or presented orally at various meetings; one receives secondhand accounts but cannot obtain original copies or transcripts. Throughout our study, we consider positions that are important, whether their sources can be cited or not; hence often we must resort to the indefinite, "Some argue . . ." The most notable study which can be cited is: Louis Janssens, "Morale conjugale et progestogènes," *Ephemerides theologicae lovanienses*, 39 (Oct.– Dec., 1963), 787–826. Another important theological study is: W. Van der Marck, O.P., "Vruchtbaarheidsregeling: poping tot antwoord op een nog open vraag," *Tijdschrift voor theologie*, 3e, #4 (Jaargang, 1963), 378–413. Semi-popular in style, but basically theological in orientation is: Louis K. Dupré, "Toward a Re-examination of the Catholic Position on Birth Control," *Cross Currents*, 14 (Winter, 1964), 63–85. Rev. Michael O'Leary, "Some Thoughts about the Oral-Steroid Pill," *Jubilee*, 11 (March, 1964), 44–46, proposes a suggestion which he believes can solve the whole problem. The body of Protestant theological literature on contraception is substantial; an introduction to it is provided by: John C. Ford, S.J., and Gerald Kelly, S.J., *Contemporary Moral Theology*, Vol. 2, *Marriage Questions* (Westminster, Md.: The Newman Press, 1963), 245–255; Norman St. John-Stevas, *Birth Control and Public Policy* (Santa Barbara, Calif.: The Fund for the Republic, Inc., 1960), 28–38.

2. Two encyclicals make clear the proper role and limits of philosophy in relation to Catholic faith: Leo XIII, *Aeterni Patris* ("On the Restoration of Christian Philosophy," August 4, 1879); Pius XII, *Humani generis* ("False Trends in Modern Teaching," August 12, 1950).

3. The popular material is much greater in bulk, and even less accessible for citation, than the theological material. A sample is: John Rock, *The Time Has Come: A Catholic Doctor's Proposals to End the Battle over Birth Control* (New York: Alfred A. Knopf, 1963); Rosemary Ruether, "Marriage, Love, Children," *Jubilee*, 11 (December, 1963), 17–20; "A Catholic Mother Tells 'Why I Believe in Birth Control,'" *Saturday Evening Post*, April 4, 1964, 12–14; Bruce Cooper, "An English Father Hopes the Council Will Act," *Jubilee*, 11 (December, 1963), 20–21; also the letters in subsequent issues of both publications. The popular attitudes also have affected theological developments; see Van der Marck, op. cit., 393–396. Dupré's article, although only citing (73) Rock once, nevertheless is considerably more intelligible if it is read *after* reading Rock's book.

4. Stanislas de Lestapis, S.J., *Family Planning and Modern Problems: A Catholic Analysis* (New York: Herder and Herder, 1961), 180–194, contrasts the technique of birth control with the self-mastery required for regulation by periodic continence.

5. Leon Joseph Suenens, *Love and Control: The Contemporary Problem* (Westminster, Md.: The Newman Press, 1961), 41–50, 81–83, 104–105, emphasizes very effectively this distinction between orgasm and incomplete sexual acts. The same point is discussed in popular fashion, against some of the opinion cited in note 3, by: Frank M. Wessling, "Is It Mature Loving?" *America*, 110 (May 2, 1964), 594–596.

6. That sexual behavior is subject to diverse meanings is almost universally admitted. See, e.g., James S. Plant, *Personality and the Cultural Pattern* (Cambridge, Mass.: Harvard University Press, 1937), 213–228. The fact is masked by statistical studies, such as Kinsey's, which consider only the quantity of behavior. Also commonly admitted by Catholic psychologists is the principle that compulsiveness and morally good action are incompatible;

to the extent an act is compulsive, it tends to fall short of being human action at all. See: Marc Oraison, O.S.B., *Man and Wife: The Physical and Spiritual Foundations of Marriage* (New York: The Macmillan Co., 1962), 69–86, 118, and passim. An interesting example of psychological theory which explains the facts is: Claire Russell and W. M. S. Russell, *Human Behaviour: A New Approach* (Boston-Toronto: Little, Brown and Company, 1961), 268–312, esp. 284–285. Henri Gibert, *Love in Marriage: The Meaning and Practice of Sexual Love in Christian Marriage* (New York and London: Hawthorn Books, Inc., 1964), 65–73, 108–113, describes in some detail the difference in attitude between sensual eroticism and communicating love.

7. The best treatment of rhythm medically considered: John Marshall, *The Infertile Period: Principles and Practice* (Baltimore: Helicon Press; London: Darton, Longmans, and Todd, 1963). Marshall writes for physicians but can be understood by laymen; his chapter on psychological aspects (81–93) is particularly relevant to our argument. I. E. Georg, *The Truth about Rhythm* (New York: P. J. Kenedy & Sons, 1962), also is an excellent presentation. It has an entire part — "Marriage, Family, and Birth Control" — devoted to putting the problem into context. Suenens, *op. cit.*, 97–105, views rhythm from the pastoral viewpoint; Lestapis, *op. cit.*, 180–214, a fuller treatment, practically oriented. Ford and Kelly, *op. cit.*, 378–459, offer an excellent theological treatment of periodic continence; they make useful remarks on psychological aspects, 437–445.

8. Raymond Pearl, *The Natural History of Population* (New York: Oxford University Press, 1939), 204–217, showed that contraceptive effort and effectiveness both increase in direct relationship with social-economic status; his findings have not been upset by subsequent research. An introduction to more recent studies, and to the Catholic problem is: Franklin J. Henry, *An Empirical Study of the Relationship of Catholic Practice and Fertility* (Washington, D. C.: The Catholic University of America Press, 1958). Henry shows that the differential between Catholic and non-Catholic fertility is greater at higher status levels where contraception is practiced more effectively (39) although on the whole he finds no very important correlation between Catholic practice and fertility (47). These findings suggest that Catholics at higher status levels meet the greatest pressures, but that many resist these pressures; it is important to remember that at least part of the similarity between the fertility of Catholics and others can be explained by the Catholic practice of continence.

9. Suenens, *op. cit.*, 11–25, begins his work by considering sociological factors, including the changed role of woman. This factor, of course, is an aspect of the feminist movement, which generally has encouraged contraceptive practice. Feminism is still a popular topic; see, e.g., Betty Friedan, "Woman: The Fourth Dimension," *The Ladies Home Journal*, June, 1964, 48–55, and the rest of the issue, which is devoted to the same topic. William B. Faherty, S.J., *The Destiny of Modern Woman in the Light of Papal Teaching* (Westminster, Md.: The Newman Press, 1950), provides a convenient collection of recent papal reactions to feminism. A masterful refutation of the feminist supposition that sex need not make a great difference is: Lucius F. Cervantes, S.J., "Differences of the Sexes," in his and Carle C. Zimmerman's *Marriage and the Family: A Text for Moderns* (Chicago: Henry Regnery Co., 1956), 137–590; contraception is treated specifically in 310–333.

10. Suenens, *loc. cit.*; John L. Thomas, S.J., *The Catholic Viewpoint on Marriage and the Family* (Garden City, N. Y.: Hanover House, 1958), 133–

174. Thomas stresses the sociological aspect of the pressure Catholics face; he specifically mentions contraception (167–168).

11. Gérard Gilleman, S.J., *The Primacy of Charity in Moral Theology* (Westminster, Md.: The Newman Press, 1961), offers a clear statement of the true nature of charity (29–48) and the relation between charity and sin (279), although the work as a whole is marred by the author's tendency toward a phenomenological view of man.

12. Ford and Kelly, *op. cit.*, mention the need for such clarification, e.g., 370–371, 373.

13. The notion of demonstration here is that of "demonstration of the reasoned fact" the stringent requirements for which are explained: Aristotle, *Posterior analytics*, 71b8–79a33.

14. Someone who interprets behavior in the light of psychoanalytic theory probably would offer a diverse, but quite analogous, explanation of my effort. The important point, of course, is: whatever my motives, my argument should be considered on its merits.

II

INADEQUATE ARGUMENTS

MANY inadequate arguments against contraception have been proposed. These arguments must be studied to see where they go wrong. This clarification will explain the general dissatisfaction with them, for bad arguments do not satisfy honest minds.

Moreover, it will help us to see why some have maintained certain indefensible positions — e.g., that one must not limit fertility even by periodic abstinence, that the common good could not require fertility regulation, or that every human faculty deserves immunity from frustration just as the procreative ability does. Such propositions might seem essential to show that contraception is immoral, although a sound proof does not require them.

Clarification of unsound arguments is most important, however, for four methodological reasons. First, in seeing where others have made mistakes we will discover where the real issue lies. In this way we will avoid struggling with confused mixtures of opposite errors which sometimes even share indefensible common ground.

Second, the inadequate arguments will illustrate the two unsound theories of moral law to be described in the next chapter. The conventional arguments came, of course, from conventional

19

natural-law theory, while the other argument has some affinity with what we shall call a "situationist" theory of moral law.

Third, the clarification of inadequate arguments will set in relief the new argument which we shall present in Chapter III. Fourth, it will undermine certain unsound defenses of pharmacological methods of contraception, defenses which depend in part on an inadequate argument against other techniques.

Arguments proceeding within the framework of conventional natural-law theory always include the following incomplete syllogism: *Contraception is intrinsically immoral because by it one engaging in intercourse prevents his act from attaining its natural end.* This syllogism can be understood and completed in various ways, and my sole concern here is to indicate clearly some inadequate ones. Hence, rather than trying to survey the literature, where the precise completion and interpretation followed is often unclear, I shall work through as many interesting possibilities as I can distinguish, criticizing them as I go.[1]

The obvious way to expand the incomplete argument into a formally valid syllogism is the following.

Major: To prevent any human act from attaining its natural end is intrinsically immoral.

Minor: Contraception prevents sexual intercourse from attaining its natural end.

Conclusion: Contraception is intrinsically immoral.

Once the argument is completed in this way it remains only to clarify the meaning of the terms in some fashion compatible both with the truth of the premises and with the unity of the middle term. Unfortunately, as we shall see, it is difficult to meet these two requirements at the same time. If the premises are understood in an obviously true sense, "natural end" becomes equivocal, and as soon as this equivocation is eliminated one of the premises is exposed to serious objections. We shall consider first the way in which the middle term becomes equivocal.

Contraception clearly does prevent sexual intercourse from attaining the end proper to it as a biological process. The sexual organs are not called "genitals" for nothing; no physiologist would treat sex except as a mode of reproductive functioning. We are dealing here with natural teleology, and although the word "teleology" is not used by modern life-scientists, the reality of functional goals is still a key in the understanding of organic processes.

From this point of view it is irrelevant that not every act of intercourse leads to conception and that the psychic drive toward sexual activity can promote it beyond functional necessity. Particularly where reproduction is concerned, the phenomenon of superabundance is common in nature. It does not in the least impede the teleological interpretation of reproductive functions.

The reproductive process is understood as a complex dynamic whole proportionate to a definite completive effect — the continuance of life in new individuals. The parts of the process are explained in terms of this whole simply because in this way maximum intelligibility is gained. Thus the sexual urge is unintelligible except as a reproductive drive, and the sexual act is unintelligible except as part of the reproductive process.

If the minor premise of the syllogism is understood in this obviously true sense, how might the major be interpreted so that its truth is equally obvious? To prevent an act from attaining the natural end of the function to which it belongs certainly would be intrinsically immoral if "natural end" refers to a good which one is morally required to seek.

There are ends of this sort. Every job or profession has a certain end which really defines the role of one who enters it. Certain actions or tasks belong to the role, and a person who accepts it is expected to perform these tasks. For him to do so only for the advantages which accrue to himself — e.g., income — while preventing the attainment of the end of the function to which his acts belong would be to defraud his employers or clients. Hence if "natural end" refers to a morally obligatory end, the major premise will have a clear meaning in which it is evidently true.

But when we couple the two premises understood in these ways the equivocation of the middle term becomes evident. To prevent one's act from attaining an end which one has a *moral obligation* to seek in exercising it is intrinsically immoral. Contraception prevents intercourse from accomplishing what *natural teleology* requires. From these two propositions nothing logically follows.

And it is important to observe the reason why. Not because "end" is being used in two senses such as *end of the agent* and *end of the work*. No, in both propositions it refers to the end which defines a certain function — i.e., the end of the work. However, "natural" has not the same meaning in the major premise, where it refers to *moral obligation*, as it does in the minor premise, where it refers to *natural conditional necessity.*[2]

As we shall see later, this equivocation between different senses of "natural" is simply an instance of a basic equivocation underlying conventional natural-law theory. We would have the same difficulty if the faculty in question were the intellect, for the mere *fact* that its end is truth does not show that we have an *obligation* to seek the truth. That we have *obligations* in both of these cases to pursue the inherent ends of the faculties has a reason, as we shall see, beyond the fact that the two faculties *have* these ends.

Of course, merely because the argument may be interpreted so that it is equivocal does not mean that it *must* be equivocal. Unlike those who are satisfied to refute only the simplest mistakes, we must proceed further to see how each of the premises might be understood in order to eliminate the equivocation and to make the argument sound. The premise, given a stronger sense, will no longer be obviously true, of course, and so we shall have to examine it closely to see whether it can be defended.

Suppose we first strengthen the minor premise and understand it to mean that contraception is the prevention of the end, procreation, which one who engages in sexual intercourse ought to achieve if it is possible. To show the truth of the premise understood in this way is a completely different matter than to show the truth of the weaker physiological proposition.[3]

To begin with, it is by no means obvious that everyone who practices contraception has a real obligation to seek the good of procreation. So far is this from being clear that all who condemn contraception agree that in some cases the right alternative is abstinence, not fruitful intercourse. Moreover, in practice, rhythm seems to negate this supposed obligation as effectively as contraception. In both cases one engages in sexual intercourse only if it probably will not be fruitful.

Further difficulties arise for this interpretation of the minor premise when we seek to understand why the good of procreation should specify so strong an obligation. Reproduction, after all, is not an unqualified good; it becomes good only if the proper education of offspring is assured. For this reason the institution of marriage has developed and reproduction outside it is considered wrong.

Will the proposition that intercourse implies an obligation to seek its natural end be strengthened if we add that the end of sexual intercourse is a common good rather than a proper one? This addition only raises the question: Whose interests or rights are being violated by contraception?

Insofar as the end is a common good of the couple themselves, the prevention of its achievement by mutual consent cannot violate the rights of either party. Everyone agrees that contraception without the consent of one's partner is wrong, but that can be explained by reference to justice alone.

Perhaps the common good in question is the life of the possible child? But the possible child has no actual right to exist, and it may be better for him as well as for the rest of the family if he does not come into being. In any case, if the common good in this sense creates a compelling obligation not to practice contraception, why does it not also create a compelling obligation not to practice periodic continence or even celibacy?

Perhaps the end in question is the common good in its most usual sense, the good of society or of mankind as a whole.[4] But, again, why should we distinguish between contraception and abstinence if social well-being is the issue? If the practice of contraception is a default on one's social duty, other methods of limiting fertility seem equally wrong. At least those with large families have done their duty sufficiently.

Besides, the present problem is not underpopulation but overpopulation, and there is no use denying this obvious truth. A reluctance to admit it is unnecessary for the defense of the ethical condemnation of contraception. Moreover, suggestions that the population problem might be solved by migration to other planets, by unexpected wars or plagues, or by improbable technological and economic accomplishments only expose a sound moral position on contraception to ridicule.

Apparently the strengthened minor premise — that contraception prevents the attainment of a morally obligatory end — cannot be supported directly if obligation and its object are understood as they are in the preceding arguments. We shall see in Chapter IV that if obligation is understood in a less legalistic sense and if its object is not assumed to be merely a definite objective performance of duty the proposition in question is perfectly true and immune to the objections alleged against it.

At present, however, we must proceed to examine indirect ways in which the proposition might be supported. These arguments will be considered only to the extent that they presuppose the same questionable notion of obligation as do the preceding arguments.

One indirect way in which the proposition might be supported is from the consequences which can follow if procreation is not treated as an obligatory end of the marital act.[5] Will not every couple employ sex for their own satisfaction while avoiding the difficulties and responsibilities of parenthood? Will not extramarital sex become licit when really certain means of contraception are used?

If so, it might seem that although procreation is not in every instance an obligatory good in itself, it must be treated as if it were in order that the pleasure of sex — the only adequate motive, so some think, for assuming the duties it leads to — shall not be separated from the responsibilities of parenthood. Someone depending on this argument also may assert that periodic continence is licit because it is sufficiently difficult and uncertain so that allowing it will not subvert the cunning strategy of nature, while contraception must be forbidden because it is too ingenious a device for cheating nature.

This kind of indirect proof is called a "generalization argument" by ethical theorists. This argument has an important place in Kantian ethics and in certain other systems but it has found little favor with Catholic philosophers. Hence I shall not go deeply into its theoretical foundations.[6]

Concretely, a reasonable system of obligations ought to allow for reasonable exceptions rather than to maintain generality at the price of irrational universality. Allowance for the practice of contraception in some difficult cases certainly need not imply that its universal practice would be good.

Indeed, rhythm itself is not an unqualified good; justifying indications are required for its use. Yet no one believes that the abuses — which will become more numerous as the rhythm method becomes more effective — ever can render the practice of rhythm intrinsically immoral. At most they might increase the obligation required by the common norm of generous fruitfulness, for if the population were declining rapidly a higher rate of fertility would be implied by this norm.

Furthermore, concern about consequences seems to lack factual grounds. In the United States, where contraception has been practiced for generations, the normal patterns of marriage, fruitful relations, and child-rearing continue to prevail. Contraception does not seem to be limiting vigorous national expansion. Of course, it has opened the way for increased extramarital sexual relations, but these might occur in any case. Moreover, they can be condemned on other grounds, and if contraception is really effective they are, from an ethical point of view, little or no worse than petting which leads to orgasm.

The proposition that contraception prevents intercourse from attaining a morally obligatory end also may be supported indirectly by deducing it from a more general principle of sexual ethics: *Any sexual activity apart from the conditions necessary for it to be suited of itself to the procreation and proper education of children is intrinsically immoral.* This principle has a substantial tradition behind it, and I believe that it is true if it is properly interpreted.[7] However, its use to support the argument against contraception is open to many objections.

To begin with, the limitation of sexual activity to procreative purposes implied by this principle seems too severe, since at least within marriage incomplete sexual acts are licit even though they are unsuited to procreation. Moreover, sexual relations between husband and wife can be morally good even when procreation is impossible.

Sometimes this general principle is thought to express the *sole* principle of sexual ethics, and it is understood to mean that any behavior of significance for reproduction must be performed under conditions of normal intercourse and within wedlock. However, if the principle is understood in this way it is too narrow, for it cannot exclude even complete solitary acts of women.

The older scholastics who thought that feminine "semination" is analogous to male ejaculation were mistaken in their physiological facts. If they had not made a mistake on this point, many of them would have been unable to show the immorality of female masturbation because it has no objective significance for the reproductive function.[8]

Besides these points, the most telling reason against using this general principle of sexual ethics to support the specific proposition about contraception is that the general principle itself is neither evident nor easily proved. Moreover, the argument that contraception may not be intrinsically immoral implies precisely that this general principle admits of exceptions. Consequently, simply to assert the general principle is to beg the question.

Of course, it is fair to point out that if the general principles which have been thought to control sexual ethics admit of exception in the case of the practice of contraception by married couples having sufficiently strong reasons, exceptions also may be required to other applications of these principles. Some homosexuals, for example, offer arguments in defense of their perversion very similar to the reasons given for allowing exceptions to the prohibition of contraception.

I fear that those who are defending the practice of contraception have not considered this implication, because they have focused on contraception in abstraction from the wider problem of developing a sound ethical theory of sexual conduct.

However, such victims of abstractionism might be willing to accept the implications of their position and to allow any perversion in really difficult cases. Or they might be able to construct some nontraditional arguments against allowing exceptions to other applications of the general principles of sexual morality.

Thus our conclusion remains that the minor premise of the original argument appears to be indefensible if it is taken in a sufficiently strong sense to eliminate equivocation in the middle term. Another set of possibilities is opened, however, if we decide to use the minor in its obviously true sense and to strengthen the major instead. Rather than understanding the major in its obviously true meaning — the prevention of the realization of an end which one ought to seek is immoral — let us take it to mean that the exercise of any human function in such a way that its given end is frustrated of attainment is intrinsically immoral.

This interpretation of the major premise yields what is called the "perverted-faculty argument."[9] This major never has seemed obvious to many although some have claimed it to be self-evident. Whether it were evident in itself or not, it would need to be explained in some way that would reveal why the natural teleology of human functions requires absolute moral respect. Simply to assume this principle against someone who is defending the liceity of contraception is to beg the question.[10]

One way to explain the major of the perverted-faculty argument is to say that the integrity of the natural design of human functions always must be respected because it was instituted by God. Yet, it is not evident that God requires that this design always be respected. If the assumption is true, however, it seems to have great force only in the sphere of sex, since other functions are interfered with in many ways without arousing moral condemnation so long as the faculty itself is not permanently damaged. Begin the list with earplugs.

Moreover, not even all interferences with the natural design of sexual intercourse are rejected as immoral. *Assisted*, as distinct from *artificial*, insemination is generally approved by moralists.[11] If one refers only to this principle, then the distinction between licit and illicit interference seems arbitrary.

Another way to explain the major is by arguing that just as the end of man determines the rightness and wrongness of his action on the whole, so the end of each of his faculties determines its right and wrong use.[12] The trouble with this argument is that it proves the wrongness of contraception only from the point of view of the sexual faculty considered in isolation. No doubt, contraception is an evil for the reproductive capacity, but this faculty is not a supposit with absolute rights of its own.

Hence it seems to follow that the good of this part can be subordinated to the good of the whole. That the principle of totality does apply to the reproductive faculty is shown by the fact that the removal of diseased generative organs for the good of the whole body is allowed.

A fortiori, the suppression of the effect of the generative function seems legitimate provided that the remaining exercise of the function and the suppression itself yield an overall benefit to the whole. If the common good is invoked at this point, the arguments previously presented may be reviewed.

Apart from these theoretical considerations, the major of the perverted-faculty argument is open to numerous objections drawn from exceptions. Walking on one's hands interferes at least temporarily with their proper function.[13] Similarly, to hang rings in one's ears or nose, by stretching them out of shape, may lessen their effectiveness. But no one objects in such cases that the faculties are being perverted.

Of course, one may argue that these counterexamples are frivolous, since the abuses themselves are insignificant. However, a defense of this sort implies the concession that it is not the perversion of the faculty but the significance of its function that is at stake. Yet our examination of the strong minor premise seems to have shown that contraception cannot be excluded in virtue of the objective good at stake.

Moreover, more significant counterexamples can be formulated easily enough. Imagine a person who ingests some food and drink by mouth for satisfaction although for medical reasons the stomach constantly is pumped so that nothing is digested. Real nourishment is given intravenously. Would any moralist object if such action seemed medically harmless and was comforting to a very ill patient?

An exceptional case? Consider smoking. Here we use the respiratory system in a way which does frustrate its proper function to a considerable extent, particularly if one inhales. We do this for no apparent reason other than for a pleasure not unlike mere sexual release. Yet no one was inclined to consider smoking seriously evil until it began to appear that it may cause permanent damage. Even now moralists hesitate to take a very severe view of it.

If these examples are not sufficiently analogous to the phenomenal pattern of contraceptive behavior to satisfy someone who cannot grasp the application of a principle except it be verified in imagination, he might reflect on the conduct of women engaged in lactation.[14]

In many cases there is excess milk and it is pumped out of the breasts and thrown away. The infant may be fed artificially during a temporary separation from his mother while she continues regularly to empty her breasts artificially and to waste their product. No one condemns this conduct nor even demands that there be a serious cause to justify it.

Yet lactation is the essential end of a very important natural faculty. And, like sex, it depends upon depositing a valuable glandular secretion in the appropriate natural receptacle. But mere convenience is a good enough reason for interfering in this process. Hence if contraception really is seriously wrong there must be some reason for its malice that has nothing to do with what these two cases have in common — i.e., preventing an important faculty from attaining its natural end.

The defender of the perverted-faculty argument may insist that even this analogy is inadequate to illustrate the mode of frustration exemplified by the practice of contraception. He may suggest that the consumption of enough of some nondigestible substance to cause death would be an acceptable parallel frustration of the function of the nutritive faculty.[15] But this suggestion evidences a failure to distinguish between the significance of permanent and irreversible contraceptive sterilization on the one hand and a single, apparently reasonable contraceptive act on the other.

Due to these difficulties, the Roman *vomitorium* has played a large role in statements of the perverted-faculty argument.[16] This repulsive practice, presumably, is a perfect parallel to contraception, since the natural function of nutrition was frustrated while the faculty was exercised for sheer delight to such an extent that periodic induced vomiting was necessary to make room for additional courses. But the analogy is unsound on two counts.

In the first place, eating cannot occur normally without reaching its nutritive end, but sexual relations most often are not generative. The user of the *vomitorium* hardly can have any motive other than gluttony, while the person who practices contraception can have the good reasons for intercourse which usually justify engaging in it during naturally sterile periods.

In the second place, as soon as there is any good reason to

induce vomiting, no objection is made to doing so. For example, even a small danger that one has consumed poison or a moderate discomfort which may be relieved by vomiting are sufficient justifications for inducing it.

Indeed, in such cases no moral issue even is raised, and this fact shows that gluttony rather than induced vomiting is what was immoral in the Roman practice. If the perverted-faculty argument only proves contraception immoral when intercourse is had out of sheer lust, however, either the argument is question-begging or it is inconclusive. In the latter case, there is room for reasonable exceptions here, just as there is in the case of induced vomiting.

From all of these arguments it clearly follows that if the major premise of the conventional argument is understood in the strong interpretation, which yields the perverted-faculty argument, that premise becomes an indefensible proposition. As a rule we rightly consider the claims of the natural ends of our various faculties only in subordination to our well-being on the whole. We shall see later why this is so, as well as how the principle of the perverted-faculty argument can be vindicated in the unique case for which it was designed — the reproductive capacity.

It is only unfortunate that those who wished to show the intrinsic immorality of contraception assumed the first logically adequate major premise which came to hand — one indefensible because it is more general than is required — instead of examining the specific nature of the contraceptive act. The many attempts over the years to show the intrinsic immorality of contraception using this faulty premise have exposed Catholic moral thought to endless ridicule and surely have caused harm in other ways.

From our examination of arguments we also can elicit a certain methodological moral. One who wishes to show the intrinsic malice of contraception must bear in mind that the alternative to the practice he condemns is abstinence. Contraception is not intrinsically evil if it is not evil in every instance, and the instances which are most plausibly defended are those in which there are very serious indications against conception. To prove contraception intrinsically evil is much more difficult than to prove permanent sterilization intrinsically evil or to prove contraception generally evil.

Often, especially in popular writings, reasons such as the following have been given for not practicing contraception. It is said to be a violation of God's will, a contamination of one's bodily temple, a practice amounting to mutual masturbation or the use of one's partner as a mere device, an intrinsically shameful practice having no reasonable end in view, a practice which will harden hearts and blind minds to higher things.

It seems to me that all these condemnations are correct and that consideration of them may provide motives for avoiding the evil of contraception. But none of them is an argument showing the malice of contraception, for every one of them presupposes that it is intrinsically evil.

Like them is the statement that contraception is wrong because it is against the natural law. This is not completely uninformative, since it asserts that the practice is immoral in itself rather than by mere imposition of authority. However, this classification, like that of contraception among sins against nature, presupposes rather than proves its immorality.

To show that contraception is against natural law we must show that it is immoral in itself. The opposite course is not open to us since natural law cannot be consulted except by examining the morality of various species of human action. Like civil law, natural law can be violated only by violating a specific precept of it, so that a violation is against the law only by being against a law.[17]

The question also is begged if one asserts that contraception is wrong because it separates sexual pleasure from reproduction. The assumption here either is that sexual pleasure as such is evil or that the pleasure of contraceptive intercourse is evil.

The former is indefensible. In practice it leads to the conclusion that since this evil is necessary one may as well enjoy it. Moreover, any sound theory will hold that the pleasure of sex has the same moral quality as the act to which it belongs, and so the very pleasure of good sexual activity itself must be considered good.[18]

It is true that one should not seek sexual pleasure for its own sake, and this is equally true of all other kinds of pleasure — they should be sought only in subordination to the functions which they perfect. However, those who defend contraception claim that contraceptive intercourse can have the same good purposes as other licit though unfruitful sexual relations.

On the other hand, to assert that the sexual pleasure of contraceptive intercourse is evil is simply to assume what needs to be proved — that contraceptive intercourse is evil. If it is so, no doubt its pleasure and the enjoyment of that pleasure also is evil.

Partly because of dissatisfaction with the arguments examined above, various authors in recent years have proposed an altogether different mode of argument against contraception. The new approach has been called "phenomenological" because it proceeds by describing the *experience* of marital intercourse and then by analyzing this description, rather than by arguing from the end of the sexual function.

Presumably this argument will show that contraception involves the violation of the intrinsic meaning of sexual relations. Its proponents sometimes have contrasted their way of arguing with the conventional way, claiming that the latter reduces sexual activity to the status of a mere function performed in view of an *extrinsic* goal.[19]

The gist of the phenomenological argument is that sexual intercourse reveals itself directly as an act in which man and wife cooperate in personal immediacy to accomplish in fleshly union the most perfect possible expression of their special conjugal love. This love primarily is a special mode of mutual benevolence, a wish to perfect one another in every possible way. Human sexuality transcends physiological utilities and instinctive drives; human sexual intercourse represents objectively the mutual, total self-giving of man and woman.

No reservations and obstacles must be allowed to interfere with the definitive and exclusive surrender of man and wife to one another. But contraception introduces such an obstacle, for it represents a limitation on the giving and receiving of selves. Hence this practice is an offense against the very meaning of the conjugal act, and for this reason it must be avoided.

One way to understand this argument is to assume at the beginning that the withholding of one's effective generative power, whether or not one's partner approves, is a withholding of part of what *ought* to be given in the mutual self-giving.[20] If the argument is understood in this way, however, it will not prove that contraception is immoral, for it proceeds on the supposition that it is.

However, this argument gives a persuasive reason for avoiding the practice of contraception if one admits it to be immoral, because it describes in concrete form how such immoral behavior corrupts the natural beauty and even the deepest satisfaction of the marital act. One who believes that contraception is wrong could hardly engage in contraceptive intercourse as an expression of genuine benevolence and affection for his partner. Cooperators in sin are not true friends, because the same selfishness which leads to sin also precludes genuine mutuality.

A second way to understand this argument is to take it as an effort to emphasize the personal and interpersonal psychological and moral function of sex apart from any direct reference to its reproductive function. Mature sexuality is an expression of the transcendence achieved in sound interpersonal relationships. It is not merely self-indulgent pleasure-seeking.

Rather it is an experience shared by mature persons who have much else to share and who enjoy feeling in a most concrete manner their total human relationship by giving one another sexual delight.[21]

If this theory is not pushed to extremes, we must concede that it has a certain value. It illuminates an aspect of sexuality which was largely neglected until this century. The psychological function of sexual activity can be of value in itself. It can render worthwhile the conduct of sexual intercourse by married couples during times of natural sterility. Moreover, the satisfaction of psychological rather than reproductive needs is the reason that human sexual association tends toward the normal pattern of permanent and exclusive union of one man with one woman.[22]

The psychological aspect of sexuality also seems to me the source of one of the pillars on which a reconstructed sexual ethics might rest. Loveless indulgence in sexual release is more directly opposed to the psychosocial function of sex than to its procreative value.

The inherent malice of masturbation, for example, is that it reduces the only bodily capacity which naturally leads one outside himself into complete and fruitful cooperation with another person to the status of a mere device for supporting self-enclosure in isolation against any genuine mutuality with others.

Masturbation, having this psychological significance, naturally accompanies a childish reluctance to assume the risks and responsibilities of adulthood. The adolescent naturally undergoes a conflict between feeling and intelligence, fear and aspiration. This conflict is a moral one, because it occurs in consciousness and must be resolved by self-commitment.

The habitual practice of masturbation generally is a clear sign that this conflict has not yet been faced squarely and resolved properly. The end of the habit is in sight when a meaningful alternative is developed to the device of diverting tension into sexual channels to be released in a displacement activity whose only satisfaction is the very release of tension itself.

The normal, mature alternative to this childish device is generous cooperation with others in a serious commitment of effort to the pursuit of values transcending the self. This "sublimation" should not be regarded as a mode of draining off into other channels energy of itself sexual, but as a return to purposeful use of the intrinsically indeterminate energy which a kind of error of psychic control often concentrates too heavily in sexual channels.[23]

This discussion of masturbation is not irrelevant to the

morality of contraception. As we saw earlier, if it is shown on other grounds that contraception is intrinsically immoral it will be clear that contraceptive intercourse between persons aware of its immorality never could be a genuine expression of love. While still pretending to express and communicate love, such perverse activity will in reality represent a kind of selfish indulgence. This experience will then substitute for real cooperation in the work and real sharing in the responsibility proper to the married state.

In other words, to those aware of the immorality of contraception, contraceptive intercourse clearly appears for what it is — a device employed by married couples which is related to their resistance to continued growth as the adolescent's masturbation is related to his resistance to adulthood.

This is not to say that contraceptive intercourse, even for those who know it to be wrong, has the same psychic quality and effects as solitary masturbation. No, an interpersonal relationship is never the same as no relationship at all. Instead, this kind of sexual experience among adults is similar to and continuous with adolescent heterosexual activities such as petting.

In such relationships there is a certain reciprocity — of exploitation. Each uses the other both as a masturbatory instrument and as a social tool. The boy's attentions prove the girl's popularity while the girl's concessions prove the boy's masculine prowess. This whole relationship, of course, also is dignified with the name "mutual love," since mutual exploitation demands the romantic mask of sentiment in order to allow each partner to feel that he is successfully exploiting without himself merely being exploited.[24]

These psychological insights into the significance of contraception, useful as they are, do not prove the act to be immoral in itself. Rather, this is assumed. Moreover, the psychological consideration of the sexual act is just as much a functional interpretation of it as is the ordinary natural-law approach.

Any serious psychological consideration of sexual experience must pass beyond the experience itself and must consider its value in terms of psychosocial dynamics. A pure phenomenological argument against contraception would have to remain strictly within the experience as such, and it should not assume that the experience under consideration is that of persons who already consider contraception wrong on other grounds.

However, such a pure phenomenological argument seems extremely weak. Why should sexual expression be limited to marriage in the first place? Might it not be appropriate also as an expression of definitive and exclusive friendship between two persons of the same sex? Assuming sexual expression is to be limited to married couples, why should contraception be ruled out? It need not imply any limitation on reciprocity if conception-prevention is agreeable to both partners, for then it will seem to them only a further evidence of their affectionate concern for one another.

Indeed, while it has been claimed by Janssens that the phenomenological argument can appeal to non-Catholics as well as to Catholics,[25] my own experience in discussions with apparently sincere Protestants has been that those who do not consider contraception wrong as such do not find any agreeable mode of contraception inconsistent with their experience of sexual relations as an expression of reciprocal love.

Nevertheless, Janssens apparently assumes that there are other adequate ways to exclude perversions and at the same time he is willing to admit the liceity of the use of inconspicuous contraceptives such as the pill. His argument, if I have grasped it, is that since man is an incarnate spirit, there must be a harmony between the naturalistic sense of his outward behavior and the spiritual meanings that he wishes to communicate. On this ground, sexual activity is restricted within marriage, since it naturally expresses conjugal love.

On the other hand, since the value of persons completely transcends the function of reproduction, there is no reason why the use of contraceptives should be excluded provided they do not alter the symbolic sense of marital intercourse as an expression of reciprocal love. This love is prior to any other value, although it need not exclude a reference of sexual activity to its appropriate fruitful result — the child as the perfect expression of love.

Conspicuous contraceptives — i.e., those which interfere with the integrity of the sexual act in its external aspects — are excluded because they interfere with the intrinsic sense of the conjugal act, to incarnate wholly the unrestricted and unreserved reciprocal abandonment of the spouses to one another.[26]

Understood in this way, the phenomenological argument seems to be related to the theory that the primary end, or at least the essential meaning, of marriage is to be found in reciprocal love and the union of two-in-one-flesh rather than in "mere reproduction."[27] This theory emphasizes the immanent value of the marital relationship at some expense to the proper transcendent good — the procreation and raising of children — which marriage normally attains by the cooperation of man and wife.

The phenomenological argument taken in this way and the theory on which it rests are open to numerous objections. In the first place, why should the physical integrity of the marital act be so important so long as it remains an exclusive and immediate experience if the protection of fertility is not really at issue? Other symbols of human relationships are extremely flexible.[28]

Again, why make such a distinction between the integrity of internal aspects of the reproductive process, which may be violated, and the external aspects of it, which are held inviolable? If the pill is permitted, why not intrauterine devices? These set up no barrier to the sexual communion; in fact, once in place, neither partner could detect the presence of the device.[29]

If intrauterine devices are licit, why not a douche? If a douche, why not foam or jelly? If these, why not a diaphragm? And if a diaphragm, why not a condom?[30] If a condom, why not withdrawal? If this, why not mutual masturbation?

If the marital act is not to be considered primarily pro-creative, then there seems to be no single plausible place to draw the line if one considers the whole spectrum of contracep-tive methods available. Apart from medical and psychological considerations, distinctions among modes of contraception are more a matter of aesthetics than anything else.

Everyone admits that many sexual acts short of orgasm are suit-able expressions of love among married persons. Why should one who is willing to admit fertility control by means of drugs balk at orgasm in a real embrace where semen is mixed in one flesh within the vagina but not within the uterus? Would Jannsens want to maintain that a couple who used a diaphragm at the beginning of a valid marriage would not have consummated their marriage, while if they had used some less conspicuous contraceptive they would have done so?[31]

In sum, Janssens' version of the phenomenological argument against conspicuous contraceptives is subject to these three devastating objections. First, he has merely asserted, he has not proved, that marital intercourse has the precise symbolic mean-ing he assigns to it. Second, if it has that meaning, Janssens has merely asserted, not proved, that conventional contraceptives violate it. Third, he also has merely assumed, not proved, that a married couple has a serious *obligation* to avoid violating the *given* symbolic sense of sexual relations.

Here we meet once again precisely the same equivocation be-tween *fact* and *obligation* from which our discussion of the conventional natural-law argument began. What is operative to conceal it is very likely nothing more substantial than the feel-ing of repulsion one naturally has in association with the phenomenal patterns of conventional, conspicuous contracep-tive behavior if those patterns are what one always has imagined when thinking of contraception as seriously wrong.

There are deeper theoretical difficulties. Is it really true that man is an incarnate spirit? This characterization is supposed to exclude Scheler's "trialism" and to assure the unity of human nature. But it smacks of residual cartesian dualism; it implies that man really has two natures rather than one and that his spiritual subjectivity must work through an essentially alien objectivity.[32] Janssens gives himself away when he explains that Scheler's trouble arose from his failure to see that we experience ourselves immediately as personal totalities who say "I" of all aspects of our composite.[33]

In other words, for Janssens, not being but consciousness is the principle of unity in man. Janssens' next sentence offers further confirmation, for he goes on to say: "Because man is an incarnate spirit, even the bodily aspects of his sexuality have an intrinsic sense diverse from that of the animals, for these aspects participate in his spiritual interiority. . . ."[34] This explanation implies, of course, the dualistic presupposition that apart from their participation in man's spiritual interiority, the bodily aspects of human sexuality are little better than animal functions.

In truth, however, man is one nature, not two, and his life is not divided between the conscious life of personality and the material processes of an organism — processes which would serve to anchor man in nature and which would be a vehicle of his spirit but which would lack any specifically human meaning of their own. On the contrary, man is an organism whose highest integration is that of rational intelligence.[35] The human act of procreation is as properly personal as is the most perfect love of man and wife for one another. Indeed, the latter has its sense only from the former.

The marital society is a human good in itself, not only a means to procreation, and marital relations do have a role in fostering and in expressing this union on its most basic psychosocial level. But the significance of love is not complete in itself and in the unity it establishes. Lovers must have a real value besides love in which to share, a value which transcends their union and for whose attainment they cooperate.[36] This is true of all love except that of God, who is His own perfection.

Marital love is a cooperation in the highest of natural vocations — participation in the creation and perfection of new human persons. Husband and wife, indeed, are children to one another as well as being parents to their children, but even in this respect the good intrinsic to the marital community and the other values it seeks to realize, even within the partners themselves, are not the same.[37]

Of course, real marriage can exist in which man and wife cooperate together for the pursuit of goods other than procreation. But these exceptional cases merely show that besides procreation other goods which transcend the marital society can be achieved by it, and that sexual relations can be helpful in perfecting a union for the pursuit of such other goods.

The exceptional cases do not by any means show that there can be any value in the marital society itself without its being subordinated to some good beyond itself. The fact that, given such subordination, the marital union is not a mere means does not make its need for subordination any the less real.

Human immanent goods, even spiritual ones like genuine conjugal love, must be subordinate to some good beyond themselves, because human subjectivity originates as an empty reflexivity. That the transcendent good, the good beyond subjective consciousness, happens in the first instance to be a material reality should not upset anyone who is not a dualist. To claim that the spirit needs no real object for its life, on the other hand, would be worse than simple dualism, for it would involve a confusion between the finite subject and God.

My conclusion, then, not only is that a pure phenomenological argument against contraception has no cogency with regard to the point it attempts to prove, but that it is connected with a very questionable philosophical theory of man and of the marital society.

The subjective and interpersonal life of the spirit is no more human than is the humblest of human functions. And it is a mistake to yield to the temptation to attribute superiority to the immanent value of marriage over the transcendent value of the procreation and education of children to which marriage is ordained. Human sexual intercourse transcends animal reproduction in the same proportion that the human child transcends the animal offspring.

It is a permanent temptation for man to seek perfection within himself. The result is always the same whether he seeks it in his own freedom and individuality or whether he seeks it in contentless interpersonal relationships.[38] Human perfection requires that man first of all submit his emptiness to the values beyond his subjectivity which alone give meaning to his existence. It is folly to ignore these values and then to complain, as so many contemporary philosophers do, that life is meaningless.

Hell is not isolation any more than it is other people. It is the permanent unwillingness of men, alone and in society, to accept perfection on the terms reality has set.

NOTES TO CHAPTER II

1. There have been few published critiques by Catholics; one is: Dupré, "Toward a Re-examination of the Catholic Position on Birth Control," *Cross Currents*, 14 (Winter, 1964), 66–73. Less penetrating on the whole, but much clearer with regard to the vital distinction between fact and obligation, and interesting in its own right, is a non-Catholic critique: Alvah W. Sulloway, *Birth Control and Catholic Doctrine* (Boston: Beacon Press, 1959), 57–78. Most valuable are a remarkable group of articles which appeared in *The (American) Ecclesiastical Review* shortly before *Casti connubii*: E. J. Mahoney, "The 'Perverted Faculty' Argument against Birth Prevention," 79 (August, 1928), 133–145; John A. Ryan, "The Immorality of Contraception," 79 (October, 1928), 408–411; John M. Cooper, "Birth Control and the 'Perverted Faculty' Argument," 79 (November, 1928), 527–533; Henry Davis, S.J., "Birth Control: The Perverted Faculty Argument," 81 (July, 1929), 54–69; "Comment by Dr. Ryan," 70–72; "Comment by Dr. Cooper," 72–79; E. J. Mahoney, "The Immorality of Contraception," 81 (July, 1929), 90–92. Much of our critique is a systematic organization of these arguments.

2. Mahoney, "The 'Perverted Faculty' Argument . . . ," 134–136, begins from a clear appreciation of the danger of this equivocation; Sulloway, *loc. cit.*, stresses its occurrence very effectively; Dupré, *loc. cit.*, begins by alluding to it somewhat less clearly.

3. Much preaching and popular writing implicitly attempt a defense of the minor by arguing that contraception is wrong *because* large families are good, because married people should procreate as many souls for heaven as possible, and so on. See: Jacques Leclercq, *Marriage and the Family: A Study in Social Philosophy*, 2 ed. (New York and Cincinnati: Frederick Pustet Co., Inc., 1942), 210–246.

4. The popular literature against contraception used to speak of "race suicide," but this slogan has lost its rhetorical value.

5. Ryan, "The Immorality of Contraception," suggests this line of argument, but does not develop it fully.

6. Marcus George Singer, *Generalization in Ethics* (New York: Alfred A.

Knopf, 1961), has presented the most plausible theoretical defense of this argument that I have seen. Unfortunately, if the generalization argument is understood as Singer explains it, *reasonable exceptions* are not excluded.

7. Thomas Aquinas, *Summa contra gentiles*, 3, ch. 122, states this principle; his explanation is not as clear as might be desired, possibly because he had not yet developed fully the theory of moral law which he later presented in the *Summa theologiae*.

8. See the commentary of Thomas de Vio Cajetan on: Thomas Aquinas, *Summa theologiae*, 2-2, q. 154, a. 12. The great scholastic concludes that female masturbation is demonstrably wrong only after a painstaking argument in the course of which he sets aside Aristotle's opinion, which happens to be true that female *seminatio* is not the analogue of male ejaculation.

9. In the articles mentioned in note 1 above, Davis defended the perverted-faculty argument, Mahoney and Ryan did not consider it sufficient by itself although they did not reject it, while Cooper criticized it very effectively.

10. This critique is based on "Comment by Dr. Cooper," 73–75.

11. Ford and Kelly, *Contemporary Moral Theology*, Vol. 2, *Marriage Questions* (Westminster, Md.: The Newman Press, 1963), 364; they explicitly raise the question of the inviolability of the conjugal act (363) and discuss it in the following pages. Of course, moralists who approve assisted insemination might argue that it does not *interfere* with the natural structure of the conjugal act.

12. Aquinas, *S. c. g.*, 3, ch. 122, proposes this explanation; Mahoney, who often refers to Aquinas, probably was attempting to recapture the precise sense of this theory in contradistinction to the perverted-faculty argument as Davis understood it.

13. Aquinas, *loc. cit.*, considers this objection; his answer at that time to our criticism of it apparently would have been that all such exceptions do represent less serious abuses which are venially wrong.

14. Cooper, *op. cit.*, 75–77, develops this counterexample; from a psychological point of view, of course, the unconscious identification of the two processes has an important meaning, but we are concerned only with their rational analogy.

15. Davis, *op. cit.*, 65, offers this argument against Cooper.

16. The role is too large to document; one example is: E. C. Messenger, *Two in One Flesh*, Vol. 3, *The Practice of Sex and Marriage* (Westminster, Md.: The Newman Press, 1948), 54–55.

17. Sulloway, *op. cit.*, 65–66, mistakenly imagines that Catholics do not recognize that this truth applies to law in general.

18. Arthurus Vermeersch, S.I., *Theologiae moralis*, Vol. 4 (Roma: Pontificia Università Gregoriana, 1944), 80, discusses this point briefly but very clearly.

19. Such critics, as we shall see in Chapter IV, are quite right in demanding that there be nonoperational or nonpragmatic value in human action; they are dead wrong, however, in supposing (with Kant) that all ends are technical objectives. An end may be a participation in a value which as participation becomes immanent but as value remains transcendent. See: Aquinas, *S. c. g.*, 3, ch. 18.

20. Lestapis, *Family Planning and Modern Problems: A Catholic Analysis* (New York: Herder and Herder, 1961), 175–177, evidently understands the argument in this way; Paul M. Quay, S.J., "Contraception and Conjugal Love," *Theological Studies*, 22 (March, 1961), 18–40, develops the argument at great length, but he also appears to beg the question (34–37).

21. The psychological function of mature sexual activity among mentally healthy persons is unquestionable today. It is extremely important to distinguish this function from the use of sex in a more or less pathological psychic process. See: Russell and Russell, *Human Behaviour: A New Approach* (Boston-Toronto: Little, Brown and Co., 1961), p. 277; Edmund Bergler, *Counterfeit-Sex: Homosexuality, Impotence, Frigidity*, 2 ed. (New York: Grune & Stratton, 1958), 12–32 and *passim*.

22. Yet these psychological aspects of sexual activity were not wholly neglected by the ancients; they recognized that a system allowing polygamy or divorce might be compatible with the needs of procreation, but that it would conflict with the secondary ends of marriage. See: Aquinas, *S. c. g.*, 3, chs. 123–124.

23. Russell and Russell, *loc. cit.*, make very clear the psychological difference between sex as displacement activity and mature sexual activity. Suenens, *Love and Control* (Westminster, Md.: The Newman Press, 1961), 77–87, indicates the important relationship between adolescent masturbation and adult problems with chastity. He also cites a book which has the most extensive psychological-ethical treatment of masturbation I have seen: Friedrich Ernst von Gagern, *The Problem of Onanism* (Westminster, Md.: The Newman Press, 1955).

24. Lester A. Kirkendall, *Premarital Intercourse and Interpersonal Relationships* (New York: The Julian Press, 1961), 229–238 and *passim*, brings out the interpersonal significance of complete adolescent relations when they are recognized as wrong. His solution seems to be to convince adolescents that such relationships are not wrong, and to remove other interfering factors. I have been able to find no serious study of the psychological significance of petting to orgasm; my observations are based on discussions with many college students interpreted in the light of general psychological principles from sources such as those cited in the previous note. See in particular: Oraison, *Man and Wife* (New York: The Macmillan Co., 1962), 110–118, 132–133; Gibert, *Love in Marriage* (New York and London: Hawthorn Books, Inc., 1964), 101–108.

25. "Morale conjugale et progestogènes," *Ephemerides theologicae lovanienses*, 39 (Oct.–Dec., 1963), 819.

26. The argument runs on 809–824; unfortunately, it is stated compactly nowhere in the article.

27. I do not mean to say that Janssens explicitly holds the condemned theory; he does not state this position anywhere. Quay, *op. cit.*, 33–34, tries to show that his milder version of the phenomenological argument does not require a denial of the traditional doctrine on the ends of marriage; Quay, of course, was not arguing in favor of inconspicuous methods of contraception. B. Lavaud, O.P., "The Interpretation of the Conjugal Act and the Theology of Marriage," *The Thomist*, 1 (October, 1939), 360–380, reveals by his sympathetic commentary precisely how the view of those who proposed inverting the ends of marriage is related to an interpretation of the conjugal act very like the one Janssens presents. Ford and Kelly, *op. cit.*, 1–165, provide a complete theological study of the question of the ends of Christian marriage; Oraison, *op. cit.*, 53–68, gives a fairly well-balanced brief treatment of the problem.

28. Dupré, *op. cit.*, considers the phenomenological argument under the heading, "Psychological Arguments." He offers the criticism (82) that man interprets natural symbols freely; unfortunately, he goes too far and suggests that subjective intention can alter the objective intention (*finis operis*) of any human act.

29. One might object to such devices on the ground that they can cause dangerous damage and that they very likely have their effect by inducing abortion: *Year Book of Obstetrics and Gynecology, 1962–1963 Series,* ed. J. P. Greenhill (Chicago: Year Book Medical Publishers, Inc.), 390–392. However, similar objections cannot be made against the douche, foam, and jelly.

30. One might make psychological objections to mutual masturbation, *coitus interruptus,* and to the condom, but the same objections hardly seem applicable to the previous items in the list.

31. I do not mean to suggest that contraceptive intercourse of any sort consummates marriage. However, Canon 1015 states: "Matrimonium baptizatorum validum dicitur *ratum,* si nondum consummatione completum est; *ratum et consummatum,* si inter coniuges locum habuerit coniugalis actus, ad quem natura sua ordinatur contractus matrimonialis et quo coniuges fiunt una caro." If procreation can be set aside, this definition seems to admit contraception by diaphragm as well as by any less conspicuous method.

32. Albert Dondeyne, *Contemporary European Thought and Christian Faith* (Pittsburgh, Pa.: Duquesne University; Louvain: E. Nauwelaerts, 1958), tried to defend as much phenomenological existentialism as he could integrate with Christian faith. Even he was forced to criticize (114–116) the phenomenological theory of man as incarnate spirit as a subtle form of dualism.

33. *Op. cit.,* 808, n. 85: "Scheler a affirmé ce 'trialisme', parce qu'il n'a, pas tenu suffisamment compte du fait que la première donnée de notre expérience est que nous nous saisissons comme une unité, comme une totalité personnelle qui dit 'je' de tous les aspects actifs et réceptifs de son comportement."

34. *Ibid.,* "Puisque l'homme est esprit incarné, même les aspects corporels de sa sexualité ont un sens intrinsèque autre que chez les animaux, car ils participent à son intériorité spirituelle et, de la sorte, ils offrent une très grande plasticité et rendent possible leur intégration dans la totalité personnelle."

35. Bernard Lonergan, S.J., *Insight: A Study of Human Understanding* (New York: Philosophical Library, 1957), 245–270, clarifies the uniqueness of human nature without sacrificing man's unity.

36. Cf. Lestapis, *op. cit.,* 150–153.

37. Ford and Kelly, *op. cit.,* 153 and *passim.*

38. David Riesman, *The Lonely Crowd* (New Haven, Conn.: Yale University Press, 1950), described the latter danger so clearly and demonstrated its contemporary power so fully that we have had fair warning. Yet "dialogue," "encounter," "mutual love," and other items in the jargon mislead us, as advertising language sometimes does, to invest in what we know is worthless.

III

THREE THEORIES OF MORAL LAW

In THIS chapter I shall describe and contrast with one another three theories of moral law — conventional natural-law theory, a theory opposed to it which I call "situationism" for want of a better name, and the theory of practical principles which I prefer to either of the others. As I remarked in the course of our examination of previous modes of argument against contraception, deeper theoretical difficulties underlie their inadequacy in meeting this particular issue.

The present chapter will clarify these fundamental theoretical difficulties. It also will be a foundation for the demonstration of the immorality of contraception. By studying the three theories side by side, we shall become able to discern the depth and breadth of what really is at stake in the present debate.

Conventional natural-law theory, which originated with Suarez, is commonly regarded as the only traditional explanation of moral law accepted by Catholic philosophers, because it often is represented as such in the textbooks.[1] It must be understood, of course, that if some treatments have subtleties not suggested here, to that extent I would not group them with the system I am considering. There is no time now to survey the literature and to treat each author with the discrimination he might deserve.

What is most characteristic of conventional natural-law theory is its notion of the objectivity of moral norms. The moral norm simply is human nature as it is given — given, of course, not to sense experience but to rational understanding. Moral goodness and badness can be discerned simply by comparing the essential patterns of possible human actions with the intelligible structure of human nature considered both in its inner complexity and in its extrinsic relationships.

When compared with human nature, actions are seen either to conform or not to conform to the requirements set by it insofar as man is vegetative, sentient, and rational in himself, and creature, fellow creature, and ruler of lower creation in his essential relationships.

The judgment whether an action conforms or not to human nature is completely objective. In fact, it is a purely speculative knowledge, enjoying the necessity of truth based on essential definitions of formal causes. The judgment registers conformity when there is consistency between action and nature. It registers nonconformity, intrinsic evil, when the action is incompatible with human nature in any of its essential aspects.

Of course, to become aware of one's obligations it is not enough to observe the nonconformity or conformity between nature and action, and so to see the badness or the possible goodness of the action. Besides this theoretical knowledge, awareness of obligation presupposes awareness of a fundamental imperative: *Avoid morally bad acts.* This basic imperative may be expressed in other ways: *Act in conformity with nature,* or: *Follow reason.*

However the basic imperative is expressed, its meaning is understood only when it is recognized as a communication to the created subject of the sovereign will of God. The *force* of obligation derives solely from this imperative will of God. Man recognizes the agreement or disagreement between possible actions and his own nature as a source of obligation only when he realizes that the norm of nature is the specific form in which the divine will is communicated to him as a rational creature.

This natural-law theory has a peculiar conception of practical reason, allowing it only an extremely limited role. The knowledge of the obligatory force of natural law belongs to natural theology while the knowledge of the badness of various species of acts depends mainly on rational psychology. Of course, natural theology has an important role here too, and so do other disciplines which contribute to man's self-understanding.

The only specific task of practical reason in elaborating precepts of natural law is the synthesis of the two theoretical premises and the deduction of the conclusion which they imply. For example, observing that suicide is contrary to the fundamental organic good of human nature and considering that God wills what nature indicates as good, we may conclude that suicide is intrinsically immoral — i.e., a forbidden evil act.

The only reason this argument and conclusion is considered practical rather than purely theoretical knowledge is that it refers to practical subject matter — that is, a possible human action — and communicates the will of the superior about that action.

Of course, the imperative will not be effective so long as it remains merely universal. Hence practical reason has the additional task of applying the precepts of natural law to particular cases. Knowing that suicide is wrong, I still must apply this knowledge to the judgment of the concrete act I am considering in order to form a proper conscience about it.

On the surface this application would seem easy, but as situations become complicated tremendous difficulties appear. Would it be suicide, for example, if I were to risk my life as a daredevil in a circus? Suppose the stunt I wish to perform has led many others to their deaths? A whole science, casuistry, developed around the discussion of problems of this kind.

The ideal of the casuist is to maintain perfect objectivity in his consideration all the way down to the particular advice a moralist may provide for a particular client and in this way to insure so far as possible the correctness of the actual judgment of conscience itself.[2]

It is easy to see why a moral system of this kind should be far more adept in issuing prohibitions than in offering affirmative guidance. Affirmative precepts bind always but not for every instance. Hence the casuist never is able to say categorically what must be done; his affirmative judgments always are subject to conditions.

Negative precepts, on the other hand, bind always and everywhere. The casuist need only assure himself that he really is dealing with an instance of a species of prohibited action in order to know immediately that everything else in the situation is irrelevant — the action being considered should not be done.

Moreover, in normative ethics, where precepts are deduced, there are additional reasons to accentuate the negative. A negative precept follows directly from the inconsistency of any species of action with the specific essence of man. But is every action consonant with specific human nature an object of obligation?

Hardly, for if this were the case all of man's life would be sealed off under definite obligations — under many incompatible definite obligations, in fact, since many acts are consistent with man's specific essence. Moreover, if every act which is good were obligatory there would be no room for individual freedom and no place for counsels of perfection.

Consequently, only certain species of action can become the objects of affirmative precepts — i.e., those kinds of action whose omission would be wrong. Since it is difficult to find instances of this sort which are both specific and certain, and which also can be prescribed with true universality, few interesting affirmative precepts belong to the body of natural laws which most of us learned.

What is the relationship between moral action and man's ultimate end in this theory? Most of human action seems to have no essential relation to the end at all. There is, as it were, a large reserved domain for individual freedom, a domain which practically is secluded from the demands of moral obligation although it is located within the jurisdiction of the moral order.

But action which falls directly under obligation assumes an altogether different importance in relation to man's ultimate end. He who does not break the law is morally good, and avoidance of moral guilt is of transcendent importance.

The reason why this avoidance is so important, even apart from any positive achievement, is that human life in itself and the actual attainments and failures which constitute it are of no real account in the long run. The long run is one's permanent condition after death, and nothing one could do in this life is a proportionate means for effectively causing eternal happiness.

Even if man's end were a merely natural one, perfect moral goodness in this life could not cause his attainment of it, anymore than his actual achievements in this life — if he died guilty — could mitigate his permanent misery. The reason for this lack of intrinsic proportion between moral goodness and the ultimate end of man is that natural law is an intelligible system only to the extent that it is based on objective, formal necessities. These are completely static; all elements of motivation must be introduced from outside.

Hence just as natural law gets its obligating force from the divine imperative in which it originates, so it gets its motivating force, or sanction, from the rewards and punishments which God allots to His subjects according to whether they have been disobedient or not.

Four main criticisms can be made against this conventional natural-law theory.

In the first place, it requires one to pass from theoretical knowledge concerning human nature to moral obligations governing human actions. This passage is supported by the theoretical proposition that God wills us to act in conformity with nature. But notice that in very many cases the determination of what agrees or does not agree with nature seems to be either arbitrary or question-begging.

If human nature is considered only to the extent that it is

an object of theoretical knowledge, the determination that a certain kind of action would not agree with it seems arbitrary, for the reality which man simply *is* does not seem to settle what he can and ought to be.

On the other hand, if human nature is considered to the extent that it already is an object of moral knowledge, the determination that a certain kind of action would not agree with it is prejudiced by the moral knowledge that is assumed. "Nature" has two senses and conventional natural-law theory rests heavily on this equivocation.[3]

In the previous chapter we noticed how both the conventional arguments, with which we began, and Janssens' argument, with which we finished, rested upon instances of this equivocation. The conventional arguments begin from an equivocation on "natural end" and then proceed by one way or another to try to reunite the facts with a strong premise — i.e., one expressing obligation.

Janssens' argument relies on the assumption that those who have intercourse should respect its "natural, intrinsic meaning." He does not try to unite the facts with a principle of obligation. Perhaps he takes his feelings about morality as sufficient. Or perhaps he is not really very interested in showing the *immorality* of any means of contraception; his main problem is to provide some *explanation* for the traditional judgment of Catholic moralists that will leave room for inconspicuous contraception.

Another criticism of conventional natural-law theory is that it involves a voluntaristic notion of obligation. If God's command that we avoid evil is essential to the existence of obligation, the proposition that we ought to do what God wants us to do is essential to the force of any particular obligation.

I shall not take up here all the theoretical difficulties this position involves. A noteworthy one, however, is that it leads to an identification between the concrete judgment of obligation and the imperative. Now imperatives normally require of a subject only a certain definite performance or nonperformance.

The consequence is that conventional natural-law theory has no real place for flexible and open-ended obligations such as we shall consider in the next chapter. Apart from the legal effects of one's acts, one cannot bring the force of obligation as conventional natural-law theory understands it upon himself.[4]

Thus this theory has no difficulty with the marriage debt, but it is hard put to explain why a married couple have an obligation to have children.[5] In regard to our problem, this weakness of conventional natural-law theory accounts for its inability to explain how the good of procreation could ground any effective obligation sufficient to exclude contraception without also excluding other modes of nonperformance of the procreative task.

A third defect of conventional natural-law theory is its negative emphasis. This kind of ethics seldom contributes anything positive to life, it has only veto power. The negative precepts of natural law keep mankind from falling into barbarism, but they do not stimulate efforts to achieve new possibilities. Some say that conventional natural-law theory is too static because it uses logical deduction. This explanation is nugatory, since a conclusion is no more static than its premises.

However, we can see that this theory naturally tends to be static just to the extent that it very strongly favors prohibition. This same bias led those who set out from conventional natural-law theory in quest of an explanation of the malice of contraception to look for a negative principle under which to categorize it. They hardly would have imagined that to show an act intrinsically evil it might be helpful to consider the *exact* good which is violated by it and the *precise* way in which that good is violated.

A fourth defect of conventional natural-law theory is its lack of any positive link between moral goodness and the ultimate end. This missing connection drives a wedge between the moral motivation of action and the goodness of the action.

Of course, good acts often have a sufficient nonmoral motive, because they are "in agreement with nature." But where the equivocation on nature is strongest, this motivation entirely fails and the prohibition of an act such as contraception seems a particularly nasty trick of a rather arbitrary divine will which endorses nature somewhat less discriminatingly than we naturally should like.

More important, the separation of moral motivation from moral goodness inclines those who think in terms of conventional natural-law theory to forget the importance of intention in their consideration of *the objective morality of acts*. For this reason, the conventional arguments against contraception never raise the question whether one who acts in this way may be unable to avoid having a bad intention regardless of the good intentions he also may have and regardless of the good consequences his action may entail.

Diametrically opposed to conventional natural-law thinking is what I shall call "situationism." This kind of ethical theory is neither a specific philosophy nor even a cohesive movement.[6] It is a trend common to many diverse recent philosophies. This trend is even more widespread than the movement called "situation-ethics," for that movement only manifests in a particular way certain aspects of situationism. The classical utilitarianism of Bentham, dialectical materialism, and the ethics of ambiguity exemplify situationist thinking.

What is most characteristic about situationism is its flexibility in judging the morality of concrete actions. For the situationist, a man's outward behavior never necessitates placing his action in a definite moral category. Even if it is assumed that the agent is well informed and is acting deliberately and freely, one never can say that a certain pattern of outward behavior is necessarily morally evil. Thus for a situationist, direct abortion, the use of torture, suicide, euthanasia, masturbation, contraception, and many other actions might be wrong generally speaking, but there can be exceptional cases in which they are morally right and even obligatory.

To understand how situationist thinking comes to this strange conclusion, the first thing we must grasp is the situationist notion of material values, because outward behavior has significance at least in its effects on bodily goods or material values. The situationist divides such values into two groups.

In one group are the merely instrumental goods which may be employed in any way one pleases. In the other group are the necessary conditions, certain special instrumental goods, which are indispensable if other morally significant possibilities are to be realized. In the latter category are such goods as human life itself and, for the few situationists who have any respect for it, the good of procreation.

For the situationist, both classes of material goods may give rise to hypothetical imperatives. The reason for this is obvious, since physical objects and our behavior both are subject to laws of nature, with the result that if we act in certain ways bodily goods will suffer certain consequences. If life is to be protected, then a situationist like any other moralist can commend to one's consideration a number of useful maxims which should be taken into account.

Moreover, certain bodily goods — human life itself is the best example — so generally deserve moral respect that certain norms which surround them are usually treated as if they were absolute, although strictly speaking they can have the logical force only of hypothetical imperatives.

One further point must be understood in order to grasp the situationist theory of material values. It is that these values are not to be allowed to influence moral thinking except to the extent that they come to be at stake in definite realizations. In other words, they are never to be allowed to function as ideals, but only as objectives of operation.

The situationist ethician never thinks about a material good as an end without thinking of it as it exists or might exist in a particular instance where its realization will depend on definite and limited means. This way of viewing material goods is aptly called "operational" or "pragmatic."

Once these points are grasped, we need only to reflect that human action takes place in a value context which can be expanded indefinitely in order to see that even the greatest of bodily goods may be open to an ethically sanctioned violation in sufficiently necessary cases. These material goods are at best necessary conditions of what are supposed to be the absolute human values. Hence they have in themselves no absolute resistance to violation.

The norms which surround them are only hypothetically binding. Therefore, they are open to exceptions if it is better that the material good be violated. The material goods themselves are only at stake in their instances, they are not ideals. Therefore they can be violated so long as the nonmaterial ideals they embody, express, incarnate, or otherwise serve are protected.

It also is true for situationism that the goodness or badness of any external action must be gauged in terms of its actual results. This may seem surprising, but it is easy to understand as soon as one remembers that the imperatives which surround material goods are never really more than hypothetical. It follows that their whole point is to conduce to conditions whose importance is solely determined by what is really morally significant.

By this time the reader undoubtedly is wondering how situationism qualifies as a theory of moral law at all. What is the "something really significant" to which material goods must give way? Is it likewise subject to submergence in sufficiently difficult cases? Or can the situationist admit an absolute principle which will give his ethics a starting point and limit the relativism evidenced by his attitude toward material goods?

The something which controls in a situationist ethics is not always described in the same way. Some situationists consider pleasure the sole value that always is sacred, others cast authenticity in this role, others self-awareness, others autonomy, others scientific method, others human affection, others what they consider to be faith or charity, and others the triumph of the proletariat.

Whatever a particular situationist theory selects as its controlling value, this key principle always has certain characteristics. It is not a material or bodily good. Even pleasure as utilitarians understand it is a subjective and personal rather than an objective and merely natural reality. What they want is a certain kind of conscious experience.

The controlling value is an absolute end in itself; it may never be subordinated to any other good. The controlling value establishes absolute moral obligations. *Seek pleasure* is not hypothetical for a hedonist. *Be authentic* allows no exceptions for Sartre. *Construct socialism* is an absolute imperative for Communists.

The reason for the absoluteness of the key value is not only that it is preferred. This fact, of course, tends to make it absolute, since one normally protects what he prefers. However, the controlling value in a situationist theory also has another privilege which is shared by none of the material values — it alone functions as an ideal.

Every situationist theory presupposes a sort of dualistic understanding of man. The preferred value is psychic, subjective, personal, or interpersonal,[7] and the part of man in which it is realized is considered sufficiently separate from mere material goods so that the latter in the end must yield to the requirements of the former. The situationist tries to make the distinction between the natural and the moral, between fact and obligation, into a division between the outer, material world and the subjective domain of consciousness.

This peculiar dualism always has the strange effect that a situationist will notice immediately if moral implications are being derived illogically from merely factual premises until his preferred value is concerned. Then he will employ the same sort of derivation he otherwise recognizes as fallacious.

Situationism can provide an affirmative and dynamic approach to life. Reason is put to work creatively seeking ways for achieving the controlling value as fully as possible and for manipulating all other goods in such a way as to promote this. The enthusiasm of a situationist is not dispersed and diverted among many ideals. The ideal he espouses is one with which he can identify himself wholly.

Thus situationist ethics is free of a difficulty we noticed in conventional natural-law theory, the lack of intrinsic link between morally significant action and the ultimate good. A situationist needs no ethical doctrine of sanctions because the moral ideal he espouses is an immanent one. This is so even if it is called the "leap of faith," for in such situationism we have a pseudo-supernaturalism which respects human freedom far more than it adores divine transcendence.[8]

Situationism also removes the problem of practical judgment. In making his moral judgment, a situationist need not be arbitrary. After all, he has an absolute, if sometimes vague, ideal which never may be violated. This absolute, being subjective itself, requires at least that a good act meet certain subjective criteria for moral goodness.

The stress of situationists on such criteria often gives their theories the appearance of being concerned only with good intentions, but the situationists' exclusive stress on actual consequences when it comes to external action seems in a way to balance this subjectivism.

When such outward behavior is concerned, a situationist can recognize legal restraints. Apart from legal restraints, however, he will admit no unexceptionable principles. He will be able to appeal from any maxim to his own higher principle and to enlarge the context of any behavior to allow other considerations to enter in. He sometimes refers to this technique as the replacement of an action previously considered too abstractly into its concrete context.

It is this convenient device that leads to the peculiarity we started from in our description of situationism — one never can say for certain that any given pattern of external behavior is evil. Situationists, of course, need not reject general ethical principles. They need only require that, so far as external acts are concerned, the indications of every principle must always be open to modification by the final practical judgment. This judgment has been attributed by various situationists to intuition, choice, guesswork, conscience, experience, and divine inspiration.

Situationist theories are open to two very serious objections.

First, the key value in any theory of this sort always is arbitrary. It represents, as its absoluteness and subjective status suggest, some formula for human self-deification. Of course, sometimes the idolatry is veiled under confusions between man's natural subjectivity and supernatural spirituality, as is the case in the pseudo-religious humanism I mentioned in the Introduction.

The falsity of such spirituality is evident the moment that love is used as a justification for submerging a bodily good such as procreation. Truly supernatural spirituality, never confusing the transcendence of subjectivity over matter with that of God over creatures, always recognizes that among finite goods even the humblest reflects divine perfection in its own unique way and so has a certain absolute character.

The arbitrariness of their key values allows ethical theories of the situationist kind to be systems in a sense in which sounder ethics never can be systematic. "Autonomy," "authenticity," or "mutual love" define a particular ethics in a way that "virtue," "nature," or "reason" do not. Moreover situationism, unlike the humanism of the ancient philosophers, has a personal character. As a perversion of Christianity, situationism retains the Christian insight that the absolute is a complete personality.

Another criticism of situationism is that it makes excessive demands on man's ability to know. First one must be able to know an absolute principle as elusive as a situationist's key value. Then he must derive a moral judgment from this theoretical principle. Further he must be able to know whatever the peculiarity of this key value requires.

Hedonists, who follow classical utilitarianism, for example, should know what will bring about the greatest happiness for the greatest number. Proponents of mutual love should know what really will promote it. Because the morality of outward behavior depends on results, a situationist ideally needs a perfect knowledge of nature to reach any definite judgment about a proposed external act.[9] Since this demand is too great for him he settles for some method of judgment that is more or less straightforwardly irrational.

When these peculiarities of situationism are considered in relation to a practice such as contraception there is no reason for surprise that contraception almost always is generally approved by situationists and always is considered unobjectionable at least in difficult cases. If his own principles were against contraception in a concrete case, a situationist would have difficulty knowing it.

As for the general question, procreation as such is only a bodily good. Therefore, for situationists it could not be an ideal. Hence it can be attained sufficiently and then the competition of other material goods will neutralize its *prima facie* claim to consideration. At this point it becomes a positive disvalue, and it is to be treated like a disease. And, of course, if a situationist's key value happens to be mutual love, then a neutralized procreative good which might interfere with sex for sentiment's sake is not worth a good second thought.

I wish to state here very emphatically that not all those who are defending the possible morality of contraception in difficult cases want to be overt situationists. But we are faced with a slight infection of which the victims themselves probably are not even aware. The infection can be contracted easily because it so completely pervades the contemporary, "post-Christian," intellectual atmosphere.

Moreover, as Catholics begin to think about moral theory, they naturally become dissatisfied with conventional natural-law theory and it is not surprising that they should become susceptible to certain well masked types of situationism. As we have seen, the two sorts of theory of moral law have certain common features. Both proceed illogically from facts to obligations. Both are voluntaristic, with natural-law theory involving the divine will while situationist theories depend on human freedom for their arbitrary starting points.

More subtly, neither type of theory considers material goods to be intrinsically related to the ultimate good of man, though they have quite different reasons for this. Situationism views material goods as necessary conditions, at best, of the true, subjective, human values. That is why it permits their violation. Conventional natural-law theory considers the whole of life a test which must be passed only in order to get an extrinsic reward. That is why it is satisfied to remain negative.

Rather than dallying any longer over the conflict between situationism and conventional natural-law theory — the one favoring contraception and the other rejecting it in a prohibition which it cannot explain — let us now move out from conventional natural-law theory and, without stopping at the halfway house of situationism, enter into a sounder shelter for our moral judgments.

This more adequate theory of moral law is to be found in the later works of Thomas Aquinas.[10] However, I do not wish to present my sketch as a historical study nor do I commend this theory because it happens to be that of a much commended author. Rather, I present the theory for consideration on its own rational merits, confident it can meet that test.

The most characteristic feature of this theory of moral law is its notion of practical reason. Reason does not become practical merely by its subject matter, nor by being moved by will or inclination. Rather reason is practical by nature just as really as it is theoretical by nature. And just as theoretical thought is by its very nature is-thinking, so practical thought is by its very nature ought-thinking.[11]

In this characterization we must notice that "ought" does not refer exclusively to legal duty or to strict obligation. Practical reason controls the entire domain of free action, not by directing or censoring it from without, but by creating its structure from within.[12] Obligation-thinking occurs in extreme cases of moral judgment, the case in which there happens to be only one good way of acting or the case in which we are interested in determining the least good way of acting that is open to us.

Hence practical reason must consider what is to be pursued

and done whether that "is to be" refers to the minimum good of strict obligation or to the more adequate good which usually is possible and always is well to do. Obligation and counsel do not differ from one another as if the one *really* is to be done and the other not. Instead they are merely different modes in which the prescriptive force of practical reason is expressed.

Once we have grasped these points we will not be surprised to discover that according to our theory the circle of free acts and that of morally significant acts are one and the same. Every deliberate act must be either good or evil. The reason is that deliberation is the work of practical reason — which can think only in modes of is-to-be — and that the degree of our control over deliberation is precisely the degree of our freedom.[13]

Unlike conventional natural-law theory, our theory is not compelled to reserve an enclave for freedom. The moral norm of practical reason need not treat freedom as something alien, because this moral norm works from within and respects the special conditions required by its place of work. It does not try to impose imperatives formed outside and based on merely formal aspects of reality.

Yet practical reason proceeds from principles. These principles are neither theoretical truths, nor facts of nature, nor are they imperatives whose rational force depends on an assumption laid down by authority. Instead they are fundamental prescriptions — basic formulations in the mode is-to-be — which practical reason itself forms for its own starting point.[14] Because the principles of practical reason are its own, it need not try to derive them by any illicit inference from facts nor need it accept them from any extrarational decree of will.

Just what are these principles of practical reason and how does practical reason form them?

To begin with, since practical reason shapes action from within, it must require the minimum conditions without which action is not possible at all. The least condition for human action is that it have some intelligible object toward which it can be directed. One cannot act deliberately without orientation; one cannot commit himself to action without some sense of what the action is to achieve.

The objective need not be a definite goal. A man can give his all for love, but even then he must have some sense of what his action means precisely in terms of its attainment of the ideal of love. The objective which practical reason requires, therefore, need only be some form of intelligible good.

Consequently, the first prescription of practical reason is that good should be pursued and that actions appropriate in that pursuit should be done, and also that actions which are not helpful in pursuit of the good or which interfere with it should be avoided.[15]

Of itself, this general norm excludes no value accessible to man. The general norm of practical reason is completely liberal and altogether open to every value that can give direction to action under the auspices of intelligence. All ethical theories take this general norm for granted. It does not conflict with any of the goods in which they may specialize.

In fact, so liberal is the general norm of practical reason that no human action can violate it directly. Only insofar as some actions violate subordinate principles are they in an indirect way opposed to its sense. Thus the *good* referred to in the general norm is not only moral goodness, the immanent perfection of human actions as such. Rather it is every good that man can attain by using his wits and his freedom.

We must be absolutely clear that this general norm of practical reason and the other basic prescriptions we shall consider shortly are not in any sense imperatives received from without. They express the necessities which reason must determine for itself if intelligent action is to be possible. Good is to be done not because God wills it, but because one must do something good if he is to act intelligently at all.[16]

Of course, metaphysics can show that the human mind has been created, and that its practical reason and the primary principles it necessarily forms are a participation in divine intelligence. God has made man able to govern his own life by his own intelligence just as God by His wisdom governs the universe as a whole.[17]

This first principle is perfectly acceptable, a reader might think, but toward what definite goods can practical reason direct human action? The first principle by itself obviously provides no direction and tells us nothing about what to do.

This question is hopelessly muddled at the outset if one tries to draw up a list of approved goods while rejecting others as unworthy of human concern. Just that sort of arbitrary selection has led to all the ethical systems which fill a philosopher's library, some of which we referred to while discussing situationism.

The proper way to understand the question rather is this. What in fact are all the goods which man can seek? What goods define the totality of human opportunity? What are all the goods which offer possibilities to human effort?

This question must be answered in such a way that no arbitrary exclusions narrow the gamut of human possibilities, precisely because it belongs to man to be open to indefinite development and to determine the course of this development by his own intelligence and freedom. The basic principles of practical reason make this openness possible, hence they cannot also restrict it.

The answer to the question, therefore, is to be found only by examining all of man's basic tendencies.[18] These prefigure everything man can achieve. It is impossible to act for anything without having an interest in it and it is impossible to become attracted to anything, and so to develop an interest in it, except to the extent that it falls within the scope of some inclination already present within oneself.

The task of discovering all of man's basic inclinations may seem impossible of fulfillment. Indeed it is not easy, but it is by no means as difficult as the theoretical confusion in ethics might lead one to suppose.

Since we are interested in the primary principles of practical reason, our question about the natural inclinations can be viewed in two distinct ways. One is the way of theoretical reflection in which we are now engaged. The other is the way of practical insight itself.

Let us first consider the theoretical question. What are all the inclinations with which man is endowed prior to acculturation or any choice of his own?

This question requires and can be settled only by empirical inquiry. Fortunately, psychologists, despite their theoretical disagreements, have come to a remarkable consensus that human motivation presupposes a number of basic inclinations.[19]

Although these inclinations are classified and named in different ways by different authors, they tend to form a list which can be summarized as follows. Man's fundamental inclinations are: the tendency to preserve life, especially by food-seeking and by self-defensive behavior; the tendency to mate and to raise his children; the tendency to seek certain experiences which are enjoyed for their own sake; the tendency to develop skills and to exercise them in play and the fine arts; the tendency to explore and to question; the tendency to seek out the company of other men and to try to gain their approval; the tendency to try to establish good relationships with unknown higher powers; and the tendency to use intelligence in guiding action.

Anthropological investigation only confirms what psychology states. In fact, these basic motives are the topics according to which anthropological investigations commonly are conducted. This is so precisely because these motives are the principles which collectively define whatever human life might be.[20]

The basic human inclinations, of whose existence and place theoretical reflection thus assures us, become the source of the primary principles of practical reason not by theoretical reflection but by practical insight. The act of practical insight itself cannot be performed discursively or communicated linguistically. However, we can reflect upon that act in an attempt to understand the precise relationship between the basic inclinations and the principles of practical reason.

The inclinations, simply as psychic facts, are not themselves principles of practical reason. Although these are facts which might *move* us to action whether we reason or not, they are of themselves no more *reasons* for action than any other facts. It is very important that we be careful here not to commit the usual error of proceeding from a preferred set of facts to an illicit conclusion that those facts imply obligation.

If, however, we do not suppose that the inclinations themselves are the principles we are seeking, what role do they play in the formation of the primary principles of practical reason? Their role in the formation of the principles is this, that our understanding grasps in the inclinations the possibilities to which they point. Since understanding is determined by the general norm which we discussed previously to direct action in pursuit of the good, intelligence prescribes every one of these objects of natural inclination.

Thus we form, naturally and without reflection, the basic principles of practical reasoning. An example is the rational principle of self-preservation. Life is a good whose requirements are to be served; actions which promote it should be done; what is opposed to it should be avoided.

All of these basic principles are affirmative. Each of them prescribes that one of the goods indicated by one of our basic inclinations is to be accepted as a guide for our action.

In thus deriving practical principles from given inclinations, our practical intelligence is operating neither rationally nor irrationally. It simply is working intelligently — that is, intuitively — using experience as a point of departure for forming its own fundamental insight. The principles are practical intelligence's interpretation of experience.[21]

The principles go beyond experience in a certain way. Indeed, interpretation always goes beyond its data. But because these are practical interpretations of human sources of motivation, the way in which they go beyond the inclinations is precisely by becoming principles of practical reason rather than by becoming mere facts about the given inclinations.

It is because they go beyond experience that these basic principles have the mode of ought-thinking even though they depend upon the given content of experience. The principles of practical reason cannot be mere forces moving one to act. They must be reasons for acting. "Is-to-be" in their statement marks the work of practical reason. Just as being is intelligible objectivity, oughtness is intelligible motivation.

It is also because the principles go beyond experience that every one of the goods prescribed in one of them takes on an intelligible form and characteristics. The felt need for food refers only to oneself and only to the concrete food one requires to satisfy hunger. But food as an object — rather, as something included in the object — of a primary practical principle is grasped as an ideal.

The food which is to be obtained and eaten is a *human* good, not merely *my* good. Hence the principle concerns every man's food and eating as well as my own. It concerns the food for unborn generations which is worrying the demographers. It concerns the food to which a good chef devotes his career. It concerns the food a glutton loves too well.

This last point is interesting, because although the glutton behaves in a repulsive fashion, his very behavior reveals most clearly what status food has as a principle of human action. It is not merely a definite good sufficiently cared for in the most efficient way by limited means. Food shows itself to be an ideal by the very fact that when a person commits himself exclusively to it he can build his whole life around it.

But how do these primary practical principles actually establish definite obligations? Do they not underlie everything that we might do, no matter what? Certainly, they seem to open the doors too liberally, for they begin from every possible basic human good and they endorse every one of these goods indiscriminately. Or perhaps it is better to say that the effect of practical reason interpreting experience in such a way as to form all of these primary affirmative principles is to invent the possibility of all human goods.

However that may be, the endorsement does seem indiscriminate, since every act ever performed for any reason at all, including every immoral act, had a good reason in these primary practical principles. If there were no good reason, an act never could be performed deliberately. Then it would not be a human act and there could be nothing moral about it. In fact, we can diagnose insanity by observing that a person's action has no intelligible reference to any basic human good at all.

The problem cannot be solved by suggesting that we restrict ourselves to natural goods. All of these basic goods are equally natural and whatever we derive from them is equally a product of our ingenuity. That is why the categories of anthropology always are being filled with diverse concrete content.[22]

Neither can the problem be solved by appealing to the general norm, because that only requires us to act for an intelligible good, and all of these principles qualify. In each of the primary principles of practical reason the general norm is present in a diverse special mode. Hence the general norm does not commend any one of the essential goods more than another to us, although it does commend each of them in a peculiarly different way, since "good" is predicated analogously of all the basic human goods.

At this point situationist theories arbitrarily prefer some of these goods to others. Some of the basic goods, we notice, are *substantive* values which can be achieved in definite material embodiments — human life and health, procreation, and certain others. Another group of the basic goods are what we might call "reflexive" values. These are specifically human and are specified by some aspect of man's subjectivity itself. These include human association, the use of reason to direct action, and others. The situationist subordinates material goods to some reflexive value despite the fact that practical reason depends equally on both.

This preference at least can appear reasonable. After all, that is how one would choose if he were in a position to make a choice, since the reflexive values considered in themselves must in some way be superior to the material ones. However, the situationist is not arbitrary only in this respect. He also arbitrarily prefers one reflexive value to all others and treats his preferred value alone as an ideal.

Even such nonmaterial but substantive values as truth, which is the object of the basic inclination we call "wonder," are regarded by a situationist as mere conditions for his ideal, because truth transcends the human and makes objective demands which could conflict with situationist subjectivism.[23]

It might seem, then, as if there is no way to derive any definite obligations from our series of primary principles. There they stand, opening the way to all human possibilities. But they do not tell us what to do. The solution to our perplexity will be at hand when we stop looking to these principles for a set of directions. They simply are not a crowd of guides able to tell us the best way to do life in one day.

The primary principles of practical reason determine action from within by shaping our experience into categories relevant to human interests, by making it possible for us to recognize that we have problems, and by stimulating us to reach intelligent solutions to our problems. They have their effect only by serving as points of departure for the development of interests, interests which lead to choices.

That is all very well, a critic might complain, but why call such a liberal set of principles a moral law? These principles are at the origin of all human actions and there is no rational way to mediate between them or to establish operational priorities among them. Even if they provide some vague positive direction, how do they exclude any moral evil?

In one sense, of course, the primary principles of practical reason do not exclude evil, since one or another of them always is available as a good reason for whatever a man deliberately does. But why should we want exclusion? Is it not enough that man be what he can be?

Certainly it is enough, and the principles demand only that the human possibilities they establish should be maintained.

All they ask of us is that we make no arbitrary selection among them, for that would be to spurn something of human value. Of course, this mild and reasonable demand itself is a certain exclusion. It means that in all of our practical reasoning each of the primary principles must be maintained and allowed to exercise its influence.

From freedom, to which the primary principles of practical reason contribute the possibility of meaningfulness, they require only a decent respect. In the will, where the principles also work, each of them demands respect from its co-workers and from the will itself. None of them is servile, and every one of them requires that its peculiar contribution to human goodness be respected.[24]

What the basic principles of practical reason exclude, in other words, is any action *against* one undertaken in order *to* *maximize* another. No one of these values is absolute, but none of them is so relative that it does not resist submergence.[25]

If he wishes man can choose one value over against the others. He always has the value he chooses as a sufficient reason for doing so, yet such choices are made at the expense of rationality, because the prescription which is degraded also is primary, underived, self-evident. It has equally valid claims upon our interest, because it has precisely the claims it gets by being represented in a primary principle.

We shall explain in greater detail in the next chapter the various ways in which basic affirmative principles of practical reason cause definite obligations. For the present, however, it is enough to grasp in general the way in which this is possible. Whenever it happens that an attitude of nonarbitrariness toward the basic human goods requires us to have a certain intention, and that intention requires a certain action or omission, then we have a definite obligation.

The point will be clearer, perhaps, if it is approached negatively. We violate a definite obligation whenever our action is not in accordance with the kind of intention that we must maintain if our intention is not to imply an irrational preference of one value over others. The insane man's action has little or no intelligible relationship to any of the essential human goods. The immoral man's action has an intelligible relationship to some of the goods but not to others. The virtuous man's action has an intelligible relationship to all of the goods.

Act in accord with reason expresses the meaning of virtue just to the extent that it tells us to hold fast to all the primary principles of practical intelligence, which we spontaneously form as the origin for all our rational deliberation.[26]

The theory of moral law which we have been considering has very definite advantages over situationism.

Our theory explains what situationist theories assume — namely, how practical reasoning begins. There is no need to invoke will at the beginning or at the end of a sound ethical theory. Only unsound ones must find a way of making facts, which are not intelligible motives, play a role in grounding obligations that they cannot really fulfill.[27]

Our theory also has an advantage over situationism in being able to provide a starting point from which really significant guidance for life can be derived. The situationist's key value becomes contentless and meaningless because situationism separates a reflexive value from substantive goods, completely subordinating the latter, especially if they are material.

Our theory keeps all of these primary values in the first rank of practical principles. Hence substantive values give definite meaning to reflexive ones, material values give psychological force to spiritual ones, and reflexive values give status as ideals to substantive ones by including them as co-aspects in the immanent perfection of human life.

Finally, our theory, unlike situationism, does not make impossible demands on man's ability to know.[28] For the goodness of action, even action affecting material values, it is enough that our intentions and choices be good; actual results are not demanded by the ideals.

Of course, this does not mean that one can disregard the facts which he can and should consider nor that action is justified by partially good intentions. If all the intentions underlying an action are sound, that can be only because the agent is guided by love of all the essential human goods.

It is obvious also that our theory of moral law is superior to conventional natural-law theory.[29] The point that our theory explains the origin of ought-thinking has been stressed sufficiently. Our theory also eliminates legalism from the notion of obligation, although legal obligations and imperatives have a place insofar as they express in certain domains the requirements of essential human goods.[30]

The negative emphasis of conventional natural-law theory also is eliminated. We begin with a series of primary principles all of which are affirmative. Our method of excluding moral evil is not basic but derivative — the exclusion of irrational preference among *essential human goods* all of which hold a primary place in the proceedings of practical reason.

But what kind of account can our theory give of the end of man? How are the essential human goods to be related to it? Will the relationship be closer than the sanction of conventional natural-law theory? The answer to this question is too complex to permit adequate treatment here.[31] However, a sketch is possible.

None of the goods to which the basic principles of practical reason direct us is sufficient to satisfy man's potentiality for goodness as such. Precisely for this reason man can disregard the prescriptions of reason and, as it were, gamble his existence on an identification of one of the goods with goodness itself. What reason requires is that all of the goods be maintained in their irreducible but not absolute positions.

In fact, it is only possible for man to love all of the goods properly if he considers each of them a participant in perfect goodness. Only in this way can he keep all of them separate from perfect goodness but irreducible to any other particular value, for only in this way will he see that each good uniquely represents the perfect good itself without ever encompassing its absolute goodness.

This complex orientation and delicate balance could provide man with a basis for establishing orderly direction in his life. Although the unity would not be monistic and although the actual achievement of goods could not be definitive, a man's love of all proportionate human goods as participations in pure goodness could guide him toward an existence both full and open.

The end of man, according to this theory, would be to achieve, insofar as possible, the goods accessible to man, and to maintain permanent openness for an even greater achievement. To this end moral action is naturally proportionate, simply because that action is morally good which is as proportioned to this end as human wits and freedom can manage.

Thus far philosophy. If the teaching of the Christian faith be considered, a further complexity is introduced. Faith teaches that the immanent value of human goods, insofar as they are obtained by human actions, can be preserved and simultaneously infinitely transformed through divine loving-kindness. Human action and its naturally suitable objects thus become divine in their value.

The result is that the perfect Good which man must love if he is to love anything well becomes actually attainable not only in Its participations but even in Itself. In this way the openness of human nature is fulfilled without any restriction. But man's natural values also are completely respected, for the Good Itself is not opposed to any of Its participations.[32]

NOTES TO CHAPTER III

1. A full and accessible presentation of the conventional theory is: Thomas J. Higgins, S.J., *Man as Man: The Science and Art of Ethics*, rev. ed. (Milwaukee: The Bruce Publishing Co., 1958), 14–146. Higgins' extensive bibliographies are a good introduction to conventional natural-law literature. The chief source is: Francisco Suarez, S.J., *De legibus ac Deo legislatore;* the most relevant passages are in: Suarez, *Selections from Three Works,* J. B. Scott, ed., *The Classics of International Law,* no. 20 (Oxford: The Clarendon Press, 1944). A good historical study of natural law which clearly divides scholastic theories from others, although synthesizing Suarezian and Thomistic theories, is: Heinrich A. Rommen, *The Natural Law: A Study in Legal and Social History and Philosophy* (St. Louis: B. Herder Book Co., 1947).

2. Casuistry of the type required by conventional natural-law theory leads to

probabilism; the latter, and its alternatives, have been criticized severely from a Thomistic point of view by: Thomas Deman, O.P., "Probabilisme," *Dictionnaire de Théologie Catholique*, 13 (Paris: Librarie Letauzey et Ané, 1936), 417–619.

3. Kai Nielsen, "An Examination of the Thomistic Theory of Natural Moral Law," *Natural Law Forum*, 4 (1959), 63–68, offers a criticism along these lines against what he mistakenly considers to be Thomistic theory; interestingly, Nielsen himself makes the error of thinking that the *fact* of decision can establish *ought*.

4. Here we see the theoretical source of legalism; attempts to escape without finding a basically different theory of obligation always lead to confusion. See, e.g.: Gilleman, *The Primacy of Charity in Moral Theology* (Westminster, Md.: The Newman Press, 1961), 253–279; Ignatius T. Eschmann, O.P., "St. Thomas's Approach to Moral Philosophy," *Proceedings of the American Catholic Philosophical Association*, 31 (1957), 25–33.

5. Ford and Kelly, *Contemporary Moral Theology*, Vol. 2, *Marriage Questions* (Westminster, Md.: The Newman Press, 1963), 389–392, indicate how little grasp there was of this point prior to 1951.

6. Ford and Kelly, *op. cit.*, Vol. 1, *Questions in Fundamental Moral Theology* (Westminster, Md.: The Newman Press, 1958), 104–140, provide an introduction to the movement called "situation-ethics," which is one mode of the general trend which I call "situationism." This trend is common to almost all post-Hegelian, secular ethics which is not deontological in character. As soon as those lacking a concept of a genuinely transcendent absolute — God, as opposed to the Hegelian spirit — seek a good and an end — not merely obligation, as in Kant — they inevitably find it in man himself. Since one thing in man's complex nature must be absolutized, because many absolutes are impossible, they always hit upon some subjective value, usually one which could be called "reflexive" — i.e., specifically rational and specified by something in man himself. There is no adequate general study of this state of affairs; the nearest approach to it is: Jacques Maritain, *Moral Philosophy* (New York: Charles Scribner's Sons, 1964), 119–447. This study includes Hegel, Marxism, Compte, Kierkegaard, Sartre, Dewey, and Bergson, but it does not systematically elucidate their common features.

7. Dondeyne, *Contemporary European Thought and Christian Faith* (Pittsburgh, Pa.: Duquesne University; Louvain: E. Nauwelaerts, 1958), 182–189, distinguishes different domains of value, separating moral values from biological, cultural, and religious ones. Respect for life and death, and love of truth are included as moral values with love, liberty, and society — somewhat inconsistently from a logical point of view, but fortunately for ethics. His opening remark about moral values is most interesting: "It is not easy to define precisely what, from the phenomenological point of view, is the original character of moral conduct. One can, however, in a general way say that our conduct will be good or bad from a moral point of view according to the extent to which it has the character of being *a concrete and effective recognition of the dignity of the human person*, or, if you will, of the value of the person as a whole. Man is called a 'person' because he appears to himself as something for-itself, that is to say, as an end in itself existing for its own good. He is a kind of 'embodied liberty.'" Dondeyne may understand his statements in some orthodox fashion, or he may not be asserting them, but they express admirably the attitude of situationism, which looks for the good *within* man himself, and puts it in a reflexive value.

8. Louis K. Dupré, *Kierkegaard as Theologian: The Dialectic of Christian Existence* (New York: Sheed and Ward, 1963), 107–109, explains why the Danish precursor of much current, "Christian" existentialism could not accept predestination: because it excludes human freedom and "disregards the subjectivity which is the very source of religion."

9. G. E. Moore, *Principia Ethica* (Cambridge: C.U.P., 1960), 142–167, faces the problems of those who require actual effects as a criterion of the goodness of external action; Moore's treatment is marked by the honesty he brings to the situationist predicament.

10. Especially in: *Summa theologiae*, 1–2; particularly relevant: qq. 90–94. Gerald Vann, O.P., *Morals and Man*, rev. ed. (New York: Sheed and Ward, 1960), is a useful, popular introduction. Antonin Gilbert Sertillanges, O.P., *La philosophie morale de saint Thomas d'Aquin* (Paris: Aubier, 1942), is the most accurate scholarly introduction.

11. John E. Naus, *The Nature of the Practical Intellect according to St. Thomas Aquinas* (Roma: Liberia Editrice dell'Università Gregoriana, 1959), has provided a useful compilation of materials on Aquinas' theory of the practical intellect. Our present point is simply that there is, for Aquinas, an innate habit of practical first principles just as there is an innate habit of speculative first principles: *S.t.*, 1, q. 79, a. 12; 1–2, q. 10, a. 1; q. 94, a. 2.

12. The work of Gregory Stevens, O.S.B., should be consulted on Aquinas and obligation; see, e.g., "The Relations of Law and Obligation," *Proceedings of the American Catholic Philosophical Association*, 29 (1955), 195–205.

13. *De malo*, q. 2, aa. 5–6, provides the best explanation; from our present position we can see why late scholasticism so much debated this Thomistic thesis.

14. Sertillanges, *op. cit.*, 91–104. The notion simply is that of natural law as Aquinas understands it: *S.t.*, 1–2, q. 94, a. 2.

15. *Ibid.* The most helpful commentaries on this point are: J. B. Schuster, S.J., "Von den ethischen Prinzipien: Eine Thomasstudie zu S. Th., I–II, qu. 94, a. 2," *Zeitschrift für Katholische Theologie*, 57 (1933), 44–65; Michael V. Murray, S.J., *Problems of Ethics* (New York: Henry Holt and Co., Inc., 1960), 220–235.

16. D. O'Donoghue, "The Thomist Conception of Natural Law," *Irish Theological Quarterly*, 22 (April, 1955), 89–109.

17. *Ibid.*; this is the meaning of the formula, "natural law is the rational creature's participation in eternal law": *S.t.*, 1–2, q. 91, a. 2.

18. *S.t.*, 1–2, q. 94, a. 2, c.

19. Ernest R. Hilgard, *Introduction to Psychology*, 3 ed. (New York and Burlingame: Harcourt, Brace, and World, Inc., 1962), 124–146, is a typical, standard introduction. The psychologists emphasize physiology, and so they distinguish by material differences drives which are unified as intelligible motives; they do not distinguish object and subject very clearly when dealing with motivation, and so they tend to multiply motives in relation to the same object. Our list compensates for both of these factors.

20. Robert H. Lowie, *An Introduction to Cultural Anthropology*, new and enl. ed. (New York: Rinehart and Co., Inc., 1940), has typical chapter headings which match very well with our list of inclinations. Alexander MacBeath, *Experiments in Living: A Study of the Nature and Foundations of Ethics or Morals in the Light of Recent Work in Social Anthropology* (London: Macmillan, 1952), shows how basic human goods are protected in diverse ways in various cultures.

21. Peter Hoenen, S.J., *Reality and Judgment according to St. Thomas* (Chicago: Henry Regnery Co., 1952), has worked out from the texts Aquinas' theory of speculative principles, emphasizing (3-35) their derivation from experience. No one has undertaken the comparable task for practical principles, but what Hoenen says can be applied, *mutatis mutandis*. See also: O'Donoghue, *op. cit.*, 95-102.

22. See: MacBeath, *op. cit.*, *passim*.

23. Thus situationism belongs to philosophies which have no place for theory in the strict sense. The significance of flight from theory is discussed by: Josef Pieper, *Leisure, the Basis of Culture*, rev. ed. (New York: Pantheon Books, 1964), 73-76.

24. P.-M. van Overbeke, O.P., "La loi naturelle et le droit naturel selon saint Thomas," *Revue Thomiste*, 57 (1957), 53-78, 450-495, presents a remarkable exposition of the chief texts in which Aquinas states his theory of moral law. Overbeke shows with particular clarity (450-458) that the same principles which are expressed as prescriptions of natural law are primary orientations of natural volition and principles of the virtues.

25. I have dealt with the metaphysics of absolute and relative in a paper, "Sketch of a Future Metaphysics," *The New Scholasticism*, 38 (July, 1964), 335-340.

26. Odon Lottin, O.S.B., *Morale fondamentale* (Tournai, Belgium: Desclée & Co., 1954), 165-173, 114-128, shows clearly how Aquinas considers reason to be the moral norm — insofar as it is informed with the first principles, which are the ends.

27. The attempt of unsound ethical theories to accomplish the impossible has led to recent metaethical theorizing by British and American philosophers; much effort is devoted to showing how unsound theories fail to accomplish what their authors supposed they were achieving. For a good critique which still misses the truth in its positive effort, see: Philip Blair Rice, *On the Knowledge of Good and Evil* (New York: Random House, 1955).

28. I have discussed the problem of moral judgment in: "The Logic of Moral Judgment," *Proceedings of the American Catholic Philosophical Association*, 36 (1962), 67-76.

29. The most complete and adequate comparison between Thomistic and Suarezian natural-law theory is: Walter Farrell, O.P., *The Natural Moral Law according to St. Thomas and Suarez* (Ditchling: St. Dominic's Press, 1930), 103-155. O'Donoghue, *loc. cit.*, also helps to clarify the difference between Thomistic and conventional theories.

30. See: Eschmann, *loc. cit.*

31. The following can be consulted: Walter Farrell, O.P., and Mortimer J. Adler, "The Theory of Democracy, Part III, The End of the State: Happiness," *The Thomist*, 4 (April, 1942), 286-308; Venant Cauchy, *Désir naturel et béatitude chez saint Thomas* (Montréal, Paris: Fides, 1958), 85-115; Jacques Maritain, *Neuf leçons sur les notions premières de la philosophie morale* (Paris: Pierre Tequi, 1951), 96-101.

32. It is well known that the Thomistic theory of analogy "makes room for" God and creatures in being; the ontological counterpart of logical analogy is the Thomistic doctrine of participation. See: Louis B. Geiger, O.P., *La participation dans la philosophie de S. Thomas d'Aquin* (Paris: Librarie J. Vrin, 1942), 31-33. See Aquinas: *De malo*, q. 5, a. 4, ad 1, where he explains that creatures do not add to divine being — it follows, of course, that the two cannot be at odds.

IV

WHY CONTRACEPTION IS IMMORAL

ACCORDING to the theory of moral law which I outlined in the previous chapter, there is a fundamental affirmative precept of moral law corresponding to each of man's basic natural inclinations. All of these precepts together provide the foundation for all practical reasoning. These precepts make the demand never to be violated directly by the will. Of course, man can choose to act against them, but he does so at the price of sacrificing part of the very source of the rationality of his free action.

To show that contraception is intrinsically immoral, therefore, we need only show it to be a direct violation of one of the basic principles. The proof of this point and the treatment of points directly related to it will be the work of this chapter. The proof itself has two parts. We first must see what basic moral principle is violated by the practice of contraception; then we must see how contraception violates this principle.

The principle violated by contraception is that procreation is a human good worthy of man's pursuit, and that human acts suited to achieve this good should be done. This is a basic moral principle. It is one of the primary sources of all human practical reasoning. It obligates all men and holds true at all times.

Of course, someone may object that it is no easy task to determine with precision what man's basic natural inclinations are. Is it not possible that the enjoyment of sexual pleasure for its own sake is natural? Is it not true that man has a natural inclination to seek more than his share? Moreover, have not many individuals or particular groups peculiar inclinations which they consider to be natural?

The answer to such objections is that it is indeed difficult to exclude candidates for the list of natural inclinations. Moreover, it is quite possible that some individuals may have abnormal inclinations which seem to them as basic and natural as any others, and that in some whole cultures certain practices may be so well entrenched that they seem natural to those within the group at least until they encounter other customs.[1]

Moreover, there is a sense in which we must call "natural" inclinations which we would want, all things considered, to exclude from the list of inclinations whose objects establish primary principles of practical reason. The inclination to want more than one's share is an example of this kind.

This last tendency is a normal incident to development; it operates just to the extent that rational control of behavior is not dominant and that the controls at the level of experience and emotion have not yet matured.[2] Thus we find it a normal attitude in infants, but it does not achieve the status of a principle of practical reason and eventually it yields its place to other principles as maturation proceeds. The proof is that even a selfish individual never attempts simply to argue, as he would if it were at all reasonable to do so, that he *deserves* more than his share.

A similar analysis may be made of the appetite for sexual pleasure as an end in itself. There does exist an instinctive demand for sense satisfaction, but practical intelligence perceives the action to which pleasure is attached as well as the feeling itself, and so it directs our efforts toward some end more meaningful than a mere detached state of consciousness.[3]

Our problem, however, is not to show what does not belong

to the basic principles of moral law, nor is it to show everything that does belong to them. It is merely to show that one such principle has the procreative good as its object.

The only difficulty we shall have if we try to prove this point is the difficulty that is inherent in dealing with the obvious. Nevertheless, there are at least three considerations that can be brought to bear on it.

The first is the fact that having children and raising them is practically a universal phenomenon.[4] Few normal people fail to marry, and few married couples who are not sterile fail to have children. And for all who do marry and have children, this dimension of life clearly is a basic and central concern.

One of the last reasons the ordinary man has for doing everything he does is to take care of the family, for the needs of the children. For many in our own society and probably for most people throughout the world and throughout history, this part of life is the chief substantive concern. Man is born, he grows, he marries, he has children and brings them up, and then he grows old and dies. One might only add that he plays a little in between times.

Someone may object that this very description indicates that procreation itself is not a fundamental human good; the basic good really is the persons who are born and raised. In one respect this objection is merely sophistic. The good which is an object of the parent's effort is strictly speaking only what the parent can attain — not the child in his totality as a person but rather the child only insofar as his being and perfection depend upon the action of his parents.

We easily become confused about this point because we assume that the relevant value is *what* is loved, and obviously the child as a whole is loved. However, persons are not among human goods as if they were values to be desired. Instead, they actualize and receive the human goods into personal existence. We love persons, including ourselves, when we will relevant values *to* the person, when we will that the person *have* the goods.[5]

Yet the objection does bring out this point, that the good in question is not procreation to the exclusion of the rearing of children. Both are joined in the object of inclination and in the object of the primary principle of practical reason with which we are concerned without any distinction being made between them.[6]

We distinguish the two clearly only because different actions are proportionate to initiating new life and to caring for the life of children once they are born. Procreation in the narrow sense is only part of the total procreative good, but it is normally an essential part and the first condition of the rest. Thus while man is inclined by the tendency in question to more than the life-giving act, he certainly is inclined by it at least to the good of procreation in the narrow sense.

The second consideration which shows that the procreative good is the object of a basic natural inclination is the fact that from a biological point of view the work of reproduction is the fullest organic realization of the living substance. Man is more than merely a living substance, of course, but still this plane of existence really does belong to him. Man is not complex in the sense that he is composed of several natures bonded together like the laminated layers of a plywood board, but still there are distinct planes of existence within his complex unity.

One of these is the organic system of nutrition, growth, and reproduction. This system is not isolated from the rest of man. Indeed, as psychosomatics shows, there are all manners of intimate relationships between it and the higher psychic and intellectual planes of man's being. Nevertheless, the organic system does have its own unity and distinctness. And for it all achievements center on reproduction. Reproduction is the act of maturity and full power. It is the act which uses the best resources of the organism. It is the act after the completion of which the life of many organisms is finished.[7]

To the extent that man truly is an organism rather than a pure spirit using a bodily medium of expression, the basic organic plane of his being inclines him to the attainment of its appropriate perfection in the good of procreation. One can explain many human interests and tendencies, but it is impossible to explain the fact that having children is practically universal except by observing that it is natural for man as an organism to reproduce.

But is the natural inclination really toward reproduction, or is it not in fact merely toward the delight of sexual functioning? Does not man seek sexual satisfaction instinctively, quite apart from any consideration of its results? This objection presupposes a faulty analysis of the mode in which even instinctive behavior is determined.[8] We remarked earlier that the notion that pleasure is an end in itself is a misinterpretation of the facts. But we shall not belabor this point.

Let us assume for the sake of argument that sexual satisfaction is a good in itself. The striking fact is that human beings do continue to reproduce and that there is no real necessity that they should do so in order to enjoy sexual satisfaction. Masturbation is always possible and is widely practiced, yet it is usually only a phase. Heterosexual experience with parenthood excluded is practically universal, for even the primitives know *coitus interruptus*, abortion, and infanticide.[9] Still people continue to have children. Even in our society with every modern means of contraception available the population continues to mount.

Someone may object that the facts can be explained by social sanctions, by moral and religious precepts and prohibitions. Quite true. But whence the social sanctions? They come about because prior to deliberation and so without the possibility of choice everyone naturally knows that procreation is a human good and that acts fit to attain it should be performed. Primitive codes as well as civilized law arise from the primary principles of practical reason.[10]

Still it may be objected that while reproduction is a human good on the biological plane, it ought not to be treated as an object of a fundamental law.[11] To this objection two replies are necessary.

In the first place, the object of the precept in question is not a merely biological good; it is the life of a human child. The inclination in question is integrally organic, psychic, and rational, and on all of these planes it exists prior to acculturation and self-determination.

It is true that the good of procreation in the narrow sense is primarily an object of organic inclination. However, organic inclination in man is human; it prefigures a good which man can attain by human action. And this good is not completely reducible to any other human good as an end.

A principle of practical reason therefore must exist to direct us toward this good. Otherwise, some possible human good would be omitted from the source of rationality in human action. This precept is just as rational and just as primary as any of the other basic precepts although the good which is its object is less exalted than some others, since mere human life is less exalted than the good life.

We cannot suppose that man's organic life is infrahuman. But may we not suppose that the life of the spirit by itself exhausts the goods to which man can attain? Is man not a spirit who attains perfection on the spiritual plane so great that it includes in an eminent mode all the perfection of organic existence? The answer is no, for the goods of organic life are not achieved by the spirit alone.

But unless we make one of these assumptions, we must consider the good of procreation as a determinant of a primary principle of practical reasoning. And all such principles are moral laws. They are, indeed, the basic moral laws from which all other moral laws take their origin.

But even if the prescription, *Procreation is a good which should be pursued*, is a basic moral principle, it hardly seems to carry sufficient force to exclude an action like contraception. Does not periodic continence also conflict with the principle just as effectively? Does not celibacy conflict with it even more? This principle is only an affirmative one, in any case, and we are accustomed to imagining that most affirmative principles do not oblige very strictly.

It is true that affirmative principles do not bind in the same way that negative ones do. Unfortunately, neither conventional natural-law ethics with its emphasis on prohibition nor situationism with its operationalist attitude toward substantive values has given much thought to the way in which affirmative principles, especially those concerned with material goods, do bind.

The first point to notice is that the principle in question does not bind one hypothetically and only up to a determinate point. As we explained in Chapter III, the objects of primary principles of practical reason always are ideals, not merely definite operational objectives. The good which is prefigured by the natural inclination toward reproductive action is grasped by reason simply as the good of procreation in itself. The good is not the number of children sufficient to bring the family up to size or to maintain the nation's population.

Nor is the procreative good even restricted to the children one can personally generate. The midwife and the obstetrician act for this good, and so does the friend who loans a honeymoon couple a cottage where they can get away for a few days to "make a baby." There are positive laws and institutions devoted to protecting the procreative good, and the present study is dedicated to defending it.

Perhaps this point will become clearer if we think about still another good which is the object of a primary principle of practical reason — truth. Truth is the object of curiosity and it defines the intellectual life. It has no proper name and is limited to no definite quantity. Yet this does not mean that truth, like the good of procreation, cannot mistakenly be reduced from the status of an ideal to that of an operational objective, a definite good to be attained once and for all by sufficient and limited means.

Philosophers seek truth but philosophers sometimes fall into dogmatism. This happens when they forget the difference between the truth which specifies the philosophic quest and the truth which is encompassed by their own particular philosophies.

The primary principle which enjoins that we seek the truth

does not specify its conditions and qualifications. The principles cannot be more definite than the inclinations in which the goods are prefigured. In a certain sense, in fact, the principles must be less definite, because the good has a status before reason only as an intelligible object, not as a felt need.

Another point follows upon this one. Affirmative principles of this kind are not to be understood as if they were positive imperatives issued by a superior. The basic moral principles indicate the goods which can be attained by human action, but they do not move us toward anything as would an act of our own will or of another's will.

Movement toward the good naturally does not originate from any command implicit in the primary principles of practical reason nor from any other external source. Rather, it originates from the natural responsiveness of human interest to the possibilities indicated by intelligence, on the basis of its comprehension of the objects of natural inclination.[12]

It follows that although these basic precepts bind everyone at all times they do not exact a merely legalistic conformity of precise performance. One cannot be acting always for all of the human goods. It is only essential, so far as action is concerned, that he be doing something toward one of them.

Since the good of procreation can be attained sufficiently for the human race to continue without every individual personally engaging in reproductive acts, there is no reason why someone who has a reason not to contribute toward this particular good should do so. Usually a sufficient reason exists if a particular individual can live a good life and achieve maturity without marrying and if he devotes himself more completely to the achievement of other goods.[13]

Yet if the goods do not require that we always be acting toward them, they do require that we never act against them with direct intent. To act directly against any of the basic human goods is to spurn one aspect of the total possibility of human perfection, and it is freely to set the will at odds with its own principle of interest in the goods open to us.

To clarify this point we must consider several ways in which the basic affirmative moral principles do bind us. Bear in mind that each of these primary principles of practical reason has as its object a distinct and irreducible essential human good.

In the first place, all of these goods bind us at least to this, that we take them into account. In our practical reasoning, we must have a permanent sensitivity to the essential goods to which primary principles direct. An attitude of simple disregard for any one of them reveals that we have set ourselves against it. Therefore, such an attitude is incompatible with our basic obligation to pursue and to act for it.

In the second place, every one of the goods demands of us that, when we can do so as easily as not, we avoid acting in ways which inhibit its realization and prefer ways of acting which contribute to its realization. This principle never can be applied legalistically, but nevertheless its use is quite common in practice in ordinary moral arguments.

"Why did you do that?" one man asks another. "You could just as well have . . ." and then follows a description which shows that some value was harmed or left unrealized gratuitously. One who does not promote the values when there is no significant consideration against doing so, not even the consideration that one already is busy or needs rest, obviously does not hold them as effective ideals.

In the third place, every one of the goods demands of us that we make an effort on its behalf when its significant realization in some person is in extreme peril. This obligation is conditioned by other obligations, it is true. Yet it frequently binds with great force.

When someone's life or knowledge of truth really is at stake in an important way, and when we are more capable of preserving it or contributing to it than anyone else, then if we fail without good excuse to do what we can, the value which is in peril is not really the object of any efficacious love of ours.

This type of obligation binds in degrees varying with the seriousness of the stake, the immediacy of the peril, and the opportunity we and others have for giving aid. When the peril is recurrent and serious the good does not fail to bind merely because someone else always is as able to help as we are ourselves. In such cases, we have an obligation, as the British say, "to do our bit."

In the fourth place, every one of the goods demands of us that we do not act directly against its realization. There are two ways in which this demand may be violated.

First, and most often, the direct sacrifice of one value seems to be urgently required by another. Thus truth is sacrificed for all sorts of reasons, murder is committed for love, and every value is subverted when fear for life prevails over rational judgment. These basic values, nevertheless, cannot be sacrificed directly if practical reason is to remain in charge of life. No good is so absolute that other basic goods can be submerged for it as if they were mere means or only necessary conditions.

Perhaps God could determine something better on the whole than what our best judgment dictates. Man lacks omniscience and has no standard beyond the first principles of his practical judgment to which he can make a rational appeal. Man simply does not know how to negate one or another value *directly* with better results on the whole and in the long run than can be achieved by holding to known principles. The reason is that man does not know "the whole" and "the long run."

Of course, it is almost impossible for man to act toward one good without in some way interfering with or inhibiting the realization of that good itself or of others. If such adverse results are unwanted but unavoidable by-products of action, then they may be permissively willed under certain conditions. This point will be discussed further in Chapter VI when we treat direct and indirect voluntariness.

There is another less ordinary way in which man directly violates one of his own basic values. This is to violate it simply for the sake of violating it, to violate it from sheer destructiveness.[14] It seems at first impossible that anyone ever should act in this way.

But such action becomes intelligible when we consider the predicament of one who has restricted himself arbitrarily to certain values and who regularly has violated others. His intelligence is permanently at odds with itself, and the evidence of obvious human goods constantly accuses him of his irrationality.

What is a person in this predicament to do but to try to forget the evidence, to deny its existence, finally to deny the validity of the values he no longer wishes to admit? Eventually, this final denial leads to the desperate measure of negation in action. Then the absurdity of freedom rejecting its own source is consummated in the absurdity of sheerly malicious action directly aimed at destroying an essential human good.

Still another, the fifth, way in which the values establish obligations is that each one of them demands of us that we keep our engagements with it. We do not have a general obligation to seek out opportunities for promoting every one of the goods. But we should pursue something good, and each person according to his individual aptitude must choose the values he will try to promote. Once this choice has been made, an investment of effort will be made which will exclude possibilities of other accomplishments. Positive sacrifices will be made too.

At the end of this process of self-limitation is a social role, a personalized share of mankind's common obligation to attain all the values accessible to human abilities. One who has such a role by that very fact has a special obligation toward the value which defines it. Having embarked upon a certain limitation of life with the intention of its appropriate basic human good as one's justification, one cannot really intend that good without accepting it sometimes as an effective and real motive of positive action.

By this principle are condemned the scholar who never pursues truth, the public official who makes no effort to improve human community, and the married couple who prefer permanent sterility to fruitfulness. In other words, the good of procreation does establish a definite obligation, and it is one which falls on persons who enter the married state.[15] This obligation is the reason why even periodic continence requires a justification, and why generous fruitfulness is a real moral norm. But since this obligation allows limitation, and is subject to many conditions, it is not this one which excludes contraception.

Before we clarify the precise obligation which does exclude the practice of contraception, let us notice our present position. We have found that affirmative precepts do have many powerful implications even though they bind in a reasonable manner and fit themselves to the peculiarities of each situation. Obligation appears only when, of all the possibilities before us, one is the *least we can do* consistent with a constant, positive love of each of the essential human goods.

This point deserves emphasis. The final control of rationality on choice is not our knowledge of the status of problems, possibilities, and results in the world beyond human action. The objective situation only provides data which moral judgment must take into account. This is the reason why therapeutic abortion, for example, and many other acts which situationist theories allow, cannot be justified even when there is nothing to be gained and much possibly to be lost by refusing to sanction them.

The final control on the rationality of choice is the entire set of essential human goods in their status as ideals. They exercise their control by way of the principles of practical reasoning which also shape the will's basic ability to be interested.[16]

For the sake of self-consistency, then, choice must include intentions consistent with its own fundamental orientation. Hence the place at which moral principles become immediately effective is in the will itself, whose every deliberate act necessarily is either a man-made absurdity or a living expression of the possibility of meaningful freedom. The latter possibility in nowise contravenes, rather it fully meets, the will's own inherent willingness toward human goods. Freedom for absurdity is valuable only because it is identical in fact with freedom for human perfection.

By this point we can see also that the obligating force of affirmative principles increases as we move toward realization. Everyone must take into account the good of procreation. Married persons sometimes must act for it unless they have good reasons for not doing so. If this good were imperiled — for example, by a sterility-causing disease — a physician especially would be bound to protect it if he could do so.

Now we are ready to consider the rather common type of case in which a person places himself directly in the focus of an affirmative principle and so brings upon himself the full force of its absolute demand.

A scholar has a general obligation to seek that truth for whose pursuit his special training has made him competent. He may select the specific areas of his inquiries. It is not wrong for him to allow personal and other nonscholarly considerations to influence this choice. But once he has undertaken a certain line of investigation, he has a new and intensified obligation toward the truth, which is now *by his own choice* more proximate to realization. Still, if he has good reasons he may discontinue his studies. But what he may never do is to carry on his work all the way to the point of publication while concealing the very truth which he has undertaken by his very profession to reveal.[17]

A scholar need not publish everything he thinks, but he must not allow any ulterior consideration to lead him to suppress the truth. To do that would be to abandon his commitment to truth, a commitment which he accepted as an absolutely compelling obligation when he made the final choice to act in a way that would of itself bring the truth to light. Once this choice has been made, it is the duty of the scholar to let the truth be known — the chips fall where they may.

I am sure it was only consciousness of this obligation which led some to publish their mistaken views on the morality of contraception. I respect their professional character as much as I regret their theoretical errors.

Consider another example. A physician has the care of a terminal cancer case. No matter what happens, the patient soon will be dead. Although the physician may not do anything to cause death, he need not employ every available means to keep the patient alive as long as possible. Neither common sense, nor professional ethics, nor any moral theory that I know of would require that. On the other hand, the physician must give ordinary competent care; his enagagement in the case requires this much.

Now let us suppose that the physician *by his own choice further engages himself* by undertaking some extraordinary measures in the way of treatment. He may do this for his own purposes. Let us say he undertakes heroic measures not for his own financial advantage, but because he wishes to learn the precise results which can be achieved. Let us imagine that he tries a new coagulant to see how it will affect the massive internal hemorrhaging from which the patient is rapidly and peacefully dying. And let us imagine that this measure is successful, so successful that the patient revives and his death agony is being prolonged indefinitely.

Can the physician now *intervene* by administering an antidote in order to prevent *his own previous* act from continuing to have its now undesired life-giving effect.[18] The answer clearly is negative, for although the physician had no obligation to administer the coagulant to begin with, once this treatment has been undertaken its benefit to the patient also must be permitted.

This is true despite the fact that the physician already has learned what he set out to discover by his experiment. It is true despite the fact that the patient may not desire the benefit, and would much prefer to die. And it is true despite the fact that the patient will soon be dead in any case and that his remaining life will be so full of pain that all other awareness is excluded — life and health are not at stake in any operationally significant way.

Once elective procedures have been undertaken, the physician must allow their life-prolonging effect to follow. For him to do otherwise, regardless of the circumstances and the purity of his intentions, would be exactly the same as if he were in the first place to have given the patient an overdose of morphine instead of a life-prolonging drug.

To allow the patient to die can be morally right; to kill the patient always is morally wrong. And to *intervene* to prevent the life-giving effect of an action *he has chosen to take*, although he had no strict obligation to take it, would be to murder the patient.

Little reflection on the principles we have been developing is needed to understand why this harsh judgment is true. To act as the physician would if he administered an anticoagulant in this case would be to go directly against life. The will of such an agent could not be oriented toward what in his very act he willingly prevents.

Whatever excuses he may have had for not acting, whatever leeway he perhaps had for permitting the effect which it is wrong to cause — those excuses and that leeway were ceded forever *when the choice to act was made.* That choice set aside indefinite possibilities of nonobligation and accepted definite obligation toward the good which stands to be achieved by the act in question.

The agent in a case such as this has brought himself to the very focus of the obligating power of an essential human good. Having brought himself to this point, he cannot avoid being transfixed by the full power of that principle. There now no longer is an alternative he could choose consistently. He can only let the good be or set himself directly against it.

Now consider contraception. Normally one has no obligation to engage in sexual relations. One may engage in them for excellent reasons which have nothing to do with procreation. Moreover, procreation is not the usual result. One may prefer, wish, hope that it will not follow. Neither feelings nor wishes of this sort are incompatible with the required love of the procreative good, anymore than they would be at odds with the required love of the good of human life if they concerned the life of a friend in prolonged death agony.

But if intercourse is carried on to the point where procreation might follow unless we act to prevent it, then the full force of obligation falls upon us. We need not act, but if we do act we may do nothing to prevent the procreative good from being realized. Positively to do any such thing by direct volition will set us absolutely at odds with the essential human good which our very action has made proximately possible of attainment.

What good reasons we may have for engaging in sexual intercourse are beside the point. What good reasons we may have for preferring that it be sterile also are beside the point. No matter what ulterior motives we may have, we cannot avoid willing contrary to a good when we directly prevent our own action from achieving it.

Not to seek that the good be realized is compatible with fundamentally loving it, for such nonintention merely is permission that the good not be. But to choose by our very action that the good not be realized is incompatible with fundamentally loving it, for such a choice is identically an unwillingness to permit the good to be. And man's basic obligation with regard to all of the essential goods is that he should be open to them, that he should be willing that they be.

Contraception, then, is a directly willed intervention of any positive kind to prevent the realization of the procreative good when it otherwise might follow from an act of sexual intercourse in which one has chosen to engage. This definition clearly indicates that the method of prevention is altogether irrelevant to the action in question.

Likewise irrelevant is the question whether the man or the woman acts to prevent conception. The primarily guilty party is he who first chooses to prevent. The other sometimes becomes a guilty cooperator, even if he is not himself primarily responsible.

Irrelevant also is the temporal sequence or simultaneity of the physical behavior of intercourse and contraception. The two external acts may occur in either sequence or they may occur at the same time. The guilt arises *at the moment one chooses* both to engage in intercourse and by one's own directly willed positive act to prevent conception.

This, then, is the malice of contraception. It is to set oneself directly against the essential human good of procreation, to place oneself in an absurd conflict between an unavoidable natural volition of that good and a free volition against it. The malice of contraception is not in the violation of any general obligation to cause conception. The malice is in the will's direct violation of the procreative good as a value in itself, as an ideal which never may be submerged. He who practices contraception acts directly against one of the principles which make human action meaningful.

How, then, is the malice of contraception intrinsic to the act? It is not primarily intrinsic to the external act in isolation, as if the distortion of the normal behavior pattern were all that is wrong. That notion is a naïve moral phenomenalism.

Still, the behavior pattern is significant to the malice of the act, because one has not practiced contraception unless he has done something to prevent conception, just as one has not killed the innocent unless he has done something to cause their death. Moreover, sound practical reason cannot ignore these implications of external action, because sound practical reason has bodily goods among its ultimate principles.

We also must bear in mind that the pattern of behavior usually associated with contraception also can be followed for other reasons, and that such behavior might violate goods other than the good of procreation. A sterile couple, for example, might engage in intercourse in a way which would violate important psychological and symbolic values. The malice of their action would not be that of contraception, although their mode of behavior would preclude fertility if they were not otherwise sterile. Our argument is not against every form of sexual vice and abuse; it is aimed specifically at that mode of action which properly is contraceptive.

There is no question that contraception can be wrong for many secondary and incidental reasons, and that some of these modes of extrinsic malice might apply in common to certain forms of contraception and to certain other types of behavior which in a strict sense are not contraceptive at all. The intrinsic malice of the act is essentially this — that one who has intercourse while preventing conception and who does both with practical knowledge and direct will puts himself in intellectual and volitional absurdity. Thus the malice is in the intention, but in an intention which is inseparable from the act, an intention which gives formal unity to its very object.

Needless to say, if the will to prevent conception is separable from contraception, then one might practice contraception without accepting its malice. With regard to this point a great deal more must be said in Chapter VI when we examine conception-preventing behavior in relation to the problems of indirect voluntariness.

There are many objections to our conclusion which we shall examine in the course of the next two chapters. But there are two points which are so directly related to our thesis that it is necessary to deal with them immediately.

First, if contraception is intrinsically evil, need it be very seriously evil?[19] After all, many intrinsically evil acts, such as petty theft, are not seriously evil. And contraception in many cases seems to have absolutely no bad effects and many good ones. Why then must a negative judgment of it be harsh?

At this point we encounter one of the unspoken but very basic doubts which have pervaded past discussions of contraception. Not only those who practice it, but even some who have no occasion for practicing it, nevertheless wonder why so much of human significance — of real, experienced importance — should depend on the question whether a couple halt their lovemaking short of orgasm or enjoy the release and satisfaction of orgasm using some innocent little barrier to prevent pregnancy (when there are excellent reasons for preferring that one should not occur). Why, the believer may ask, should heaven or hell hang on a little matter of this sort?

This objection has different aspects. With some of them we dealt in the Introduction; with others we shall deal in later chapters. Let us focus on only one question. Must the intrinsic evil of contraception lead to the judgment that it is seriously immoral? Might it not be only slightly evil in itself?

Once we see that contraception is intrinsically evil, there is no way to avoid branding it seriously immoral. In the first place, contraception is directly contrary to an essential human good, and it is against this good in a manner which is not subject to degree. To prevent procreation is to act against its whole possibility of realization, not in the sense that to undergo permanent sterilization is to act against the whole potentiality of the generative powers, but in the sense that to prevent a conception completely prevents the initiation of a particular life. Each such life is of indefinite importance in itself, and we must be extremely careful not to set ourselves against it.

The objection that the unconceived child has no actual rights is narrow-minded legalism. Contraception, of course, is not an injustice, but its malice, like the malice of every intrinsically evil act, is measured by the value which the good it violates would have to the person in whom it would be realized. In this case it would be a great value, since it is the very beginning of being.[20] Hence the malice of contraception cannot be slight. To try to justify it by appealing to personal values, therefore, is to select quite arbitrarily among persons as well as among values.

In those matters of justice, by contrast, which often admit insignificance of matter in acts intrinsically evil, the goods at stake are themselves of small degree and they are only indirectly related to an essential human good. Thus it is possible to steal a small amount, provided the theft does no important harm to anyone, with deliberate intent and direct will without setting oneself directly against any of the goods to which man has a basic natural inclination.

Furthermore, once we are aware that contraception is intrinsically evil, the significance of contraceptive intercourse for other values changes considerably. As we saw in the second chapter, if a married couple has contraceptive intercourse despite the fact that they know it to be wrong, their action takes on the significance of mutual masturbation rather than the value of genuine communication.

Man and wife cannot express love in any genuine sense if they know they are cooperating in an evil act. Hence such cooperation renders the sexual act for those who practice contraception while knowing it to be evil an offense against marital love as well as an offense against procreation. It follows that contraceptive intercourse is at least as seriously evil as masturbation.

The last question we must consider in our study of the intrinsic malice of contraception is whether an act intended only to render conception less probable, without wholly eliminating its possibility, should be considered morally contraceptive in the same way as an act which is thought to be fully effective in preventing conception.[21] For example, if it were possible to reduce the number of spermatozoa in the semen without completely eliminating fertility, would the act causing such a reduction be an act of contraception from an ethical point of view?

The answer is that if the limitation of fertility is caused by any positive act directly intended for the purpose of reducing the probability of conception, then the act is contraceptive in exactly the same sense, ethically speaking, as an act thought to be perfectly contraceptive. The reason is that one who directly wills a positive act which physiologically is semicontraceptive sets himself against the procreative good no less directly than one who wills similarly but chooses a more effective means.

The moral status of such an act is like that of pointing at one's head and firing a revolver which contains only a single bullet. If one does this with the direct purpose of risking his own death, then the act is suicide although the means used is not certainly efficacious. However, confusion is likely to arise in the case of contraception for two reasons.

In the first place, since the semicontraceptive act does not surely prevent conception, it may seem similar to the noncontraceptive method of limiting fertility by periodic abstinence.

Precisely how rhythm and contraception differ will be discussed at length in the latter part of Chapter VI. However, they evidently do not necessarily differ in effectiveness, since rhythm carefully practiced can be highly effective while many contraceptives — in fact, all of them — are subject to a certain percentage of failure.[22]

For the present, it should be sufficient to state that we have not found the malice of contraception to consist in the mere desire that conception should not occur. Even those who totally abstain from sexual relations have this wish. The malice of contraception rather consists in the opposition to the procreative good which cannot be avoided in the intention of one who directly wills a positive act aimed against the fruitfulness of his own engagement in intercourse.

Whether the positive act is only a partly effective contraceptive from a physiological point of view is beside the point. Its directly willed performance presupposes the same opposition between the intention of the will and the procreative good as does the use of a more efficient method.

In the second place, since the semicontraceptive act is likely to be more complex in its effects than a simply contraceptive act would be, there is a much greater likelihood that the act in question may be willed only indirectly.

In that case, under certain conditions, which we shall consider in Chapter VI, the fertility-limiting act might not be contraception in the ethical sense at all. But this analysis will apply equally whether the indirectly willed restriction of fertility is total or partial.

Hence it will be useful to consider a few examples in which the distinction between directly and indirectly willed fertility-limiting behavior is fairly clear. In every one of these examples, we assume that intercourse itself is directly willed. As we have seen, the full obligating force of the procreative good falls only on one who chooses to have intercourse.

1. A condom with a perforation in the tip sometimes is used in otherwise normal intercourse to collect a sample of

semen for medical analysis.[23] The opening permits part of the
semen to enter and remain in the vagina, so that true though
limited intercourse actually occurs. When this procedure is used
for good medical reasons, it is morally unobjectionable in itself,
because although the likelihood of conception is lessened sub-
stantially, this effect can be indirectly willed. If the same procedure were used merely to limit the likelihood of conception,
however, it clearly would be contraception.

2. It has been suggested that some climates or some types
of clothing may be more conducive to fertility than others.[24]
Here again there may be many factors which provide grounds
for choosing a certain climate or garb, all of which could leave
open the possibility that one's act implies only an indirect willing of its fertility-limiting effects. However, to move to a less
fertile region or to wear fertility-limiting clothing merely for
the purpose of rendering conception less probable clearly would
be a directly willed positive act contrary to the procreative good.

3. Someone has proposed that in the future there might be a
method for eliminating all of the spermatozoa capable of leading to a conception of one or the other sex.[25] This procedure
could be used by those who wished to have a child of certain
sex. Its use in such a case might be morally questionable on
other grounds, but our only question is whether it would be
contraceptive. Clearly we would have a positive act which limits
fertility, but if the couple are *attempting* to conceive, the limitation seems to be only indirectly willed. Hence this procedure
would not be contraceptive unless it were used simply in order
to reduce the probability of conception.

4. One position in sexual intercourse may be more conducive
to fertilization than another. If this is so, may a couple use the
position least conducive to fertilization? Evidently there may be
other reasons for preferring a certain position — e.g., that it is
more pleasant. If it is used for such a reason, the fact that it
also limits fertility is willed only indirectly. However, if there
is no reason for choosing one position except to render conception less probable, then the use of this position would seem

to be a directly willed positive intervention at odds with the procreative good.[26]

All these examples serve to emphasize that the malice of contraception is neither in the mere purpose of avoiding pregnancy nor in the mere performance of outward behavior by which conception is more or less surely prevented. Instead, as we have explained, the malice of contraception is in the unavoidable opposition of free volition to the procreative good on the part of one who engages in sexual intercourse and yet who commits himself to a positive act intended to be at odds with the realization of the procreative good.

Having completed our study of the intrinsic malice of contraception, we shall round out this chapter with a comparison between our analysis and the arguments based on conventional natural-law theory which we criticized in Chapter II.

Those arguments, we saw, began from an incomplete syllogism expressed in the proposition: *Contraception is intrinsically immoral because by it one engaging in intercourse prevents his act from attaining its natural end.* Our analysis of the intrinsic malice of contraception also can be viewed as a completion and interpretation of this syllogism.

The formally valid expression of our explanation would be the following:

Major: For one who has sexual intercourse to act in a way which presupposes an intention opposed to the procreative good is intrinsically immoral.

Minor: Contraception is an act — the prevention or lessening of the likelihood of conception by any positive deed directly willed for this purpose — of one who has sexual intercourse which presupposes an intention opposed to the procreative good.

Conclusion: Contraception is intrinsically immoral.

The entire discussion of this chapter and the last one has been aimed at making evident the truth of these two premises and at clarifying the meaning of their terms. Of course, "directly willed" and "positive act" have been used without clarification but they will be treated more fully in Chapter VI.

Someone might suppose that by formulating the explanation of the malice of contraception in this way we have contradicted our earlier assertion that the immoral act of contraception is against a primary affirmative principle rather than against a derived negative one. But this supposition is mistaken. Of course, by using familiar logical devices it is possible to formulate any precept either affirmatively or negatively.

The important question about whether precepts are derived or not, however, does not concern the possibilities of logical manipulation but the relationship of a particular action to an essential human good.[27] The immoral act of contraception is *directly* against the procreative good. It is not merely against some condition of its attainment or some institution which has developed to support its pursuit.

The syllogistic statement of the malice of contraception makes it clear that those who practice contraception are not merely violating a rule, *Do not practice contraception.* Nor are they violating anything in reality except the procreative good itself. Our syllogism merely places these facts in a suitable form for clear and orderly theoretical expression. Its conclusion that contraception is intrinsically immoral is a theoretical truth rather than a precept, although, of course, it presupposes the primary affirmative precept which contraception violates.

In our expansion of the incomplete argument, the expression "natural end" is replaced by "procreative good." The two expressions, of course, refer to the same thing, but our preference for the latter is not merely linguistic.

"Natural end" in the conventional natural-law arguments was found to be susceptible to equivocation, and the equivocation in question was traced eventually to the theoretical basis of conventional natural-law thinking, where "nature" is used equivocally to refer both to the specific essence of man and to the moral norm. Partly under the covering of this equivocation, "ought" is derived in an illogical way from every fact of teleology discovered in theoretical studies of man.

In our description of a sounder ethical theory, we explained how man's basic inclinations do provide the experiential material from which underived principles of practical reason are formed. We also have seen that the procreative good as an object of a primary practical principle must be understood as an ideal, not merely as an operational objective. Hence, while it is not true of all natural ends, it does happen to be true of the natural end of sexual intercourse, the procreative good, that it grounds moral obligations.

Thus we prefer the expression "procreative good," both because it is fully precise and because our previous explanations should have made it clear that the expression is being used in both premises to designate the object of the primary principle of practical reason. This object is what is violated by one who practices contraception, since the act is immoral only because it is contrary to a morally obligatory good.

Once this point is understood, it will be clear how our argument is related to the perverted-faculty argument which we criticized so severely. The perverted-faculty argument depended upon the defense of the general proposition that the prevention of any act from reaching the end proper to an act of its faculty is intrinsically immoral.

This proposition we found to be indefensible even when it was taken with restrictions. The truth of the matter is that the proposition does accurately indicate the reason why contraception is wrong, but it does not apply to any other faculty. Consequently, our argument uses the principle of the perverted-faculty argument only after limiting it to the sexual faculty.

In the case of any other faculty, the effects of frustrating an act from its natural end are judged in terms of their relationship to human life and health as a whole rather than in relation to the end of the particular faculty. The reason for this is that human life and health is an essential human good, but the isolated end of each particular faculty, such as respiration or nutrition, is not.

In the case of generation a different principle applies simply because the procreative good is in itself an essential human good. Perhaps this was in the minds of those who suggested that the frustration of sexual acts from attaining their natural end is *sui generis* because that end is a common good.

Besides restricting the major premise of the perverted-faculty argument to the only faculty for which it is true, our use of the premise also differs in the explanation we give of it. The emphasis of our explanation is on the procreative good as a principle of practical reasoning, and hence as a moral ideal, rather than merely on the generative power and its natural teleology.

It should be clear by now also to what extent those who rejected contraception as an interference with the integrity of the marital act were headed in the right direction. To the extent that contraception is indeed an act which distorts the natural design of sexual relations by introducing a *morally forbidden* factor — the positive intervention by which conception is prevented or rendered less likely — it is an interference with the integrity of the marital act itself.

The naturalness or artificiality of this interference, however, indeed even the *fact* of the interference itself, is not what makes contraception immoral. Rather, it is the free volition against the procreative good which interference of this particular kind necessarily presupposes. For this reason it is nugatory to argue that every interference in the integrity of the marital act which would be allowed to promote fertility should be allowed to limit fertility. A medicine likely to kill a patient may be used as the last resort to heal a patient, but not to kill him.

If we recall the defense of the conventional natural-law argument which tried to strengthen the minor proposition, we can also see precisely how it failed even though it was on the right track. All of those arguments assumed that the proper end of sexual intercourse is a good toward which there is a definite obligation on the part of those engaging in intercourse. With this view our argument agrees.

However, those arguments failed to make a clear distinction between the procreative good as an operational objective — e.g., the limited number of children sufficient to fulfill the obligation to generous fruitfulness — and the procreative good as a principle of moral obligation. Only in the latter capacity, as a moral ideal, is it always violated by contraception.[28]

Moreover, those arguments did not use a sufficiently clear notion of obligation. In many cases, they presupposed that the obligation in question would be similar to a legal debt or to a duty to carry out the imperative of a legitimate superior. We have seen that the obligation in question is strictly a moral one.

Although it conceivably could be related to justice as well, the contraceptive act of itself surely is not a matter of injustice or disobedience. The obligation it violates is simply the obligation to promote the procreative good, and this obligation is violated by one who practices contraception only because by engaging in sexual intercourse he has brought upon himself the full obligating force of this good.

This inadequacy of conventional natural-law arguments in support of the strengthened minor premise appeared most clearly when we considered the relevance of the fact that the procreative good is a common good rather than a proper one. Clearly this point is correct, and it also is important because it is this fact which makes marriage and the marital act necessary.

Moreover, it is no coincidence that the procreative good is the only object of a single natural function which is one of the essential human goods and that it is the only object of a single natural function which is a common good. Both facts arise from this, that reproduction is the fullest perfection proper to an organism. For this reason reproduction is a perfection in which the organism transcends itself and it also is a perfection which is not simply subsumed by any higher grade of being in man, although man is an organism that is more than merely organic.

However, the common good of no particular community, except the marital union itself, need suffer as a result of contraception. And the only reason why the common good of marriage itself suffers is that contraception is a violation of the procreative good. Insofar as the procreative good really is violated, and insofar as this good is the common good of husband and wife, the good of the marriage is violated itself, and the act of contraceptive intercourse can hardly be an expression of mutual love.

The fact, on the other hand, that the procreative good also is a good of the child, the very beginning of his life, is the basic reason why the intrinsically immoral act of contraception must be considered seriously immoral. But here, as we have seen, no right is at stake and no violation of a common good seems to be involved.

A final difference between our argument and conventional natural-law arguments may be indicated for the benefit of those who are interested in niceties of methodology. In the conventional arguments the middle term always had a wider extension than the subject. As we now have seen, many of the difficulties of the conventional arguments arise from their need to defend what is implied by this excess extension of the middle term.

In our argument, the middle term is simply a precise definition of the *moral act* of contraception. This difference has great value for the argument, because it frees the defense of our thesis from having to argue a whole series of irrelevant issues. In argument it is always best to defend as little ground as necessary.[29]

The important point to bear in mind about our demonstration is that the syllogism formulated above must not be removed from the context of our whole study and then considered in isolation as if it were a demonstration of the immorality of contraception. The most powerful demonstrations always have this characteristic, that outside their proper context they appear to be merely conventional definitions. Clearly, the formulation of our argument will not demonstrate without all the preceding explanations, since the syllogism is only a summary of what already was completed by the time it was formulated.

NOTES TO CHAPTER IV

1. Aquinas, *S.t.*, 1–2, q. 94, a. 4; *In libros Ethicorum Aristotelis*, 5, lect, 12, already suggested this possibility. A similar account has been arrived at by a contemporary sociologist who has carefully studied the problem of cultural relativism — Morris Ginsberg, "On the Diversity of Morals," in: Jones, Sontag, Beckner, and Fogelin, *Approaches to Ethics: Representative Selections from Classical Times to the Present* (New York: McGraw-Hill Book Company, Inc., 1962), 484–494.

2. Rudolf Allers, *The Psychology of Character* (New York: Sheed and Ward, Inc., 1935), 63–66; Oraison, *Man and Wife* (New York: The Macmillan Co., 1962), 43–47.

3. See: ch. 2, note 23; Alexander A. Schneiders, *The Psychology of Adolescence* (Milwaukee: The Bruce Publishing Co., 1951), 191–208; Magda B. Arnold, John A. Gasson, S.J., *et alii*, *The Human Person: An Approach to an Integral Theory of Personality* (New York: The Ronald Press Co., 1954), 472–476. Interestingly, Freud himself considered the separation between pleasure and reproduction to be the hallmark of perversion: *A General Introduction to Psychoanalysis* (New York: 1920), 273.

4. Bronislaw Malinowski, "Marriage," *Encyclopaedia Brittanica*, 14 (Chicago: Encyclopaedia Brittanica, Inc., 1962), 940–950.

5. This is the distinction between love of friendship — willing a good to SOMEONE — and love of concupiscence — willing a GOOD to someone: *S.t.*, 1, q. 60, a. 3; 1–2, q. 2, a. 7, ad 2; q. 66, a. 6, ad 2. The important point to notice is that both loves are included in every act of love; when we are selfish, the good we love and the one to whom it is willed remain distinct.

6. At the level of inclination, the two are closely related; see: Hilgard, *Introduction to Psychology*, 3 ed. (New York and Burlingame: Harcourt, Brace, and World, Inc., 1962), 135–137, mating and rearing offspring are two aspects of the same continuous process. Ford and Kelly, *Contemporary Moral Theology*, Vol. 2, *Marriage Questions* (Westminster, Md.: The Newman Press, 1963), 47 and *passim*, point out that the procreation and rearing of children, which together constitute parenthood, are primary ends of marriage.

7. Oraison, *op. cit.*, 11–18. This, of course, is looking at matters from the point of view of sexual reproduction, where the reproductive act is quite distinct from other functions. If one looks at life as a whole, one might ask whether reproduction is so much a distinct function as simply the overflow and continuousness of life. For this point and the related discussion, see: Lestapis, *Family Planning and Modern Problems* (New York: Herder and Herder, 1961), 147–160.

8. Russell and Russell, *Human Behaviour* (Boston-Toronto: Little, Brown and Co., 1961); M. Esther Harding, *Psychic Energy: Its Source and Transformation* (New York: Bolligen Series, 10, Pantheon Books, 1947), 117–122; Arnold and Gasson, *loc. cit.*

9. See: Frank H. Hankins, "Birth Control," *Encyclopedia of the Social Sciences*, 2 (New York: The Macmillan Co., 1953), 559; George Devereux, *A Study of Abortion in Primitive Societies* (New York: The Julian Press, 1955), 24–26 and *passim*.

10. Ginsberg, *loc. cit.*; Bronislaw Malinowski, *Sex and Repression in Savage Society* (London: Routledge & Kegan Paul, Ltd., 1927), 193–200, illustrates this point quite well. Aquinas was aware that the human law based on positive law includes more than formal enactments: *S.t.*, 1–2, q. 97, a. 3.

11. Dupré, "Toward a Re-examination . . . ," *Cross Currents*, 14 (Winter, 1964), 69–70, seems to have some such objection in mind.

12. G. C. de Menasce, *The Dynamics of Morality* (New York: Sheed and Ward, 1961), is a remarkable effort to show how goods provide the sufficient motivation *to be good*. Montessori education proceeds on the same principle.

13. Thus the traditional defense of the legitimacy of clerical celibacy and religious virginity — e.g., *S.c.g.*, 3, chs. 136–137. Our present point should be taken in conjunction with the fifth of the ways mentioned below in which goods oblige.

14. Cf. Dietrich von Hildebrand, *Christian Ethics* (New York: David McKay and Co., Inc., 1953), 443–444, where "satanic pride" is discussed.

15. This obligation is discussed at length from a theological point of view: Ford and Kelly, *op. cit.*, 396–430.

16. *S.t.*, 2–2, q. 47, a. 6, Aquinas explains how the ends naturally given to the will and intellect serve as the point of departure for prudence; cf. Overbeke, "La loi naturelle et le droit naturel selon saint Thomas," *Revue Thomiste*, 57 (1957), 450–458; G. P. Klubertanz, S.J., "The Root of Freedom in St. Thomas' Later Works," *Gregorianum*, 42 (1961), 714–715, mentions the priority of natural love to free choice and provides bibliography.

17. We are not merely saying that a scholar may not lie, nor are we claiming that he is obliged to publish everything he knows. If he does publish on a certain subject he has an obligation to tell not only the truth and nothing but the truth, but even the *whole truth*, to the extent that he knows it and can tell it. The concealment which is allowable in other cases is not allowable for scholars publishing their findings.

18. We do not ask whether the physician can desist from extraordinary measures; as we shall see in Chapter VI, that would be analogous to rhythm. The question is whether he can *act* to eliminate the consequences of his previous act.

19. This question is discussed surprisingly little. Dupré, *op. cit.*, 67, simply assumes *non datur parvitas materiae* settles everything — a strange oversight in one who asks many questions. August Adam, *The Primacy of Love* (Westminster, Md.: The Newman Press, 1958), 137–157, has an extensive theological discussion of this "principle." Clearly, there can be venial sins *ex obiecto* against chastity in marriage. Unfortunately, Adam's treatment is not as scholarly as one might wish. Cooper, "Comment by Dr. Cooper," *The (American) Ecclesiastical Review*, 81 (July, 1929), 72–79, presses the question of seriousness against Davis.

20. *S.c.g.*, 3, ch. 122, where Aquinas considers sexual sin next to homicide, should be read in the light of his distinction between mortal and venial sins: *S.t.*, 1–2, q. 72, a. 5; q. 88, a. 1, a. 2.

21. Ford and Kelly, *op. cit.*, 364 ff., discuss some of these problems.

22. Lestapis, *op. cit.*, 55–56. It is well known that all the conventional contraceptives fail, but is this true also of the pill? The answer must be yes, when we consider that a missed pill is a contraceptive failure. Human error should not be excluded here — it is strange how some proponents of contraception always discount human error except where rhythm is concerned.

23. Ford and Kelly, *op. cit.*, p. 364, provide an introduction to the literature.

24. *Ibid.*, 362–363, note 31. The view referred to seems to us to open the door to all but total contraception.

25. Francis J. Connell, C.SS.R., discussed this question; cited in Ford and Kelly, *op. cit.*, 364, note 32.

26. Undoubtedly, at this point the distinctions must be drawn very finely, because it is not easy to say what is and what is not a positive act. A couple can omit to act, and can stop short of acting as fully as they might, without counteracting the effect of their action. *Copula dimidiata* (*ibid.*, 220–224) seems to me to be a limitation of action rather than a positive act to prevent conception; the choice of position seems to me less a limit on action than a counteraction.

27. Aquinas (*S.t.*, 1–2, q. 94, aa. 4–6) likes to consider the secondary precepts as *quasi-deduced* conclusions from the primary ones; his view is clarified considerably when his early discussion (*In 4 Sent.*, d. 33, q. 1, aa. 1–2) is taken into account, for there he explains what he apparently takes for granted in *S.t.* that the secondary precepts concern subordinate goods and ends, and that procreation is primary while the relational value of sex is secondary.

28. *S.c.g.*, 3, ch. 122, should be reread in the light of this conclusion. When Aquinas is understood in terms of his own doctrine of values and obligation this argument, though overly brief, begins to make sense.

29. But apart from dialectical advantages, the restriction of the middle term to a definition of the act, and the use of a primary principle to explain the major premise of our argument have the effect of making it a demonstration according to the requirements of Aristotelian logic. It is, in fact, a *propter quid* demonstration, which is called a "demonstration of the reasoned fact." See: *Posterior analytics*, 71b8–79a33. The important point about this kind of demonstration is that it not only shows its conclusion to be true, but also reveals the reason why the conclusion is true by indicating in the middle term the proper cause of the fact expressed by the conclusion.

V

THEORETICAL OBJECTIONS

AGAINST our conclusion that contraception is intrinsically immoral so many theoretical objections could be made that one treatise hardly can examine and respond to all of them. Yet certain objections both are so sure to arise and are so plausible that it is necessary to consider them. In this chapter we shall examine objections which are connected with the theory of moral law, while in the next one we shall deal with the question of whether the universal prescription which prohibits contraception might not be subject to exceptions.

The first objection is that our argument merely shows that contraception violates a certain human good, while the real question is whether it is a sin or not.[1] As a philosopher I cannot respond completely to this objection, because it depends on the concept of sin, which is theological rather than philosophical. Nevertheless, some remarks can be made.

In the first place, our argument shows that contraception is something more than a violation of the physiological end of the reproductive function. That point is a fundamental one, but clearly not every frustration of a natural process is morally evil. Our argument has come to its conclusion through the evidence that the procreative good really is one of the essential human goods. From this we inferred that it deserves a place among the objects of the primary principles of practical reasoning and that it has a role to play in the natural determination of volition.

Moreover, I tried to show in the latter part of Chapter II and in the description of situationism in Chapter III that the invidious comparison sometimes made between the "merely biological" good of reproduction and the human values of the spirit presupposes a faulty theory of man. The procreative good is essentially human because man's organic nature is not merely an instrument or a necessary condition of his personal subjectivity.

While there can be distinctions between higher and lower aspects of man's integral nature, nothing which belongs to man is merely natural and absolutely at man's disposal in the way that everything in lower nature is. The good of procreation in actual fact is the coming into existence of a human infant, and such a good is properly human rather than being merely natural, even though "mere existence" is at stake.

Perhaps more deeply underlying this objection than confusions of this kind is the notion that moral issues concern only certain matters and that contraception is not one of them. This confusion is not present only in the simple mind which cannot see a moral issue except in those areas which involve shame and feelings of guilt. Rather a similar confusion in a more sophisticated form is common among our educated contemporaries.

Those who have reflected upon morality and who have adopted some mode of situationism become able to see moral issues at two points. On the one hand, there clearly is a moral issue when their preferred reflexive[2] value is at stake. Thus the hedonist sees a moral issue not only when pleasure is reduced operationally but even when it is not respected as an ideal. Similarly, the theologically oriented situationist sees a moral issue, even apart from consequences, where what he imagines to be the spirit of faith or of charity seems to be missing.

On the other hand, a situationist will recognize a moral issue in the effects of external action on some material good (or, for that matter, of any effective action on any substantive good) only if he considers the results themselves to be important for his preferred reflexive value. For this reason the situationist may be able to discern the moral issue in many cases of injustice because unjust action often has actual bad effects for the reflexive values situationists espouse.

But a situationist cannot see a moral issue where no outward harm is done and where his preferred value does not seem to be involved. Thus one even hears Catholics who have been influenced more than they realize by situationism ask: "What harm does contraception do? Often, apparently, none. Then how is it at odds with what is essential to a Christian life? It does not seem to be against any theological virtue."

The assumption here is that there are no other modes in which actions could become immoral. But, in fact, there is another way, since the situationist division among values is not sound. An action which does little or no objective damage and which is neither directly against a reflexive value such as friendship nor directly against a supernatural value such as charity may be directly against a substantive good.

Substantive goods demand not only effective protection but even a certain absolute respect. As we have seen, those material goods which are essential and irreducible goods of man are not to be considered merely operational objectives, concrete goals of action to be achieved sufficiently by definite and limited means. Although they may take on this aspect in their particular instances, these goods are primarily ideals or moral norms which, together with the other primary principles of practical reason, mark out before human ingenuity all the possibilities of human perfection.

Because material goods such as human life itself have an irreplaceable role to play in whatever man can be, then, there is no reasonable way to circumvent their demand for respect. Hence we can never justify a direct will opposed to them. It is for this reason that therapeutic abortion and euthanasia can

never be approved, although the refusal to permit these procedures in some cases gains nothing — and might even lose
something — operationally significant for life.

The procreative good, like human life as such, is an essential
human value which extends beyond all its exemplifications when
they are considered from a merely pragmatic viewpoint. The
distinction between the operational objective and the ideal is
not easy to notice so long as there is no conflict between the
demands of the ideal value upon categorical moral reasoning
and the regulation by the operational objective of conditional
technical reasoning — for example, when morality and the obvious requirements of competent medical practice coincide.

In certain cases the two roles which substantive values play
can become separated from one another, as they do for instance
where there appear to be medical indications for therapeutic
abortion. Similarly, contraception now appears to be a "necessity."[3] But the moral force of the substantive values remains
unimpaired when such a divergence occurs. Thus the population problem does not affect the immorality of contraception,
because its essential immorality never did depend upon the
population trends and the need of societies for unrestricted
reproduction.

Hence, to deny that any material good should be regarded as
an ideal moral norm is simply to plunge into situationism. This
plunge evidently has been taken by those who offer all the old
utilitarian arguments for contraception as a method to regulate
population. They assume that morality requires nothing more
than necessity and efficiency. Contrary to situationism, however, the truth is that we have no way by which we might
determine when the exigencies of other goods are sufficiently
great to outbalance the claims of any primary human good so
that we would be reasonable in directly violating it.

The whole problem can be seen to come down to this one
point. If we are to use freedom meaningfully, we must judge
what to do. But since we lack angelic intuition, we must reason
in order to judge, and reasoning either goes around in circles

or it goes back to basic principles. Once it has gone as far as the very first principles, there is no place further to which it reasonably can go. First principles themselves cannot be judged.

Nor can they be played off one against another, because by the very fact that they are many and yet primary it is clear that they are incommensurable with one another. If there were a single standard to which they could be compared, it rather than they would be really primary. To try to arbitrate among first principles without any standard, moreover, is simply to be arbitrary.

The procreative good happens to be one of the values which is an object of a primary practical principle. Undoubtedly the reason this is so is that man does have an organic plane of existence and that reproduction is an essential function on that plane. It is this fact which underlies the natural inclination toward procreation which reason naturally accepts as a clue when it is forming principles.

If this good were completely absorbed by goods at higher planes of human existence, it would not lead to a basic principle. But it is not thus absorbed — the plane of organic being possesses a certain perfection not duplicated in any other aspect of human existence. The most brilliant mind never gave birth to a single child. Moreover, if the human spirit completely encompassed the perfection of the other planes of man's existence, sexual activity would have no necessary place in human love.[4]

Since, then, we have no reasonable basis on which to judge that any one of our basic principles of practical reasoning should be violated, our only reasonable course is to abide by every one of the principles and to hope for the best.

If it were possible to consider all things together, we might come to a different conclusion. But such a manner of consideration becomes possible for us only by subordinating all other first practical principles to some one of them, as situationism does, or by putting aside rational judgment altogether in favor of mere feeling. We all are tempted to take the latter course when, as in contraception, feeling has a strong case and reason lacks pragmatic counterweights.

In difficult situations, it is easy enough for us to imagine that God would see things differently than our most reasonable judgment dictates. And, indeed, it is possible that He does, but still He has made us able to direct our own lives by our own intelligence.[5] It would be most rash of us to imagine that an arbitrary judgment of ours would be nearer to divine wisdom than the ability God has given us as a share in His wisdom — our rational intelligence with its naturally evident first principles.

Of course, since human intelligence is limited, and since our freedom is not restricted to any particular good — not even to the good our best judgment can indicate — it always is possible for us to find some plausible pretext for abandoning our reason in the use of our freedom. But to do this is, precisely, from an ethical point of view, to act immorally. Thus contraception really is immoral, not merely against a natural good.

Still someone may object that although contraception is incompatible with an essential human good, perhaps it is compatible with man's attainment of his ultimate end. After all, is it not the ultimate end rather than any more limited good, however essential it may be, which determines morality?[6]

It is not sufficient to respond to this objection by saying that morally bad action must be avoided if the ultimate end is to be attained. That answer either would beg the question, if it meant that contraception is wrong in relation to the ultimate end, or it would imply that the ultimate end has no real effect on what is good and what is bad.

In fact, the essential goods prescribed by the primary affirmative principles of moral law in themselves and simply as such cannot be man's ultimate end, for they are multiple and irreducible to any single intelligible principle. The ultimate end, however, must be single and simple.

Moreover, if the ultimate end is imagined to be something lacking all intrinsic relationship to life, merely annexed to it by God as a reward for passing the moral test, then indeed it will be impossible to be certain about the morality or immorality of any action except by considering whether it has been prohibited or demanded by a divine edict.

For this reason, some theological theories of sin, which separate it completely from substantive human values, may allow contraception — or any other mode of behavior — on the principle that the leap of faith or the demand of grace, communicated personally to the conscience of each believer, requires the transvaluation of all natural values and the cancellation of merely finite goods. Personally, I do not accept such theology, and as a philosopher all I can say is that I see no good reason to accept it.

Primarily, I would answer the objection concerning the ultimate end in a traditional way. The ultimate end of man, whatever it is, includes or presupposes that man must direct his life according to the dictates of right reason.[7] Contraception, as we have seen, involves an unavoidable irrationality in human action. Hence, it must be incompatible with the ultimate end. This argument shows that the act in question must be considered immoral in the full sense in which immorality means contrariety to the ultimate end.

However, this argument does not show why the violation of a particular good which is not itself the ultimate end of man should imply also the violation of that final good. It is possible to explain the reason for this in two different ways.

First, let us consider the matter negatively. Since the good which is violated is one of the irreducible principles of our practical judgment, the only reasonable way to transcend it would be by appealing to the supreme value of the ultimate end itself. Actually, however, we cannot do this, so one who violates the procreative good must be treating some other good — e.g., "mutual love" — as if it were the highest good.

However, this substitution, as we remarked in our criticism of situationism in Chapter III, is a kind of idolatry. Thus the direct violation of a limited good involves an implicit violation of the ultimate end, because only an excessive regard for some other limited good could have led us to approve such a violation.[8]

If we wish to look at the matter positively, we must consider that none of the essential human goods should be regarded as merely extrinsic means to man's ultimate perfection. These goods mark the limit of man's inherent abilities and inclinations.

Hence although beyond all of them man still desires goodness as such, this desire is not one which he has the natural ability to fulfill except to the extent that the goods he can attain participate in the perfect goodness he only can conceive as beyond his abilities. From a philosophical point of view, then, we must think of the end of man as perfect goodness insofar as that is attained by a progressive participation through the gradual and increasing achievement of proportionate, natural goods.[9]

Although this theory of the end of man does not concern the supernatural perfection which Christian faith proposes to mankind, our theory by no means conflicts with the teaching of faith. About this point, however, enough was said in Chapter III at the end of the description of our theory of moral law.

Therefore if the end of man itself is attained only in and through the attainment of the essential human goods, it follows that a direct rejection of any one of these also is a rejection of the end to which man's very nature directs him.

Once this point has been grasped, it should be clear why it is fallacious to object that the total prohibition of contraception absolutizes one aspect of man's nature — the biological — at the expense of other aspects such as the personal goods of mutual love or personality development. The rejection of contraception does not really absolutize those essential human goods which are material values, it simply resists relativizing them in favor of the others.[10]

What really must be done to preserve and promote mutual love surely should be done. Yet the prevention of conception, precisely as such, certainly does not of itself contribute to mutual love or to any other value. On the other hand, it is directly against the procreative good.

To defend contraception on the ground that the biological value of procreation is not absolute, therefore, is simply to accept the situationist position that all material values are nothing but more or less essential means to reflexive ones. In that case, clearly, it is the reflexive values which are being absolutized, and none of them deserves to be identified with the absolute good itself anymore than does the humblest of basic material goods.

This kind of objection also falsifies the facts about what leads to the practice of contraception, by locating the tension where it does not exist. The problem is not that mutual love and biological values are at odds with one another. The problem rather is that psychic demands for sexual release exceed a reasonable judgment based on the good of procreation and other relevant values. These other values already have influenced judgment since it is not the procreative good itself which has indicated that fertility should be limited.

There is little use for a proponent of contraception to appeal to psychology at this point. Some psychologists have been influenced by their own ideology with regard to sexual activity and also by various situationist philosophical views. More relevant is the almost universal agreement of the sages that the psychic drive for sexual release must be mastered if man is to become fully human.[11] Surely this common view must be correct, although some have added to it various unsound explanations.[12] Certain recent ideas disagree with this traditional notion, but human nature has not changed so much that the psyche need no longer yield to reason.

Yet is it not true that human nature changes?[13] Modern man is not the same as medieval or ancient man; Christian man is not the same as pre-Christian man; civilized man is not the same as primitive man. Perhaps contraception has been wrong in the past, but will not continue to be so.

We cannot respond to this objection merely by denying essential change in man and insisting that all of the changes in him are only accidental.

In organic nature apart from man the process of evolution leads to the development of new species. When a new species appears, we can never say that a nature has changed, for the moment we find any really significant development we consider that we are confronted with a new and different nature.

So long as we find sufficient sameness of anatomical and physiological character among a group of individuals to regard them as members of one single species, on the other hand we also discover sameness in instinctive behavior, in the good which are concretely sought through this behavior, and — apart from interfering factors — in goods actually achieved. Nature is creative of new species but natural beings, other than man, are not self-creative of new realizations of their own nature.

Think, for example, how little of significance there is to distinguish the life of one robin from that of another. Any interesting differences are caused by conditions external to the individual animals or by genetic mutations which are nearly always unfortunate and which are always accidents from the point of view of the individual robin.

Compare man. What is most interesting and most important in man is what depends on the unique fact that he has an open, creative, and free spirit.[14] From this abundant spring arises almost everything that is really interesting about man — knowledge, society, the arts, technology, and, to a certain extent, religion. With regard to every one of these specifically human fields of achievement there are significant differences to be found between cultures and among men of the same culture. We nevertheless recognize that all of our fellows form with us a common human species.

These facts can be interpreted in various ways. From one point of view it is clear that if all men fully used their unique potentialities, at the limit every single human being would differ from every one of his fellows in ways both fully intelligible and completely unique. Cultural pluralism would reach the point where each person within a common culture would have his own complete personal culture. Then every single man could have a really interesting biography of his own. In that case each man would be like a natural species by himself.

But short of this ideal situation the facts can be arranged in another familiar pattern. Man lives in a world which is determined by cultural space and time, a world where simultaneity is identical with effective communication. Thus pockets of primitive humanity survive even to the present, but as communication begins such primitives rapidly become contemporary. In the cultural world those who are contemporary with one another always display some striking similarities. For this reason we can speak of "classic man" and "modern man."

Moreover, the cultural ancestors and descendents of any culturally unified group of men always show both significant differences from them and significant similarities with them in such a way that the processes of human change can be fitted into an evolutionary pattern. Man continues within the unity of his species at the level of culture the evolutionary process which occurs so differently in subhuman nature.[15]

In man we find an evolution not of organism but of spirit. In the course of history, in the medium of culture, man's open, creative, and free spirit is unfolding itself and working out its fullest potentialities. This Hegelian-sounding formula need not be regarded as exclusively Hegelian property; cleansed of the excesses of absolute idealism, the evolutionary conception of human culture has become a permanent acquisition. It belongs to every sophisticated philosophical anthropology of the present day.[16]

Only those whose philosophy of man remains a set of theses rather than a confrontation with the problems of human reality have failed to see and to accept the fact that human nature really is changing. Moreover, this fact can be fitted into a sound metaphysics which recognizes the irreducible individuality of each human person and the utter diversity between the created and limited human spirit and the uncreated and infinite divine reality.

But if human nature really belongs to evolving reality, and

if morality depends upon human nature, it seems to follow that moral law too must be in evolution. Hence we might suppose that while contraception was immoral for our ancestors and perhaps remained so even as late as 1930, it may not be immoral for our descendents or perhaps even as soon as tomorrow.

The first point to notice in untangling the knot of this objection is that it is most effective against the simplest forms of conventional natural-law theory. That theory presupposes a specific essence in an unchanging nature, and it tries to discover moral law by a simple comparison between the essence of the human act to be judged and some aspect of human nature. If this unsophisticated realism about moral law is annexed to an evolutionary conception of man the conclusion will be evolving morality.

Nor will there be any way of knowing the proper points at which to expect change. It still might seem that something in man must be stable, but the stable factor will turn out to be the specific essence and such a principle is merely formal, merely universal, merely an abstraction. Where conventional natural-law theory looks to find the specifically human there is in fact only the mere possibility of a humanity whose every realization is a diverse historical and cultural reality.

Thus it might be true always and everywhere that man should be just, but the diverse possibilities for the realization of justice in diverse cultures make its concrete reality differ greatly. Hence it would seem true, too, that while man always should be chaste, the real requirements of chastity must be expected to change. In fact, not only may contraception become good, but perhaps even marriage itself will become bad.

Of course, no Catholic proponent of contraception has carried his insight into the evolutionary aspect of human nature that far. Nor is it my intention to suggest that anyone is about to do so. I do not even want to make capital of the fact that those who talk of changing human nature have failed to indicate up to now where the implications of their theories can be limited. This point, while it is a sound counterobjection, would take us too far afield, and would make little direct contribution to the defense of the conclusion we reached earlier.

Our strategy rather must be to admit that human nature changes, but to deny that its changes can affect the truth of our thesis.[17] Since no one has shown the contrary, this denial in all strictness should be a sufficient answer to the objection according to the sound old principle, *What is asserted gratuitously is denied equally gratuitously.*

However, rather than holding our objector to the strict justice of dialectical exchange — he might claim after all that human nature has changed so much that the old principle about gratuitous assertions no longer applies — we shall offer some further considerations in favor of the distinction we are asserting.

Let us begin by noticing the obvious distinction between the overall pattern of human culture, which evidently changes, and the underlying constants without which such change could not occur. These two factors are not to be understood as particular realization and universal species nor are they to be imagined as if they were two things bonded together.

They really are two aspects of the same thing, human nature, and they must be included in its universal concept just as they are present in its concrete reality.[18] Yet these two factors are in truth quite distinct, and this point can be shown easily merely by examining the correct assertion that human nature does change.

If man's nature changes, then what man now is must not be exactly the same as it was before. Still if there is real difference, clearly it really is *man* who differs, it is *man* who is not the same now as before. The fact that man changes demonstrates one eternally unchanging truth about him — he is a species for whom such change is possible, a species whose real essence is a potentiality for constant development. And since this development occurs only through freedom, the conditions necessary for any possible exercise of human freedom belong to immutable human nature.

But among the conditions without which human freedom simply cannot begin its creative work are the primary principles of practical reason which constitute the universal prescriptions of the moral law. These principles are indispensable conditions of freedom because it is only by their light that the will becomes oriented toward the whole range of possibilities open before man, the very range of possibilities which make cultural evolution possible.

It is only in virtue of the influence of these principles on the will that man becomes able to take an intellectually directed interest in anything, to conceive that he might become something which he is not already. It is only through these principles that man becomes able to engage his freedom in the possibilities presented by surrounding reality and so to bring forth into actuality his given, merely potential subjectivity. And among these primary principles is the fundamental prescription which contraception directly violates.

Still it might be objected that these basic prescriptions of moral law are merely abstract while the real issue with regard to contraception is concerned with the concrete. To this I would respond that as such the prescription of the procreative good indeed is an object of intelligence, but it arises from a constant inclination, and it determines the orientation of the will. If man does not arbitrarily restrict his own possibilities by suppressing some of the potential effects of these fundamental prescriptions, they become fully actualized in the achievements of his life. Considered in this light, a basic precept of practical reason is as much as anything else truly a concrete reality — an existentially significant fact.

On the other hand, if someone wants to object that these prescriptions are abstract in the quite different sense that they are only one of the factors which together constitute the whole reality of real human life, this objection may be granted. The factor of one's freedom and the factor of one's situation also have their own contributions to make.

Yet these factors do not come together as if each of them

brought its own primary principles of practical reason with it. Only reason comes equipped with principles, although each of the other factors introduces something just as important or even more so. The modes in which the various factors contribute to the constitution of the actual process of human existence are more diverse from one another than the modes in which the parts of any other complex whole contribute to its unity. And just as there are facts in the situation that cannot be changed and there is freedom in the self which cannot be suppressed, so there are the primary principles of cultural development which cannot be transcended.

Hence, the basic prescriptions of practical reason are not modified by the other factors which join with them in the reality of life. Or better, if man presiding over his own synthesis in freedom attempts to modify or even so much as to qualify in the slightest way the primary principles which make it possible for him to exercise his freedom, then he must suffer the consequences of this irrationality in his life as a whole. The irrationality might hardly be noticed because it can be only partial, but partial irrationality is a partial abandonment of freedom itself.

Still it may be objected that the evolution of man belongs to his spirit, and that a mere organic function has no right to such dignity that it deserves respect even against the claims and needs of higher goods. The real trouble with the ban on contraception is that it interferes with spiritual values such as mutual love and personal development. Though these were not recognized as important in the Middle Ages, they have come to be seen in our day in all their splendor, and hence they must be fostered through a contraceptive practice which would indeed have been immoral when these values were not at stake.

But this objection only takes us back to our old problems with the situationists. They hold on principle that substantive values, and especially material ones, must yield under sufficiently great necessity. Situationists have no absolute respect for such values; they are regarded only as operational objectives, not as ideals. We hold on the contrary that nothing human may be regarded as instrumental to a human personality, and that to subordinate the procreative value by acting directly against it in the way contraception demands is to sacrifice an essential human good.

The spirit of man is doubtless of greater worth than his organic life, but the reality of man is not that of an incarnate spirit, and the procreative good of man is not a merely biological one.[19] Human reproduction also belongs to the life of the spirit, and if procreation seldom belongs to the spirit as truly and as fully as it might, this fact chiefly indicates the inhuman dualism which is presupposed both by contraception and by every consistent theory capable of defending it.

In any case, as we have observed before, the actual difficulties many married couples experience which tempt them to commit themselves to contraceptive practice do not arise from any straightforward conflict between the demands of the spirit and the demands of the procreative good. If man were a pure spirit there clearly would be no problem about contraception.

There could be no conflict without the appearance of a third factor — the psychic effects of abstinence. These effects include painful tension and frustration which in turn can lead to other difficulties. This group of evils — I call them "evils" not in the moral sense, but because that is precisely how we feel them in our experience — can be dealt with in several different ways. One of them is by having intercourse with contraception, but as we have seen this "solution" involves the direct opposition by freedom against the good of procreation which helps to make freedom possible.

This conflict, therefore, is not between flesh and spirit. It is between the reasonable requirements of organic nature for the respect appropriate to it and the unreasonable demands of un-disciplined sensuality for an unrestricted access to the tension-releasing experience of orgasm. There is nothing novel about this conflict except the modern tendency to imagine that ethics should allow the appeasement of sensuality instead of insisting on the necessity for self-control and genuine development of the personality.[20]

But if all this is true, what really was conceded when we admitted that human nature changes and that in some way morality changes with it? Has not this admission been rendered vacuous by our unwavering insistence on the immutability of the primary practical principles? My answer, of course, is negative. In a number of ways it is highly significant to recall the truth that human nature changes.[21]

In the first place, man's nature is becoming more spiritualized, less restricted by matter. As this process goes on, the force of the higher inclinations assumes more definite shape and so the precepts which derive from them gradually become clearer and more effective.

Because of this progress man is acquiring an appreciation of skill, of beauty, of freedom, and of truth which he did not always have — we can actually observe the transition from primitive cultures centered on physical necessity to civilized ones which open the possibilities of higher culture and its continuous advancement. Because of this development we consider superstition and obscurantism to be immoral. These same attitudes in our primitive ancestors were hardly worthy of condemnation.

In the second place, man's nature is becoming more socialized. This does not mean that the individual is more enmeshed by the restrictions of society; indeed, the primitive was almost wholly absorbed by his society. Rather it means that in at least some societies, at their best, a genuine pluralistic community is beginning to appear, an open order in which the uniqueness and freedom of each person can be achieved within the cooperating system of interpersonal relationships.

The tendency is toward a recapturing by reason in large societies of the personal adaptability and mutuality of immediate relationships. In this way there will be more diversity and a higher and more perfect unity. Whatever its supernatural significance, a matter beyond philosophic competence to judge, Christianity certainly marks an important epoch in this transition. Christian man has an awareness both of personal dignity and of social solidarity which — however distorted it may be by naturalizing heresies such as communism — pre-Christian man simply did not have.

In the third place, modern man is creating a whole new order of reality over against himself, an objective system like nature but one which is the result of intelligent design and more or less integrated planning. This new order of reality is the technological system. It constitutes a new environment for man. It is not itself human and it can be recalcitrant. However, it opens boundless possibilities.

Other aspects of human evolution might be mentioned, but these three should be sufficient for our point, which is twofold. On the one hand, the basic principles of practical reason are becoming progressively clearer and more definite, not by becoming more restricted, but by revealing more fully their indefinite potentialities.

On the other hand, when we think of moral law it is not usually these basic and stable conditions of human progress that we have in mind. Rather we are thinking of all the more concrete precepts, the taboos and the laws which characterize diverse cultures and demarcate different stages of man's increasing humanity.

Thus it is true to observe that slavery has become immoral because man has changed. It is true that "usury" — the taking of interest as such — has become moral because modern man is not the same as premodern man in regard to the realities which are expressed in modern business and a technologically grounded economy.

It is true to say that obscurantism in relation to theoretical truth is becoming very seriously immoral. These examples could be multiplied endlessly, because the body of *derived* principles of the moral law is vast, and this entire body is potentially subject to change.

Yet amid all this change the basic principles always remain firm, for they make the change possible. Even the process of clarification and definition which applies to them affects most those which are reflexive — i.e., the ones based upon human freedom. The need for the preservation of life is little altered in itself, and the good of procreation seems to have been as well understood by the primitives as it is by us.

But could not this basic inclination change and the precept based upon it give way? If man can remain human while ceasing to be an organism, if man can remain an organism while ceasing to be reproductive, then the answer will be affirmative.

I would not rule out a priori the possibility of such changes, although it is not easy to imagine what such men would be like.[22] Discussion of this point is not likely to be profitable because the change certainly has not occurred so far.

In conclusion, it is worth noticing that the changes which in fact have occurred in human nature have affected the morality of sexual conduct just as they have affected the morality of other spheres of action. Divorce and polygamy once were not seriously wrong because the mutuality in human friendship which Christian man's sexual activity requires apparently was not required by the sexual activity of pre-Christian man. Our newer humanity makes greater psychological demands, and these indicate the necessity that the sexual relationship between man and wife be perpetual and exclusive.

This is a clear example, but it is not the only one. Sexual activity, as the supreme function of organic life, had a special role in some primitive cultures in binding up the social whole and in uniting it to superior powers which it no longer has in civilized cultures. The intellectual devices of poetry, rhetoric, and dialectic begin to play this role when the power of intelligence as a life-force — its existential significance as practical reason — begins to be recognized in clear, self-conscious awareness.

Finally, it seems clear that the change induced in the human situation through the coming to be of modern man requires the use of intelligence in family planning although premodern man had not the same need to regulate fertility. Yet this change does not imply contraception, which is still wrong. Rather, this development justifies the use of complete or periodic continence, which might have been wrong for our medieval forefathers, but need not be wrong for us.

But about periodic continence we shall have more to say at the end of Chapter VI, where its difference from contraception will be considered.

NOTES TO CHAPTER V

1. Dupré, "Toward a Re-examination . . . ," *Cross Currents*, 14 (Winter, 1964), 73, insistently states the ambiguous question whether the use of contraceptives "is *destructive of an absolute value of man*," with the implication that it is not, and so may be legitimate in some cases. This question is related to his remarks (69) about natural-law arguments: "Such a way of reasoning about nature . . . confuses man's biological structure with his human nature." How this objection is to be understood is not clear to me; therefore, in the following pages I shall deal with several clear objections which are inspired by Dupré's remarks, but I do not claim that they are precisely his objections. My view is that the procreative good is an *ideal* or moral norm, not merely an operational objective, and that it is not necessary *directly* to violate the absolute good (God) to commit serious moral evil.

2. A "reflexive value" is a good which is specifically human and which is specified by something immanent in man's subjectivity itself — e.g., friendship, freedom, practical wisdom, and moral virtue in general, and such partial values as love, authenticity, dialogue, and so on. The theological virtues are treated as reflexive values by immanentist theologies; pleasure is treated as a reflexive value by hedonists. The full and true reflexive values are genuine human goods, but they are vitiated by being identified with the absolute — i.e., by being idolized — as we explained in our treatment of situationism in Chapter III.

3. Lestapis, *Family Planning and Modern Problems* (New York: Herder and Herder, 1961), 239–258, throws considerable light on the alleged "necessity," without denying the need for limiting population increase.

4. Oraison, *Man and Wife* (New York: The Macmillan Co., 1962), 22 and 77–83.

5. This theme runs all through Aquinas; it is beautifully illustrated by his answer to the question (*S.t.*, 1–2, q. 19, a. 10): "Whether it is necessary for the human will, if it is to be good, to agree with the divine will as regards what is willed?" What some who do not read Aquinas carefully do not see is that this doctrine is not a license for arbitrariness, but a natural complement of his doctrine of moral law.

6. *S.t.*, 1–2, q. 88, a. 1.

7. *S.t.*, 1–2, q. 71, a. 2; q. 75, aa. 1–2; 2–2, q. 47, a. 6. See: Lottin, *Morale fondamentale* (Tournai, Belgium: Desclée et Cie, 1954), 114–128, 165–173.

8. Aquinas explains this point briefly: *S.c.g.*, 3, ch. 122. At the beginning of the following chapter he makes the classic remark: "For God is not offended by us except from this that we act against our own good." Whereas Augustine *Contra Faustum*, xxii, 28 (P.L., 42, 419) — describes sin primarily as a turning away from God toward the creature, Aquinas describes it — *De malo*,

q. 2, a. 7, ad 1 — as a turning *toward* the creature, *away* from God. Even the sinner is rationally unreasonable, not just arbitrary, at least to begin with.

9. See: ch. III, note 31, above.

10. Of course, the procreative good is a relative value in comparison with divine goodness, but it is not merely an operational objective to be considered pragmatically. If the attack on its absoluteness were sustained, what should we say of the value of life — "It is not absolute, and so it may be violated when there is a necessity for a therapeutic abortion, or euthanasia, or convenience in spying, or . . ."? Aquinas had good reason for using Ulpian's notion of natural law — what nature teaches all animals — rather than Gratian's — what is in the law and the gospels — as his own point of departure: Odon Lottin, O.S.B., *Le droit naturel chez saint Thomas et ses prédécesseurs*, 2 ed. (Bruges: Charles Beyaert, 1931), 61–65.

11. Oraison, *op. cit.*, 131–137, synthesizes the traditional view and expresses it in modern psychological terms. It must be remembered that even Freud is something of a traditionalist, since by his theory all that is best in culture has resulted from sublimation.

12. Janssens, "Morale conjugale . . . ," *Ephemerides theologicae lovanienses*, 39 (Oct.–Dec., 1963), 793–804, argues at length that pessimist and rigorist tendencies which determined the sexual ethics of the Stoics, neo-Pythagoreans, Essenes, and Gnostics strongly influenced the thought of many Church Fathers. Lestapis, *op. cit.*, 163, note 5, provides some material for a historical refutation. More to the point philosophically is that the consensus is more widespread than the dualist-spiritualist view of man.

13. Dupré, *op. cit.*, 69–71, makes the suggestion that human nature, and natural law with it, changes; the implication, not explicitly stated, is that perhaps contraception is or is about to become morally licit.

14. Ernest Cassirer, *An Essay on Man: An Introduction to a Philosophy of Human Culture* (New Haven: Yale University Press, 1944), 222–228, states the case in a striking way. Not all scientific anthropologists have heeded this point sufficiently. David Bidney, *Theoretical Anthropology* (New York: Columbia University Press, 1953), 120–124, states a nuanced conception of freedom; in the following chapters he develops a balanced theory of cultural evolution.

15. This notion is a commonplace in modern anthropology; see the works cited in the previous note; an introduction to the literature with extensive bibliography: A. Irving Hallowell, "Self, Society, and Culture in Phylogenetic Perspective," *Evolution after Darwin*, Vol. 2, *The Evolution of Man*, Sol Tax, ed. (Chicago: University of Chicago Press, 1960), 309–371.

16. Pierre Teilhard de Chardin, S.J., *The Phenomenon of Man* (New York: Harper and Bros., 1959), has brought the evolutionary perspective to the awareness of Catholics; however, the work of Bidney (note 14, above) shows how widespread is some form of this conception.

17. Even Aquinas remarks that human nature changes, but this remark must be understood accurately: M. B. Crowe, "Human Nature — Immutable or Mutable," *Irish Theological Quarterly*, 30 (July, 1963), 204–231, offers a study of the relevant texts, a review of recent work by Catholics on the problem, and a cautious appraisal.

18. Margaret Mead, "Some Anthropological Considerations concerning Natural Law," *Natural Law Forum*, 6 (1961), 51–64; see also the references cited, ch. IV, note 10, above.

19. Lestapis, *op. cit.*, 156–160; Oraison, *op. cit.*, 47–52, 27–33.

20. Oraison, *op. cit.*, 132–137; Suenens, *Love and Control* (Westminster, Md.: The Newman Press, 1961), 51–65; Gibert, *Love in Marriage* (New York: Hawthorn, 1964), 56–65.

21. Charles Fay, "Human Evolution: A Challenge to Thomistic Ethics," *International Philosophical Quarterly*, 2 (February, 1962), 50–80, provided the inspiration for much of what follows, although I do not always follow his treatment. In particular, he seems (63–64) to view the constants as *universals*; in one sense, this is true, since they hold for all men at all times, but they are also concrete realities in the order of potentiality. The potencies which are the same in men are no more abstract than are the acts which vary.

22. Oraison, *op. cit.*, 77–79, points out that sexual capacity will not be functional in eternal life according to Christian eschatology.

VI

"DIRECTLY WILLED, POSITIVE ACT"

BESIDES the objections which can be alleged against the theoretical foundations of our thesis, questions can be raised about the manner in which the moral prescription against contraception should be applied in practice. Does it exclude all behavior which could tend to prevent conception? Does it also exclude the use of the rhythm system of periodic continence? Until these questions are adequately clarified, a theoretical study of the objective morality of contraception cannot be considered complete.

Let us begin by examining a very general proposal for voiding in practice the prescription against contraception. Some have suggested that although contraception is intrinsically immoral as a matter of abstract principle, its morality in the concrete may be quite different.[1]

This suggestion could mean only that some who practice contraception may not be aware of the evil of their acts or may not be acting with full deliberation and freedom of choice. If this is the only import of the suggestion, it can be accepted. In Chapter VIII we shall examine questions concerning the subjective aspects of the morality of contraception. There we shall see that by no means are all who practice contraception fully responsible for acting in a seriously immoral way.

But the suggestion could have a quite different meaning. Perhaps what really is meant is that the immorality of contraception is subject to exceptions in practice. After all, many ethical maxims have only a general force. Exceptional circumstances give the right and even impose the obligation that we violate them.

There are indeed moral maxims which hold true only generally. Such maxims are those which express the conditions normally required for attaining the essential values themselves or which formulate the needs of institutions that have been established for the pursuit or the preservation of the essential values. These maxims, in other words, are only secondary or derived prescriptions of the moral law.

Many precepts of justice belong to this category. The value to which they are directly related is not one of the basic human goods, but is instead a derived and supporting, or contributory, good — e.g., property. Such values can yield under pressure from the more basic goods.[2] However, the procreative good is not a derived value. Hence, unless one wishes to defend the situationist position that all substantive values must yield under sufficient pressure, there can be no allowance for exceptions to the moral prescription against the practice of contraception.

It is mere rhetoric, not philosophical argument, to condemn an ethics which insists on the universality of primary moral principles for dealing in mere abstractions and to insist that there be room for an appeal from principles to the requirements of the concrete, human situation. Every ethical consideration of any moral issue is abstract, because it is impossible to think and to communicate in language except by working with abstractions.

Among the most abstract treatises on moral issues are situationist discussions of problems such as contraception. A few impressive facts are pointed out and many vague or even meaningless questions are raised. Attention carefully is distracted from the implications which agreement with situationism with regard to contraception would have for all other areas of morality. And so, finally, the claim is made to appear plausible that since pro-creation is not an absolute value, it should yield under the pressure of other values when in really difficult situations the lack of operational stakes seems to favor its yielding.

Such a conclusion is pure situationism, and it is no less vicious, but rather more so, if it is wrapped in pious references to Christian responsibility. Moreover, it is no defense to claim that situation-ethics in the technical sense begins only when all force is denied to every universal principle.[3] Situation-ethics is only one expression of the more widespread situationist theoretical schema.

Situationism is realized just as effectively whether basic material values are altogether denied a place among the determinants of moral reasoning or whether such values are represented by maxims which hold for the most part but which are denied the universal force appropriate to primary principles. If moral judgment can transcend a prescription in any one case, that prescription never really is a basic source for moral reasoning. Rather, such a prescription merely is an instrument used by moral judgment in the service of its actual source.

Still it may be argued that not every action which adversely affects a basic human good is objectively wrong. After all, life is a basic good, and yet in some cases killing is ethically allowed. In regard to the procreative good, also, everyone admits that some acts which do prevent conception, such as the removal of diseased genital organs, are morally allowed if they are medically indicated. Even if one refuses to admit exceptions to primary moral principles, then, clearly there are cases in which conception-preventing behavior is not wrong.

How can these be explained? Is the correct explanation perhaps this, that the exceptional circumstances can alter the moral significance of objective behavior to such an extent that one with an upright intention can consistently maintain his orientation toward the procreative good even though he occasionally acts in a way which affects it adversely?

If this proposal means that the morality of the practice of contraception must be judged by one's life as a whole rather than by a few isolated acts which have the effect of preventing conception, then it must be answered with a distinction.

On the one hand, the moral condition of persons who practice contraception differs greatly in different instances. Whether the practice is a permanent feature of one's life or an exceptional act into which one has fallen under the stress of severe temptation makes a great difference to the moral state and general value-orientation of those who use contraceptives. But this point will be considered at length in Chapter VIII when we will examine the subjective aspects of the morality of contraception.

On the other hand, the objective immorality of contraception is found not only in a permanent habit of acting in this way but also in each particular choice to have contraceptive intercourse.[4] Every single choice, however insignificant it may seem when viewed in the pattern of an entire life, to some extent invests one's freedom in a certain definite self-realization with an inescapable orientation in respect to the essential human goods.

There are two reasons why this point may not be grasped. One is that the commission of an isolated intrinsically evil action is easily confused with the isolated performance of some behavior which is not intrinsically evil but whose regular performance would be related to essential values in a different way, a way which would make regular performance intrinsically evil.

Thus, to overeat occasionally is not intrinsically evil but to do so regularly is dangerous to one's health and so it is wrong in itself. Again, to refuse in any particular instance to "do one's bit" need not be intrinsically evil, but never to "do one's bit" is wrong in itself. Again, occasionally to drink to a point just short of intoxication is not intrinsically wrong, but to do so regularly, knowing that this practice is likely to lead to alcoholism, would be wrong in itself.

In cases such as these, frequency itself changes the moral significance of action because the regularity of behavior itself necessarily implies a wrong intention which may be absent in acts of similar, but isolated, behavior. However, as we have shown, contraception in each occasion of its performance presupposes an intention directly at odds with the procreative good. The whole of this good also is violated even by one act of contraception.

The other reason why some do not see that even the occasional practice of contraception is wrong is that situationist assumptions may distort insight into the source of evil in particular actions. Situationist systems require only that their controlling values be maintained. If the controlling value in a particular mode of situationism is a certain psychic condition which itself is defined in terms of a developmental trend, hardly any single human act can have great moral importance. If the controlling value is a state or quality which may be absent or present in single instances, then acts which are decisive for it will be regarded as important in isolation.

But the common attitude of situationists toward material values assures that no single contraceptive act could be of decisive importance for any controlling value. Of course, the permanent practice of contraception could violate some norm — e.g., social duty — which a particular mode of situationism might recognize.

In fact, however, every single act has moral significance according to its relationship to the basic human goods. Each new deliberate self-commitment which implies a proper orientation toward such goods makes one better. And the converse also is true.

This is not to deny, as I have said, that the long-range trends in moral action are more important than isolated acts. If I choose to live a life of crime, that commitment is both more significant than the multitude of decisions which implement it and more important than an isolated criminal act performed by a usually law-abiding person.[5]

Still each single decision by which the hardened criminal carries out the general commitment of his life has at least an additional marginal significance, not only because of its objective consequences but also because it establishes his commitment more firmly in reality and makes his reformation more improbable. Similarly, the isolated wrong act done by the normally good person has some importance because it sets him against the good, and this disorientation will initiate a vicious trend unless it is altered by a subsequent free act.

A couple who practice contraception only once a month but who do it regularly of fixed will are set as immovably against the procreative good as they would be if they practiced contraception every day. Still each additional act renders their orientation even more definite. A couple who practice contraception for the first time also have turned against the procreative good, but their orientation will be more easily altered. Still, it must be altered if the wrong orientation is not to remain indefinitely.

Before proceeding further, let us take stock of the point at which we have arrived. Some conception-preventing behavior, responsibly undertaken, is nevertheless considered morally licit. Examples would be the removal of diseased genital organs, as mentioned above, or the effort to avoid fertilization by a woman who has been raped. On the other hand, ethical exceptions to the principle that contraception is intrinsically immoral cannot be made for particular cases, no matter how difficult particular "human situations" may be.

Moreover, we are certain from our previous argument that contraception really is intrinsically immoral. In fact, we have grasped the reason why this is so. How, then, are we to exempt the behavior in question from the judgment that it is seriously wrong?

The answer to this question will differ somewhat depending

upon whether the conception-preventing behavior is a positive act or an omission. First we must consider why certain positive acts which have a contraceptive effect can be considered morally licit, and then we must examine how the rhythm system of fertility control by periodic continence differs from contraception.

At the beginning of this consideration it may be useful to recall that our proof of the intrinsic immorality of contraception really was a demonstration that one who both chooses to have intercourse and desires to prevent its fruitfulness by a positive act cannot avoid having an intention adverse to the procreative good. Neither the conception-preventing behavior alone nor the desire to avoid pregnancy alone would have been sufficient ground on which to rest our demonstration that contraception is intrinsically evil.

The solution to the first question — how certain positive acts which have contraceptive effects can be morally licit — will consist in an explanation of the principles of indirect voluntariness and their application to the problems before us.[6]

Our will can be related to an object in three different ways.[7]

In one way, when we will that the object be (not be) or occur (not occur), whether we desire this for its own sake — the intention of the end — or whether we select it as a way to accomplish our end — the choice of a means. Any external means which we can choose always becomes an actual means only in an action of our own. While potential actions may have some definite relationship to essential human goods apart from our choice of them, clearly it is only by our choice that we take upon ourselves that relationship between actions and goods and engage our will in its positive or negative orientation in respect to the values.

In this first way, the will is said to be related "directly" to its object, since the object in this case is precisely what is willed — the end intended and the means chosen. From this is derived the expression, "direct voluntariness," which designates the acts and state of such direct volition.

In a second way our will is related to whatever could be its object in the first way but in fact is not. Thus it is related to actions which are possible, but which are not performed, and to side effects of actions performed which could be prevented, at least by omitting the action, but which are permitted to occur.

In this second way, the will is somehow related to the object, because there is at least a potential relationship, and yet the object is not precisely what is willed. Still, not to will something while foreseeing the consequences of omission or to will something while anticipating the effects of action is to be willing that such consequences or effects should occur. Hence the will is said to be related "indirectly" to such objects, since the object in this case depends upon willingness although it is not directly willed. From this is derived the expression, "indirect voluntariness," which designates the state of such indirect volition. "Permissive willingness" and "permission" also sometimes are used to name indirect voluntariness.

Finally, our will is "related" to an object with whose being or occurrence we simply are not concerned. Such an object is anything really irrelevant to us, such that we could not will it as an end, and anything which cannot be embodied in an action of ours, such that we could not will it as a means.

In this third way, the will is not really related to the object at all, and this lack of volition in relation to such objects is simple nonvoluntariness.

Now it is clear that we are not wholly without responsibility for objects of our indirect will, for sometimes we have a definite obligation to act. Then an omission, although only permitted, would be wrong. Similarly, side effects of our actions, despite the fact that they do not fall under our intention or choice, in certain circumstances must be prevented even if that means the omission of an otherwise good action. Failure to prevent bad side effects — assuming that we reasonably should anticipate them — can be serious negligence.

However, it is clear likewise that we do not have the same responsibility for the objects of our indirect will that we have for the objects of our direct will. The fundamental reason for this is that indirect voluntariness does not necessarily involve a definite orientation of the will toward or against the values, since it is possible to permit what we could forestall without actually engaging our will in it at all.[8]

Nor does anyone doubt that the responsibility for direct and for indirect voluntariness differs, since no one can act to any great extent without in some way adversely affecting some values and no one can act in every possible way favorable to all values. The complexity and intractability of the world, on the one hand, and the limitation of human power, on the other, require us to permit much which it would be wrong directly to will.

The problem, therefore, is: to find the criteria according to which we can distinguish what is directly willed from what is only indirectly willed, and to determine the conditions under which we may permit what we are morally forbidden to will directly.

One traditional, though only partial, solution to this problem is called the "principle of double effect."[9] According to this principle, whatever follows from our action, but is neither the actual behavior included in our action, nor the effect which we wish to bring about through our action, nor in the direct line of causality between the two, may be regarded as a side effect. Such side effects, if not desired on their own account, clearly are willed indirectly, since they could be prevented if we decided not to act.

According to the principle of double effect, we may choose an action having side effects, willing them indirectly even though it would be wrong to will them directly, if the following conditions are fulfilled: (1) The action itself which we choose must be a good one, since otherwise it ought not to be chosen in any case. (2) The side effect must not be separable from the action, or avoidable by reasonable effort, since otherwise we ought to avoid what it would be wrong to do. (3) Between the good our action brings about and the adverse effects which its side effects cause there should be reasonable proportionality. What "reasonable proportionality" means simply is that the *operational results* ought to be for the best, since otherwise it would be foolish to choose the action.

The fact that this third criterion is used may make it appear that this traditional principle is not far from the situationism which we have criticized so severely. Indeed, to the extent that they both make use of the criterion of operational effects, they agree. However, situationism, besides the fact that it accepts a different system of values, allows this criterion a far wider scope, since it is applied indiscriminately to direct and indirect voluntariness, whereas the traditional principle only uses it as one of a set of criteria which constitute a norm for indirect voluntariness.

In effect, for situationism the pragmatic criterion is the necessary and sufficient condition for judging the morality of external action, whereas in the traditional principle it is only one necessary condition. If even the requirements of operational objectives are not met by our action, surely it is unreasonable, but the fact that they are met does not assure that it is fully reasonable.

It is important to notice that side effects which may be permitted according to the principle of double effect are not merely undesirable and regrettable occurrences. Rather, they are occurrences which it would be wrong for us to will directly, whether as means or as end. The principle of double effect usually is called into play, in fact, when directly willing the side effect would be seriously and intrinsically wrong. Thus, for example, the principle is applied to cases which involve the incidental killing of the innocent, since to kill them with direct will would be intrinsically and very seriously wrong.

It follows that conception-prevention, although intrinsically evil when directly willed, may at times result from indirect will, and in such cases the behavior which prevents conception may be morally licit. This fact will not show that there are any exceptions to the prohibition of contraception as intrinsically evil but simply will show that there are cases in which conception-preventing behavior is not directly willed as such.

The justification we have for using the principle of double effect is that where its use is appropriate, we are doing what we can to act for the essential goods and *we are not setting ourselves directly against them*.

The last phrase is true, despite the application of the criterion of operational effects, because the adverse effect is only against some particular realization of the value in question. That is to say, the value which is damaged is damaged only in its capacity as an operational objective. It is not violated in its role as an ideal, because the intention and choice of the will are not directed against it.

Once this principle is understood, it is clear how some behavior which adversely affects essential human values can be regarded as morally right. Striking out against a sudden and unjustified attacker to preserve oneself from the results of violence is justifiable according to this principle, even though the necessary means of one's defense also hurt or even kill the attacker.[10] The use of medically indicated treatments for diseased conditions also can be justified by this principle even though such treatments have the side effect of preventing conception.[11]

Thus we have one case in which conception-preventing behavior is not contraception. The reason is that the prevention of conception in this case is only permitted — that is, willed only indirectly — and there is sufficient reason to will it in this way.

As we said in Chapter IV in our proof of the intrinsic malice of contraception, it need not be incompatible with a right orientation toward the procreative good if we permit it not to be realized, but it is necessarily incompatible with a right orientation if, while acting in a way conducive to it, we will not permit it to be realized — that is, if we set our will directly against it.

The use of a cleansing and semen-removing douche by a woman who has been raped commonly has been regarded as an extension of self-defense, since the placing of the semen by the attacker is part of his violation of the raped woman. The douche itself can be regarded as a secondary line of defense; a woman who is being raped certainly should try to make her attacker ejaculate outside her vagina, and only if this primary defense fails will there be occasion to resort to a douche.

Clearly, the first line of defense as well as the second is a positive act which tends to prevent conception, but a woman who is being raped has no obligation not to interfere in such a manner. Thus this behavior, while it prevents conception, also repels violence, and does not have the moral significance of contraception. Because she has not chosen to engage in sexual intercourse, the victim of rape has not brought upon herself the full obligating force of the procreative good. For this reason her conception-preventing behavior is able to be directly intended as self-defensive and only indirectly willed as an inhibition of the possible realization of the procreative good.

It is an easy step from this position to the view that a woman who is in danger of being raped may prepare herself in advance with suitable defenses. Thus, surely, she may wear special clothing or appliances so that her attacker will find it impossible to carry out his intent perfectly. If this line of defense either is not feasible or is not expected to be adequate, there seems to be no reason why a diaphragm or similar contraceptive device might not be worn.

From this, the further step to the use of anovulant drugs is not a very great one. Thus the use of these drugs by a woman in danger of rape may be justifiable under the principle of double effect. In this case, such a use would be *self-defensive* rather than contraceptive.[12]

Not every instance in which conception-preventing behavior must be regarded as morally allowable can be explained as an application of the principle of double effect, however. Consider the case in which diseased genital organs are removed, or even the case in which healthy gonads are excised to prevent them from secreting hormones which are aggravating a diseased condition elsewhere in the body. Cases of this kind commonly are explained by the application of another principle — the principle of totality.[13]

The principle of totality simply is that parts of the body, even genital organs, may be sacrificed when the health of the whole requires it. Of course, proportionality must be observed. Moreover, the desirable effect must follow directly. For this reason, one would not be justified by the principle of totality in removing healthy gonads in order to prevent ill effects to the health of the whole body which would not happen except as a result of conception, for in that case the direct effect of the operation would be to prevent conception rather than to cure any existing disease.

Now the principle of totality obviously is another specification of the general requirements of indirect voluntariness. What this principle tells us is that behavior which it would be wrong to will directly, since it implies restriction of life and suppression of function, nevertheless can be willed insofar as it is health-giving or life-preserving.

Yet under the principle of totality many actions are licit which could not be justified according to the principle of two-fold effect. Hence it is clear that indirect voluntariness and double effect are not identical, as they have been thought generally to be.[14]

There are some other traditionally accepted principles which express in a restricted way the requirements of indirect voluntariness. One of these is the principle that the common good may be protected against unjust violations by a system of criminal law involving the imposition of punishments proportionate to crimes. Among accepted punishments for serious offenses have been the death penalty and the lesser punishment of bodily mutilation.

The use of the death penalty obviously involves a deliberate act which is destructive to the essential human good of life. But just as clearly the principle of the common good presupposes that the destruction of human life is willed only indirectly while the execution of justice alone is willed directly.[15] Otherwise the will of all those who support the system of criminal law would be set directly against the essential good of human life. Furthermore, there is no possibility that capital punishment could be justified by the principle of double effect, since the execution of the sentence actually is an essential part of the intended workings of justice.

Among the mutilations which have been proposed as appropriate legal penalties is sterilization. If the death penalty can be inflicted, surely this much lighter punishment also can be inflicted. The conception-preventing effect of the execution of a legal sentence is as much beside the point in this case as is the conception-preventing effect of medical therapy which is justified according to the principle of totality.

Of course, we are assuming that sterilization really would be an appropriate legal penalty, a point easily questionable since those sentenced to this punishment often would not regard their inability to reproduce as a serious personal loss. Also we are assuming that sterilization really would be intended as a punishment, a point easily questionable since laws inflicting it would be likely to use it merely as an absolute contraceptive inflicted on sexual delinquents and mental defectives to save the community part of its welfare costs.

At this point it appears that an easy solution is now at hand to many arguments against the thesis that contraception is intrinsically evil. The arguments are those which allege that since sometimes conception-preventing behavior is permitted, contraception is not wrong in itself.[16]

The solution, of course, is that contraception is intrinsically evil, but conception-preventing behavior is not necessarily contraception, since it may be only indirectly voluntary. This indirectly voluntary prevention of conception may be justified either according to the principle of double effect, or according to the principle of totality, or according to the principle of the common good.

Clearly none of these permits much conception-preventing

behavior. The first requires a distinct effect which really demands that the prevention of conception be permitted incidentally. The second requires a diseased condition directly treated by the behavior which prevents conception, rather than by the nonoccurrence of conception. And the third requires a real crime serious enough to warrant a sentence of mutilation, rather than merely a socially advantageous program of absolute contraception.

In what follows, positive conception-preventing behavior permitted by these recognized principles will be considered extraordinary. All other positive, conception-preventing behavior will be called "ordinary."

Now, it is precisely at this point that the difficulties of indirect voluntariness really begin. For as soon as it is realized that the principle of double effect is not the only mode in which indirect voluntariness can be expressed, the proposal is sure to arise that perhaps a great deal of ordinary conception-prevention can be permitted under some new principle of indirect voluntariness.[17]

The merit of this idea is difficult to judge because there exists no general theory of indirect voluntariness. The criteria indicated by the principle of double effect, we can be certain, are sufficient to insure that nothing wrong will be directly willed, but we can be equally certain that these criteria are not necessary in every case for indirect voluntariness — the existence of the other modes of indirect voluntariness proves at least this much.

At this point we must discuss the proposal of W. Van der Marck, O.P. He, like Janssens, thinks that contraceptives have been condemned traditionally because of their interference with the integrity of the external marital act.[18] We criticized this distinction among methods of contraception in Chapter II.

However, it is not really essential to Van der Marck's central idea. For his proposal is that much ordinary conception-prevention should be viewed not as contraception, but as fertility-regulation. Although he does not express himself in this way, Van der Marck's actual view is that indirect voluntariness can be applied much more broadly than it has been traditionally. But let us first consider this proposal in its own terms.

Van der Marck begins[19] by reviewing the history of an altogether different moral problem, the question of organic transplantation. This procedure seems to involve an illicit mutilation of a healthy person, since it cannot be justified by the principle of totality. Many moralists consequently first took a dim view of such operations. Still one would suppose intuitively that this procedure should be allowed. The principle which can justify its acceptance has not yet been agreed upon, but the consensus in favor of the procedure nevertheless has become very strong.

Van der Marck next proceeds to point to what he considers to be the fundamental problem. How is a moral question to be posed? If the question is whether a bad act can be elected as a means to a good end, the answer already is predetermined to the negative. However, the object of the human act is not defined by the relationships of cause and effect in nature or by those of means and ends in technique. This object rather is defined by one's intention. Man gives the meaning to his own acts.

Thus, Van der Marck claims, it is intention which determines what one is doing, for intention defines a certain end and also delimits as means those proportionate acts chosen to achieve this end. Van der Marck denies emphatically that this position implies that good intentions are enough to justify bad actions. Rather, one's intention determines how his action should be categorized; and once it is properly categorized, the action must be judged according to the kind of action it is.

This analysis is applied to the problem of organic transplantation. Such a procedure is intended neither as a mutilation of oneself nor as a treatment for one's own benefit. Rather, it is meant to be an assistance to one's neighbor.

For this reason the act should not be understood as if it were a mutilation which seeks justification in an ulterior good effect. Rather, the means chosen is an operative procedure which from the very beginning is transplantation. Since the end is a good one, and the proportionate means is not to be judged intrinsically evil, Van der Marck considers this procedure licit.

The same analysis is applied to the question of conception-preventing behavior. Such procedures need not be intended precisely as contraceptive acts. Rather they may be meant as fertility-regulating acts, or simply as acts suitable for expressing love without having another pregnancy follow immediately. Since the end is a good one in this case too, and since there are now proportionate means which do not seem to be intrinsically evil on other grounds, Van der Marck also is inclined to consider this procedure licit.

Van der Marck is at least partially correct when he stresses the importance of the meaning-giving function of man in regard to his own moral action. A moral act is not simply an outward performance, as it might be considered by a behavioral psychologist, apart from its human significance. Rather, the moral act is precisely that which deliberation constructs as a possibility for realization or rejection by freedom. Hence the same behavior can often have two quite different moral values because it has two quite different human meanings.[20] This is an important fact which conventional natural-law theory tended to ignore.

However, Van der Marck falls into error because he fails to notice that there are very great limitations for our formulations. Meaning-giving is not an altogether free process.[21] Imagine that I am beating my two-year-old child over the head with a base-ball bat. Do not be distracted by the fact that I might lack the subjective conditions of imputability — i.e., knowledge of the facts and ability to choose. Van der Marck's thesis concerns the object of the act, not its subjective morality.

In the situation mentioned, I could say that what I am doing is making a scientific experiment to determine the resistance of the human skull or that I am checking the efficiency of the law-enforcement process. I could say so, but that will not alter the fact that whether I like it or not my act has another and quite different meaning. Moreover, that meaning, which arises from the physical significance of the act, is morally determinative so far as the malice of my will goes.

The reason for this limitation on our freedom in giving meaning is that the act in question has an immediate and natural relation to an essential human good — the preservation of human life. The act in question may have other morally relevant meanings, but this act necessarily would become a definite act with a definite meaning simply through this relevance. It is a relevance I am not free to ignore in giving meaning to my act.

When we come to think of it, it is clear that Van der Marck's position is absurd, for he leaves everyone with a little ingenuity free to do anything without malice. It is always possible so to define action that the moral judgment which will be passed on it would have to be favorable. As a matter of fact, we often attempt this maneuver when we want to do something wrong. We have an innate gift for this method of rationalization; we do not even require theological instruction to learn how to do it. Of course, we do not usually do it well, for we only occasionally are able to confuse even ourselves.

What Van der Marck's apparently innocent suggestion amounts to is that only the directly voluntary be considered morally significant. This suggestion ignores the problem which a general theory of indirect voluntariness must settle — under what conditions are we justified in permitting what we may not will directly.

Moreover, as we have seen, Van der Marck himself has not been clear about the prior question — which is far more difficult than he suggests — how does one distinguish the directly willed from the indirectly willed. Clearly, the directly willed includes the means and the end of the human act, but what must be included in these? Our meaning-giving simply is not completely free.

A first approach to a more adequate theory of indirect voluntariness would be to require that the conditions for the application of the principle of double effect be fulfilled, even though the principle itself is too restricted for a general theory. Thus, one must at least have a sincerely good intention, a real necessity to permit evil to occur, and the justification of proportionality.

These three principles were explained above, and each of them seems clear and broad enough to hold true in a general theory. These three principles probably would be sufficient to exclude scientific experiments which involve the crushing of skulls of live two-year-old infants — one could use corpses and it would be difficult to satisfy the principle of proportionality.

However, these three principles alone are not enough for an adequate theory of indirect voluntariness, because they do not exclude many other kinds of action which situationists tend to approve but which we are quite sure must be rejected — e.g., euthanasia, therapeutic abortion, the use of torture or suicide in warfare, and so on.

A second approach to a general theory of indirect voluntariness can be made by considering modes of indirect voluntariness which are not reducible to the principle of twofold effect. We can look at the principle of totality, the principle of the common good, and the thus-far undetermined principle which justifies organic transplantation.

The principle of totality presupposes that the three general requirements are satisfied. Also, it applies only to cases in which there are no problems with regard to justice between one person and another. Further, the same value is at stake in both meanings of the behavior having ambiguous significance which the principle is designed to cover. Moreover, exactly the same behavior has the good and the bad meanings.

Clearly, what we are faced with here is something very like the principle of double effect, except that the doubleness is in the meanings of the same behavior which is equally and directly defined in different ways in relation to one value. Since the predominant meaning in terms of proportionality is life-preserving, the sacrifices involved are justified. It is important that the value is the very same, because this fact makes it possible to compare gain and loss according to the same standard.

The undetermined principle which justifies organic transplantation must be very similar to the principle of totality. It is not the same principle, for two men are not one body, and the simple application of the principle of totality to a social unit would have totalitarian implications — e.g. that an unimportant citizen, though innocent, might be put to death for the sake of an important public objective.

However, we are still dealing with a single value. The value, as an ideal, is not limited to any single person's well-being, and so it can define behavior without regard to the differences between persons. Clearly, however, since each person has more responsibility for his own well-being than for that of others, there are limits to which one may go in sacrificing organs for the benefit of another person. Moreover, one hardly could be justly compelled to make any such sacrifice.

The mode of indirect voluntariness involved in the principle of the common good obviously is more complex. Different values are at stake, so there is no commensuration. However, the act of the state in punishing criminals can be viewed as a social extension of the application of the principle of double effect to cases of self-defense. Yet the traditional principle does not seem really to apply — the execution is too pointedly a means in the sense of "means-ends" envisaged in the traditional principle of double effect. Evidently, some leeway in defining the action of the state is allowable here.

The reason for this certainly centers on two facts: that the criminal really is guilty and that the state really has a primary responsibility for public peace and order. The guilt of the criminal has removed him from the cooperative relationships normally owed to each member by others in the society. The responsibility of the state both allows it leeway to define its action in terms of the values which define its primary responsibility and demands that those whose refusal to cooperate becomes a general threat be coerced in order to minimize the damage they will do.

Consequently, the act of the state in punishing a criminal seems to be definable in terms of the values of peace and order because the criminal's own action has drawn upon himself a community response *unavoidably* formulated in those terms. The only question one might ask is whether the *degree* of response is justified.

This second approach to a general theory does not go very far toward providing one. What it does indicate are some conditions which a sound theory should consider.

One of these is that there is greater latitude for interpretation where only a single value is at stake, since the ambiguous meanings even of the same behavior then will be commensurate with one another, and the use of proportionality will not lead to the submergence of one value by another.

Another of the conditions is that innocent persons are to be favored in interpreting acts of ambiguous meanings. Only the principle of double effect has been used to justify the destruction of the innocent.

Neither of these conditions favors the view that conception-preventing behavior not currently recognized as licit by some established mode of indirect voluntariness can be viewed as licit according to a new mode. The procreative good is not itself immediately advanced by conception-preventing behavior except in a few instances — e.g., ovulation rebound — which probably also can be justified by the principle of double effect.

The possible person in whom the procreative good might be realized if conception were not prevented certainly is innocent. If from a narrow legalistic viewpoint the possible person has no actual rights, he nevertheless has great potential value and this value does not call for nonrecognition from others, since the possible person in himself neither injures nor threatens anyone.

But there are other powerful considerations, short of the development of a general theory of indirect voluntariness, which indicate very strongly that there can be no exceptions to the general assessment of ordinary conception-preventing behavior as contraception.

In the first place, the act of preventing conception and the act of sexual intercourse itself are easily separated — in fact, they are linked together only by our own choice. All the good effects of intercourse can be had without contraception; all the ill effects of noncontraceptive intercourse can be avoided without contraception.

Although both possibilities cannot be realized simultaneously, this fact about the structure of the behavior sharply distinguishes the problem of contraception from many other problems — e.g., from that of organic transplantation. There the good results can be achieved *only* through the first part of the operation. Here, it is human choice itself which solidifies the act of contraceptive intercourse.

For a couple to undertake the use of contraceptives requires a special decision, simply because the marital office and act are not of themselves conception-preventive. It follows that precisely the act which prevents conception, not the act of intercourse as such, is the one in which conception-prevention must be found to be indirectly willed if it is to be so at all.

But the conception-preventing act in itself has absolutely no value. It leads to goods only in virtue of some of the consequences of nonconception. For example, the limitation of the family to a suitable size is a condition for the avoidance of whatever evils would follow if the family were to become too large. It is clear that we are here faced with a sequence of cause and effect in some sense and that in this sense the preventive act is a cause and the *nonoccurrence* of undesired results is the sole effect.

In considering this sequence, I do not see how it can be understood as a relationship in nature. Nor is it a relationship merely in technique. The impression is inescapable that it is precisely as a chosen *means in a human act* that the conception-preventing behavior is a cause here. But if this is so, conception-prevention is directly willed, since the means in human action is directly willed in being chosen just as the end is directly willed in being intended.

In the second place, our very argument to demonstrate the intrinsic malice of directly willed contraception indicates that apart from cases in which double effect or totality clearly apply, ordinary conception-preventing behavior cannot be only indirectly voluntary contraception. It would have been sufficient for our argument merely to indicate that the prevention of conception is a positive act opposed to the procreative good. We might simply have compared it with euthanasia.

However, we chose to deal with the point that obligation becomes more intense as the agent approaches more nearly the engagement of choice through which the value will be realized. We used this point to argue that one who chooses both to have intercourse and to prevent its effect by a positive act does something intrinsically wrong. We compared contraception with a closely parallel case in which a physician, having used elective procedures, is tempted to intervene to prevent their life-giving effect.

Now this line of argument was more convincing than merely indicating that conception-prevention is contrary to the procreative good, because this line of argument sets in relief the violation of obligation, and the consequent inconsistency of will, necessarily presupposed by the use of contraceptives.

In fact, our argument neatly precludes all admitted cases of indirectly willed conception-prevention except those which can be handled by commonly accepted applications of the principles of double effect and of totality. When these principles can be employed, it is clear that the conception-preventing behavior justified by them is susceptible to another meaning, since it really has another distinct aspect to its natural or technical entity.

Thus a person who undergoes a medically indicated treatment which incidentally prevents conception very plausibly can say: "I did not choose both to have intercourse and to avoid conception. I merely chose to have intercourse and to treat my illness, although I knew that conception would be impossible and I was willing to permit this."

On the other hand, a person who chooses both to engage in intercourse and to perform a conception-preventing act whose only significant point, so far as he is concerned, is gained by its effectiveness in preventing conception cannot very plausibly say: "I merely chose both to have intercourse and to prevent the troubles that would follow from conception. I did not choose precisely to prevent conception, although I knew my action had only this effect and I was willing to permit it."

This statement would be implausible in the circumstances not because of its second sentence in isolation, which might be uttered by a victim of rape, but because the opening phrase, "I chose to have intercourse," defines the initial behavior in the situation and excludes as unintelligible an attempt to give any meaning other than conception-prevention to the behavior whose whole point depends on its conception-preventing effectiveness.

In the third place, we certainly cannot define as one act for the purpose of indirect voluntariness a behavioral sequence which includes two *human acts*, one leading to another. Thus we cannot consider the use of terror in warfare simply an application of force having two effects, because the procedure works only if our terroristic act leads to a suitably terrorized response on the part of the enemy.

Clearly the terroristic act must be viewed as a means in the moral sense, because it is a link in the chain of human action itself. Nothing good is gained in our act; everything of value is in the subsequent free choice — or, perhaps, only potentially free choice — of the enemy. Somewhere there must be limits to what we can consider as included in one act. Clearly this is one of them, that nothing belongs to one human act which exists only in a distinct human act to which the first is intended to lead.

The most plausible justifications for contraception depend on claims which are made concerning the dire effects of abstinence. But no one has shown that the effects of abstinence seriously harm any essential human good except through additional human acts, or at least through behavior which is potentially subject to human control.

If prolonged abstinence from sexual intercourse among married persons led of itself to serious illness or even death, perhaps the act might plausibly be viewed primarily as a life-preserving one, and then conception-prevention might seem incidental and only indirectly willed. Thinking along these lines, I searched for evidence that abstinence by married couples of itself leads to serious consequences. Evidently, the only serious effects would be psychic ones.

Those who have written about psychiatric medicine seem to have given little consideration to our problem. I have been able to find no real evidence that abstinence among the married *directly* and *of itself* leads to serious psychic consequences.[22] I also have talked with a number of practitioners in this field. Their view seems to be that for prolonged abstinence, strong motivation and careful avoidance of erotic stimuli are required if frustration is not to lead to neurosis. However, given sufficient motivation, it is possible to reduce frustration by reducing erotic tension. This judgment sounds so much like traditional ascetic wisdom that it is almost disappointing.

What is clear, however, is that abstinence can lead to tension, frustration, and hostility *if it is permitted to do so*. And hostility adversely affects the relationship between husband and wife as well as that between parents and children. Thus the consequences of abstinence which are invoked to justify the use of contraception are in ulterior acts which are at least potentially subject to the control of freedom. To claim that this potentiality for self-control — i.e., not simply restraint from overt sexual action but also elimination of the painful tension — cannot be realized is fashionable, but the claim seems to be undemonstrated. The belief in the impossibility or the avoidability of this achievement, of course, insures failure.[23]

It also is important to bear in mind that unless masturbation as well as contraception is sanctioned, the most difficult cases requiring prolonged abstinence remain unresolved. These are cases in which one partner is frigid or impotent.

Moreover, in all marriages there occur periods of two months or so — e.g., at the time of childbirth — when the couple continue to live in close intimacy while intercourse is excluded. The exclusion of contraception seldom means that abstinence will be required for such a long period.

Finally it must be remembered that if absolute avoidance of conception is indicated, it can be assured only by surgical sterilization or by complete avoidance of genital contact. Even the anovulant drugs, which are the most effective contraceptives so far, are subject to human error, and this factor must be considered in judging the practical effectiveness of any means of preventing conception.

Our third consideration, then, was that a behavior sequence consisting of two human acts in which one is ordered to another cannot be considered a simple human act for the purposes of determining indirect voluntariness. Our conclusion from this consideration is that ordinary, positive, conception-preventing behavior cannot be interpreted as an indirectly willed aspect of the very same human act in which are realized in virtue of tension-reduction the important values for interpersonal relations in the family, since these good effects are achieved in subsequent behavior which itself either is a distinct human act or is at least potentially subject to voluntary control.

It should be noticed that these three considerations which tend to indicate that ordinary, positive, conception-preventing behavior cannot be merely indirectly willed contraception are independent of one another. Their force, consequently, is cumulative, and it would not be destroyed completely by the overturning of any one of them.

The results of this entire discussion of indirect voluntariness may be summarized as follows.

1. All admitted cases in which positive conception-prevention is licit are accounted for by some admitted principle, and all

such principles seem to be various modes of indirect voluntariness.

2. Indirect voluntariness extends beyond the principle of double effect. Lacking a general theory of indirect voluntariness, we cannot demonstrate rigorously that some conception-preventing behavior presently considered contraceptive may not be subject to an interpretation according to which it could be licitly willed indirectly.

3. Van der Marck's suggestion that much ordinary, positive conception-preventing behavior might be considered fertility-regulation and accepted as licit lacks a theoretical foundation, for he offers no criteria limiting freedom in meaning-giving and he offers no criteria of responsibility for what is indirectly willed.

4. The desired criteria must be more restrictive than the rules of application of the principle of twofold effect. These are necessary, but not sufficient, conditions of the uprightness of action.

5. The peculiar conditions which permit other relevant recognized modes of indirect voluntariness to extend beyond the principle of double effect are not consonant with the notion that ordinary, positive, conception-preventing behavior can be defined otherwise than as contraception.

6. Three considerations with regard to the structure of the behavior of contraceptive intercourse and its relationships to human intentions clearly show that apart from already recognized exceptions, ordinary, positive, conception-preventing behavior can reasonably be interpreted only in such a way that the prevention of conception is willed directly.

Since we demonstrated previously that this act is intrinsically evil, the inescapable conclusion is that such behavior cannot be carried on deliberately and freely without entailing serious moral evil. When we consider the subjective morality of the practice of contraception in Chapter VIII, however, we shall see that it is quite possible that many who practice contraception may do so in good faith, not knowing in the relevant way that their action is evil.

While we have many good reasons for wishing we could

practice contraception there is one superior reason for not willing to do so. That reason is that this practice sets us against
an essential human good and initiates a complex of irrationality
within our freedom.

If the behavior involved were structured otherwise, perhaps
the prevention of conception might be willed only indirectly.
If the only choice were between contraceptive intercourse and
no intercourse at all, or if the only choice were between contraceptive intercourse and fruitful intercourse, then ordinary, positive, conception-preventing behavior might be susceptible to
meanings other than the one it has.

In fact, as we shall see, those who practice contraception in
good faith tend to look at their action in this way, because so
far as practical knowledge is concerned they forget that it was
a previous free choice which limited alternatives.

We may face these facts with a certain regret, wishing that
nature had made other provisions. However, the real "guilty"
party is our own intelligence, which has its own way of constructing action. It is the "fault" of our rational intelligence
that we must proceed from principles in the first place, and
it is the further "fault" of our analytic intelligence that it makes
distinctions even while constructing the potential human action
which freedom must approve or veto.

Catholics, furthermore, are "burdened" with a tradition of
ethical reflection which has discovered and clarified many distinctions and a teaching authority which insists upon recalling
them. Hence the alternative to the limits reasonable judgment
imposes is not so much a different disposition in nature as a
less acute awareness of moral truth.

Those who see less well have less responsibility, and we may
regard them as being, in a certain sense, more "fortunate" than
ourselves. But if we try to achieve this alternative by our own
choice, that choice is irrational. Irrationality itself has much to
recommend it. The only thing really to be said against it is
that it is inhuman.

Having concluded our study of the distinction between contraception and indirectly willed, positive, conception-preventing behavior, we now can turn to the difference between contraception and the rhythm method of periodic abstinence. It must be noted that we are not undertaking a complete study of the ethics of rhythm.[24] The only question which concerns us is whether rhythm is ethically the same as contraception or not.

Janssens has argued that rhythm and contraception by anovulants are ethically similar. For him both are positive ways of preventing conception, but both respect the integrity of the marital act. Consequently, both can be approved.[25] We argued in Chapter II against Janssens' distinction between modes of contraception, and our proof of the intrinsic immorality of contraception does not allow for Janssens' distinction among methods. Moreover, we shall consider in Chapter VII and in the Appendix how the anovulant drugs do not open a way around the judgment that contraception is intrinsically evil.

Therefore, if we were to accept Janssens' analysis of rhythm, we would be forced to regard it too as contraception. Hence we must examine his argument on this point. Otherwise, a serious objection — i.e., that we condemn as intrinsically evil a mode of behavior widely regarded as sometimes licit — would be made against our conclusion.

Janssens presents the argument in question when he is considering the view that contraception is wrong because by it conception is positively excluded.[26] To this view he answers that the practice of rhythm includes the same positive exclusion. For rhythm surely excludes procreation from one's intention, and it also excludes it from the means chosen, which is the external act. What one chooses is not simply an act of intercourse but precisely an act of intercourse at a carefully determined time of sterility.

Now, Janssens argues, the order of means precisely is that of concrete reality. Hence the means receives its character from the factors which make up this concrete state of affairs. The element of time is capital among these factors. Especially for living beings whose existence is a history, time is a *positive*

factor. Hence, one who practices rhythm positively excludes
procreation by his action, effectively preventing it by a temporal
barrier just as mechanical contraceptives prevent it by a spatial
barrier. Of course, the two differ because rhythm does not
deform the marital act as mechanical contraception does.

Janssens adds to this argument the point that in the practice
of rhythm the period of abstinence is carefully calculated to
allow the egg to pass out without being fertilized; only when
there is assurance that the ripened egg has been lost is intercourse again resumed. The conclusion is the same; a positive
temporal barrier is being set up to prevent conception.[27] Thus,
only the preservation of the integrity of the external marital
act distinguishes rhythm from contraception.

For us, of course, the point that the external marital act does
keep its integrity has some psychological importance, but it does
not distinguish rhythm from contraception. If we are not to
consider rhythm ethically equivalent to contraception, we must
show in what sense Janssens is mistaken when he insists that
mechanical contraception and rhythm are alike in *positively*
excluding conception.

The first point to notice about Janssens' argument is that he
has a peculiar way of making the distinction between the intention of the end and the choice of the means. He thinks the
second is concerned with the concrete, outer world where behavior goes on, while the first seems to be on the side of subjectivity alone.

We would say rather that the end intended is first an object
of cognition, but if action is successfully completed it is realized,
and its actuality may be in the external world.

Thus the intention to procreate is realized in the infant; on
the other hand, the intention to understand the ethics of contraception can be realized only in the intellect. As for the
means, they too primarily exist as objects of cognition formed
in the process of deliberation. Subsequently, depending upon
the kind of end which we are trying to attain, the means sometimes comes to realization through our behavior in the world.

Once this distinction is understood, it is clear that Janssens' argument rests on an assumption which need not be true — namely, that because (on his view) the concrete world is the arena of means, the main factors which are positive conditions of the concrete world also enter as positive elements of the means insofar as it is a human act. Thus, inasmuch as time is a positive factor in the concrete world, Janssens considers it a positive factor in the human act which is performed when rhythm is practiced, since rhythm depends upon establishing a temporal "barrier" between sperm and egg.

However, not everything which is positive in our behavior considered as part of the world is positive behavior considered as moral action. Only those factors which must be willed as such if the action is to be performed necessarily are positive factors in our behavior considered as moral action. It is true in Janssens' personal meaning of "positive" that both rhythm and contraception involve a "positive exclusion" of conception; but we shall see that in another, and more relevant, meaning of "positive," rhythm need not involve any positive act which prevents conception.

Once these preliminary points have been made, we must clarify what precisely is done by one who practices rhythm. It might seem that the difference between contraception and rhythm is the fact that the latter is mere omission while the former is action. But this observation is not adequate.

The fact is that those who practice rhythm choose, and must repeatedly choose, not to engage in intercourse, and this choice itself is a human act and a means even though it does not lead to outward behavior. Even if the practitioner of rhythm is so habituated that he no longer has occasion to choose not to act, his omission is equivalently the same as action, for one is responsible for not choosing when he can and should do so.

But here is the precise question. Does the person who practices rhythm have an obligation at the time he abstains to engage in sexual intercourse? The answer to this question cannot be a simple yes or no. As we have seen, the very state of marriage imposes some obligation to act for the value which defines it — procreation.

Thus sometimes it may be the case that rhythm has the *same essential malice* as contraception. Both *can be* chosen in defiance of a binding obligation that we act for the procreative good, and such defiance would set the will directly against the good. Moreover, the fact that we cannot say in general and cannot easily judge in the particular when this obligation is fully operative does not mean that it never can be so.

Still, not everyone who practices rhythm sets himself against the procreative good in the way that the person who practices contraception necessarily does so. Janssens suggests that the intention is the same in either case. But if what he says were true, both would directly will conception-prevention *as an end.*

The truth is that while both wish to avoid conception and do avoid it purposely, neither is likely to will the avoidance of conception itself as if it were an end. Both intend, in the strict sense of "intend," some other positive good.[28] Therefore, generally speaking, neither primarily and directly wills what ought not to be directly willed on this account — generally speaking, for someone simply might consider conception-prevention a good in and of itself. The problem primarily concerns choice. Those who decide to use rhythm, unlike those who decide to practice contraception, need not choose conception-avoidance as a means in any of their human acts.

Thus, those who practice contraception can avoid directly willing in their choice of means what ought not to be directly willed only by being confused about what they are choosing. Those who use rhythm can avoid directly willing what ought not to be directly willed in their choice of means simply by being clear in their thinking, assuming they are upright in their intention — "intention" in the strict sense. To see why this is so, we must examine the two modes of conduct and compare them with one another so far as the will-acts involved are concerned.

The practice of rhythm is a complicated moral act. It involves choices at two levels of generality. At the lower level, one who practices rhythm chooses on particular occasions to have intercourse or to abstain.

He chooses to engage in intercourse during sterile periods. His sole *intention* in having intercourse should not be that it will be sterile, for in that case his act could hardly be anything but a malicious gesture against the procreative good. Presumably, he will *intend* some good end — e.g., the psychological value of intercourse.

Of course, he would not have intercourse unless he thinks it will be sterile, but there is a difference between a condition without which one would not be willing to act and the precise reason for one's act. One need not directly will the conditions without which he would not be willing to act. One need not intend them precisely as his reason for acting; one need not choose them precisely as his means in acting. Thus a physician willing to administer a certain treatment only in desperate cases need not directly will the desperateness of the cases.

The person who practices rhythm also chooses not to engage in intercourse during times of fertility. This choice can be wrong, as we have said. Yet married persons can have sufficient reasons for choosing to abstain from fruitful intercourse. Such choices to abstain are choices to omit action which would further the procreative good, but this inhibition of the good can be willed only indirectly.

The reason for this is that the omission, not being expressed in definite behavior, is open to interpretation according to other categories than simple conception-prevention. Inasmuch as it is the only alternative to fruitful intercourse, abstinence can be understood, for example, as a choice to preserve or to contribute to some other good.

Moreover, the choice to abstain really may have this other meaning, whereas overt, conception-preventing behavior does not of itself contribute to anything. Still, if merely a negative will with respect to procreation is present, then conception-prevention is directly willed. In such a case the practice of rhythm would have the same intrinsic malice as contraception.

Besides the single choices to have intercourse during sterile periods and to abstain from it during fertile periods, one who uses rhythm also chooses this practice as such. This choice is on a different level from the other acts, since it is a choice of a certain pattern of choosing. This kind of act might be called a "policy decision," since it does not directly concern the behavior it ultimately controls but only the way future choices are to be made.

Like any moral act, a policy act has its moral character primarily from the value of what is chosen (and done) in it. The contents of this policy act are the choices previously discussed. If they are unobjectionable, then to that extent the policy to choose thus also will be unobjectionable.

The intention especially attached to the policy act, however, is not necessarily beyond question even if the act is not objectionable from the point of view of its content. If the act is to be good, the intention must not be conception-prevention; it must be some other good with this effect only an object of will indirectly.

Also, circumstances of the choice — e.g., the unwillingness of either partner to follow the system or to abstain from orgasm altogether during fertile periods — may make the policy decision wrong. But if there is nothing questionable about intention or circumstances, then the act itself, because it does not necessarily involve any act directed against the procreative good, can be licit.

The whole issue rests on the fact that indirect voluntariness has room to operate here in a way that is impossible where there is overt conception-preventing behavior, for those who choose the practice of rhythm need not do so precisely insofar as they also place themselves in the full obligatory focus of the procreative good. Consequently, they have reasonable grounds to interpret their behavior, which indeed does prevent conception, as having primarily another meaning.

If it seems unlikely that this requirement for a good intention ever is realized, this may be because the meanings of "wish" and "intend" are so easily confused. One who practices rhythm wishes to avoid conception, but his action does not demand this as its primary meaning.

It may be objected that the practice of rhythm as such also involves some overt behavior — e.g., the keeping of a calendar or the graphing of temperatures. It is quite true that this behavior belongs to the practice of rhythm. Of itself, however, this behavior does not prevent conception. In fact, it is not directly involved in the acts of intercourse or abstinence at all.

This overt behavior is part of the choice-making process; it represents part of the execution of the policy decision to practice rhythm. The acts in question, therefore, although overt, positive behavior are not appropriately interpreted as conception-preventing behavior; they are appropriately interpreted as decision-making behavior.

In the practice of contraception, similar elements of analysis must be distinguished. Here the contraceptive acts individually are immoral, and so the policy act also is immoral. The intention of this policy act might have been good, at least in the first instance. But the choice is bad. And in a way this bad choice redounds to vitiate the intention as well, since it implies some basic disorder in willingness.

Yet it must be noticed that if the individual acts were not immoral, the decision to practice contraception could be precisely like the decision to practice rhythm. We shall return to this point when we consider the subjective morality of contraception. If the immorality of the individual acts is known, the policy act to practice contraception must be immoral, since its object is immoral. No good reason, as we have seen, can alter this fact.

Janssens tends to confuse the whole question by not distinguishing between individual acts and policy acts, and by not considering separately the individual acts of abstinence and intercourse in the case of those practicing rhythm. If these acts are all viewed confusedly, no doubt the practice of rhythm must appear to be simply another method of contraception.

Indeed, it can be so, but for those who have discovered — or been instructed — how to make the requisite and *completely reasonable* distinctions and who meet the other important conditions rhythm need not be a method of contraception. Their desire to preserve and promote certain goods leads them only to permit the nonrealization of the procreative good. Their wish that procreation should not occur is like the wish of a man who hopes his suffering friend will soon die. Nothing against the good is *chosen* because it is loved too well to be directly violated.

Janssens' argument that rhythm includes the positive prevention of conception because time is a real factor in the concrete world is nugatory. He might have pointed out just as well that rhythm includes a positive spatial barrier, because periodic continence avoids conception by seeing to it that sperm and egg do not meet — a matter of space as much as of time. But this point would have made it easier to notice where his argument goes wrong.

The spatiotemporal "barrier" in rhythm is not really a barrier at all. It simply is a real condition of this external behavior to be thus related in space and time to fertility. The meeting which does not occur need not be as such the directly willed object of any act on the part of those who practice rhythm. Nonfertilization is not *something we cause* in order to prevent conception. Rather, it simply is the facticity of the objective state of affairs interpreted in relation to the policy act by which we decide to practice rhythm.

The fact that rhythm is so easily interpreted as conception-prevention reveals what one *wishes* who practices it. But it does not demonstrate what one *intends*, as Janssens imagines. If intention were so easily determined the whole study of indirect voluntariness above would have been unnecessary, since it is self-evident that he who uses a contraceptive *wishes* to avoid conception. But Janssens consistently uses "intend" in a loose sense, as equivalent to "wish."

We do not deny, of course, that time is an important aspect

of the world. It does enter into and condition human action in important ways. One who practices rhythm has intercourse at a certain time, and that time always is an important circumstance of his act. However, the time itself need never be willed precisely as a preventive of conception, because it is never posited to accomplish or to prevent anything. It is only one of the carefully considered circumstances of the act which is chosen and posited.

The greatest significance of time so far as rhythm is concerned, however, is that time makes possible distinct human acts — choices to have intercourse for good reasons and choices to abstain for good reasons. If there were no temporal succession, one would have to choose one or the other. Or, like those who have no patience with time, one would have to practice contraception — i.e., one would have to choose both to have intercourse and not to have it at the same time. A spatial difference does not open the same possibility of acting and omitting.

The general solution to Janssens' argument, then, is that although the practice of periodic continence contains many positive factors, none of them necessarily has these two damning characteristics — to be objectively opposed to the procreative good and unavoidably to be directly willed in that capacity. As we argued very carefully above, the practice of contraception, on the other hand, does contain a factor, the conception-preventing act, which has these two characteristics.

One who practices contraception must intend — or, better, choose — precisely to prevent conception. One who practices rhythm need not thus set himself against the procreative good. In this sense, contraception includes *positive* prevention of conception and rhythm does not. Janssens in this case, as in his distinction between modes of contraception, seems to embrace a kind of phenomenalism which obscures the most relevant factors. Moreover, his ambiguous language promotes confusion rather than analytic clarification.

A comparison of the distinction between rhythm and contraception with the distinction between limitation of treatment and euthanasia will confirm our conclusion. In our argument in Chapter IV against contraception, we considered the case of a physician who is tempted to give an antidote in order to prevent the life-giving effects of an extraordinary treatment he had freely undertaken. Suppose, in that case, the question had been whether it would be licit for him to discontinue the application of the extraordinary means of sustaining life in order to allow the suffering patient to die peacefully. Then the judgment would have been quite different, since by ceasing to apply extraordinary means the physician only would be abstaining from doing what he has no strict obligation to do.

In general, too, a physician might make a policy decision that he will not resort to extraordinary elective procedures to sustain life. He will allow patients to die; but he will do nothing to hasten death. Such a policy would be similar to the decision to practice rhythm. One need not directly will the death-dealing effect of the omission, even if the omission involved the discontinuance of certain external behavior — e.g., the disconnection of a heart-lung machine. But one cannot help directly willing the death-dealing effect of a positive action which tends of itself only to cause death — e.g., the use of the anticoagulant in our example, or the administration of the conventional overdose of morphine.

Someone may object that the practice of rhythm nevertheless seems as unnatural as the practice of contraception, since both lead to the same frustration of nature. However, contraception is not wrong because it is artificial nor is rhythm different from contraception by being "natural." Both involve a certain technique. But the two primarily need not presuppose the same choice, and they eventually imply a difference of intention. The ethics of the matter is not settled by how extensively nature is frustrated. It is settled by whether particular modes of behavior necessarily presuppose a vicious will. Rhythm can be wrong; contraception cannot be right.

Contraception and rhythm need not be merely different outward behavior aimed at executing exactly the same volition.[29] This widely accepted view simply assumes that there is no important ethical distinction between them. However, the use of contraception, if one knows clearly what he is doing, presupposes the assumption that fertility is an evil which must be controlled.

Of course, the factor opposing reasonable judgment which requires control is not fertility but erotic tension. Fertility is an intelligible good which may be realized or not by choice; it also is an objective fact which appears to be an evil to any couple who are not willing to limit the frequency of orgasm.

The use of rhythm, if one knows clearly what he is doing and wills only what is right, presupposes the assumption that sexual activity must be subordinated primarily to the procreative good and then also to other values. Needless to say, this partial truth will lead to grief unless one also realizes that erotic tension must be reduced, for without this realization frustration will become painful.

NOTES TO CHAPTER VI

1. Dupré, "Toward a Re-examination . . . ," *Cross Currents*, 14 (Winter, 1964), 71–72 and *passim*, contrasts the abstract principle with the concrete application; his precise point is unclear. He specifically denies (71) that he means to accept situation-ethics. He interprets S.t., 1–2, q. 94, a. 4, as a distinction between general principles "and the conclusions, the practical applications, which, derived from these principles, are true only *ut in pluribus*." Needless to say, the phrase "practical applications" suggests a peculiar interpretation of the text, the accuracy of which each reader may judge for himself. Dupré goes on to say that application of a general principle seems automatically to place it among "conclusions" in a situation where opposite principles meet. But then he seems to reverse ground by denying that every concrete ethical rule admits of exceptions. Dupré makes a great deal (72, note 9) of the fact that Aquinas considers *some precepts* concerned with man's sexual life to be secondary rather than primary. But one need only read the passages cited (*S.t.*, 3, sup., q. 65, aa. 1–2 — *In 4 Sent.*, d. 33, q. 1, aa. 1–2) without Dupré's editing, to see that the precept violated by contraception *is primary* for Aquinas. See also: S.c.g., 3, chs. 122–124; S.t., 2–2, q. 154, aa. 11–12.

2. Crowe, "Human Nature — Immutable or Mutable," *Irish Theological Quarterly*, 30 (July, 1963), 204–231, in discussing passages where Aquinas remarks that human nature changes, mentions the classic example of precepts which admit of exception — S.t., 2–2, q. 57, a. 2, ad 1 — the matter of returning a deposit of weapons to someone who intends to make bad use of it. Even very good commentators — e.g., Overbeke, "La loi naturelle et le droit

naturel selon saint Thomas," *Revue Thomiste*, 57 (1957), 474–490 — try to treat derived precepts as if they were really indefectible. This view is consistent with conventional natural-law theory, but alien to Aquinas, who does admit exceptions to secondary precepts: *S.t.*, 1–2, q. 94, a. 4. However, even his early works (e.g., *In 3 Sent.*, d. 37, a. 3) indicate that the primary precepts are *not mere abstractions*; the *S.t.* treatise on law leaves no doubt that primary precepts effectively bind: 1–2, q. 100, a. 8, where the precepts of the decalogue (they belong to the law of nature, a. 1) are said to bind indispensably. Cf. Liam Ryan, "The Indissolubility of Marriage in Natural Law," *Irish Theological Quarterly*, 30 (October, 1963), 309–310.

3. It is by no means clear that situation-ethics in the technical sense begins only when the force of general norms in particular cases is totally denied. Ford and Kelly, *Contemporary Moral Theology*, Vol. I, *Questions in Fundamental Moral Theology* (Westminster, Md.: The Newman Press, 1958), 116: "The primary distinctive mark of the new morality is its attitude toward moral laws. It either denies the existence of objective moral laws or at least it subordinates these laws to what it calls personality values. In a word, the moral law, if it exists at all, does not have a universal and absolute character." This is a part of a paraphrase of an allocution of Pius XII, April 18, 1952, to the International Congress of the World Federation of Catholic Young Women — *AAS*, 44 (1952), 413–419.

4. The vicious act is worse than the vicious habit absolutely speaking: *S.t.*, 1–2, q. 71, a. 3. Henri Rondet, S.J., *The Theology of Sin* (Notre Dame, Ind.: Fides Publishers Association, 1960), 90, states the essential theology of this point.

5. Oraison, *Man and Wife* (New York: The Macmillan Co., 1962), 131–133, contrasts the morality of goals with the morality of acts; this is perfectly acceptable if we realize that the difference is between more and less important *moral acts*. The long-range trends in moral life are established by our more significant moral acts — e.g., the decision to try to live a certain sort of life.

6. Herbert G. Kramer, C.PP.S., *The Indirect Voluntary or Voluntarium in Causa* (Washington, D. C.: The Catholic University of America, 1935), is a useful introduction to the traditional doctrine on this subject.

7. See: Kramer, *op. cit.*, 53–63. Our exposition is based on a number of Thomistic texts, but it represents a synthesis of their content: *S.t.*, 1–2, q. 1, a. 3, ad 3; q. 6, a. 3; q. 71, a. 5, c. and ad 2; q. 77, a. 7; 2–2, q. 46, a. 2, ad 2; q. 64, a. 8; q. 79, a. 3, ad 3. The prime source for the notions of *intention* of end and *election* of means is *S.t.*, 1–2, qq. 12–13.

8. Whether or not the will is engaged in the evil object is not merely a technicality, it is all-important. Aquinas explains that in tolerating evil we can be following the good example of divine providence — *S.t.*, 2–2, q. 10, a. 11; God is absolutely incapable of willing evil — *S.c.g.*, 1, ch. 95 — yet providence does not altogether exclude evil from things, 3, ch. 71. Reflection on this point should remove any notion that the necessity of sometimes willing evil indirectly arises only from a lack of technical proficiency on man's part; it is inherent in any effort to achieve good in complexity.

9. Kramer, *op. cit.*, 74–83, outlines the principle and its rules of application rather more fully than is usual; J. T. Mangan, "An Historical Analysis of the Principle of Double Effect," *Theological Studies*, 10 (March, 1949), 41–46, shows how the principle developed in some texts. Lottin, *Morale fondamentale* (Tournai, Belgium: Desclée et Cie, 1954), 262–268, 281–295, discusses the principle, especially in reference to Aquinas, and treats some applications. Joseph

J. Farraher, S.J., "Notes on Moral Theology," *Theological Studies*, 24 (March, 1963), 69–78, summarizes and discusses some recent controversies involving the principle.

10. This was the chief case for which Aquinas stated the principle: *S.t.*, 2–2, q. 64, a. 7.

11. Ford and Kelly, *op. cit.*, Vol. 2, *Marriage Questions*, 341–342, 345–346; Dupré, *op. cit.*, 74, remarks on the fact that intention rather than behavior is determinative in such cases, as if this were a recent development.

12. Ford and Kelly, *op. cit.*, Vol. 2, 365–367, provide an introduction and bibliographical notes. See also: Farraher, *op. cit.*, 81–85.

13. Ford and Kelly, *op. cit.*, Vol. 2, 318–327; the *locus classicus* is: *S.t.*, 2–2, q. 65, a. 1.

14. A study of the texts in Aquinas which we have been citing should be enough to convince anyone of this point. Omission certainly can be indirectly willed, yet the principle of double effect does not apply to omission as such. Also, the explanation of the principle of totality — *S.t.*, 2–2, q. 65, a. 1 — especially the end of the response and ad 1, show that the very same behavior would be evil if special conditions did not obtain.

15. Aquinas nowhere says this, but he always seems to assume it; see: *S.t.*, 1–2, q. 1, a. 3, ad 3; 2–2, q. 25, a. 6, ad 2; q. 64, a. 2.

16. O'Leary, "Some Thoughts about the Oral-Steroid Pill," *Jubilee* 11 (March, 1964), 44–46, argues that since sometimes sterilization is permitted, the use of anovulants need not be considered wrong in itself.

17. Although they do not state matters in this way, Dupré, *op. cit.*, 74–76, and Janssens, "Morale conjugale . . . ," *Ephemerides theologicae lovanienses*, 39 (Oct.–Dec., 1963), 824 (read in the light of 788–789), make remarks which suggest that they perhaps have in mind some such proposal. Unfortunately, both are unclear as to precisely where the issues over indirect voluntariness must be met. Van der Marck, as we shall see, has the merit of having proposed a fairly clear idea along this line.

18. Van der Marck, "Vruchtbaarheidsregeling . . . ," *Tijdschrift voor theologie*, 3e, #4 (Jaargang, 1963), 409–410.

19. *Ibid.*, 397; the section we are summarizing runs to 403.

20. Van der Marck (401, *note* 92) rightly cites Aquinas: *S.t.*, 1–2, q. 12, a. 3, ad 2; he also notes other passages, including q. 20, a. 6, but he does not deal with a. 2 of the same question.

21. Although the goodness of will depends upon the object willed (*S.t.*, 1–2, q. 19, aa. 1–2) so that in a certain sense everything depends on a right intention (a. 7), the intention relates to an object which has its own suitability or unsuitability to reason (q. 18, a. 5 and following articles). In other words, human meaning-giving is bound (q. 20, a. 2) by the real reference of what we do to the primary principles of practical reason (*De malo*, q. 2, a. 4).

22. Of course, one can find all sorts of *opinions* on this topic, but I have found no solid *evidence*. The view of some psychoanalysts that regular orgasm is essential to health does not seem to be the consensus of the profession. If one wants opinions, Oraison, *Man and Wife* (New York: The Macmillan Co., 1962), 135–136, says: "It is amazing how many women and men there are, deeply Christian in other respects, who are inclined to consider the sex urge as a categorical imperative mandated by some biological organism or other, and who cannot agree that it may readily be overridden with a pliable effort when the joint good of a married couple calls for self-renunciation." Oraison is trained in psychiatry, and his whole book develops this idea. Robert P.

Odenwald, M.D., "Too Many Children?" *The Sign*, 41 (March, 1962), 16–17, 77–80, remarks (80): "The belief that adults simply must have sexual intercourse is a purely secular belief that seems to have been sold to all modern men and women — Catholic and non-Catholic." Odenwald, a psychiatrist, then goes on to explain that it is difficult, but psychologically not impossible, to practice *total* abstinence.

23. Suenens, *Love and Control* (Westminister, Md.: The Newman Press, 1961), 59–61, remarks on this point in a brief but striking way.

24. See: ch. I, note 7, above.

25. Janssens, *op. cit.*, 824.

26. *Ibid.*, 817–818.

27. *Ibid.*, 820–823.

28. *S.t.*, 1–2, q. 12, a. 1: intention in the strict sense is an act of the will with regard to the end insofar as it is a principle to which action is directed. In this sense, obviously, not everything wished for is intended, since if we do not directly will something or do not will it as a principle of the ordination of action, we do not intend it.

29. Lestapis, *Family Planning and Modern Problems* (New York: Herder & Herder, 1961), 180–194, has emphasized the difference between the two as much as anyone.

VII

PROBLEMS IN THE USE
OF DRUGS

EVEN if our theoretical conclusions are accepted, it will be pointed out that the development of drugs having a contraceptive effect introduces a new complexity into the ethics of contraception. This point must be admitted. The new drugs do complicate the whole question, but we must notice precisely how they do so.

It is not that these new drugs modify the intrinsic immorality of the contraceptive act. As we have seen, this act is immoral because one who chooses to engage in intercourse cannot choose to perform an action which achieves nothing good except through preventing conception without directly setting his will against one of its own basic principles — the procreative good.

The real reason why the new drugs introduce new complexity is that they can achieve many effects other than simply preventing conception, and so they have many good uses. For this reason the principles of indirect voluntariness come very much into play.

A discussion of possible uses of various drugs, consequently, must employ the principles we have been examining in a very precise and technical manner. We have placed this discussion in an appendix, since it will not be interesting to many readers.

But Janssens' specific arguments for the liceity of using hormone-like drugs to prevent conception have aroused general interest. Hence we shall treat these arguments here. What Janssens has suggested is that this use of drugs may be approved under almost the same conditions which commonly are accepted as adequate justification for the use of rhythm.[1]

Janssens' first argument is that the use of conception-preventing drugs does not interfere with the nature and structure of the marital act.[2] This point must be granted to the extent that the drugs do not alter the external aspects of sexual intercourse. However, it is obvious that they do alter — or, more precisely, corrupt — the nature of the conjugal act to the extent that they preclude its fruitfulness.[3]

The fact that the drugs do not alter the experienced aspects of the marital act render their effect inconspicuous and remove certain psychological dangers which can arise from the use of other methods of contraception. No doubt an act which can violate two goods is more seriously wrong than an act which violates only one good.

If the anovulant drugs do not have any other important effects, therefore, their use as contraceptives is less seriously wrong than the use of other methods of conception-prevention. However, the if-clause is not yet demonstrated, and even if it is true, the contraceptive act as such remains seriously immoral.

Insofar as the new method renders the fact of contraception inconspicuous, it easily leads those who do not reflect to suppose that it is not contraception at all. Such persons cannot distinguish the phenomena of the behavior pattern from the morally significant elements involved in it.

Janssens' second point is that just as rhythm can be abused or properly used, so the conception-preventing drugs can be used to avoid generous fruitfulness or they can be used according to that norm.[4] The point with respect to the possible abuse of rhythm must be granted. It certainly can be employed to violate the norm which should govern the decision of a married couple about the size of their family. Moreover, as we said above, to practice rhythm directly willing the prevention of conception has the same intrinsic malice as contraception.

However, rhythm can be employed to promote or protect other goods while the prevention of conception is only indirectly willed. We must insist again that to wish or to hope for something, even to arrange for it by one's omission, does not necessarily imply that one *intends it as an end* or *chooses it as a means*.

Those who practice contraception without ill will — and how this occurs we shall consider in the next chapter — certainly might employ the drugs in question according to proper norms. However, the same can be said for the use by such persons of other methods of contraception. Thus, for example, Protestants who practice contraception with an upright conscience should not be condemned because they employ the means prescribed by their physicians — very likely, a diaphragm and jelly.

The use of anovulants as contraceptives is no more capable of being understood primarily as other than conception-preventing, and so willed only indirectly, than is the use of other means of contraception. Unlike the use of rhythm, as our analysis in Chapter VI showed, positive conception-preventing behavior which has no other significant effect except through the prevention of conception demands interpretation as a human act of contraception. Intervention by drugs as well as by mechanical means requires this meaning, but nothing done in the practice of rhythm *necessarily* requires it.[5]

Janssens' third point is that the use of the conception-preventing drugs should not be considered direct sterilization.[6] His argument for this point has two phases. In the first he recalls his position that rhythm positively excludes fecundity. Both in the act chosen and in the intention, Janssens claims, rhythm is a human intervention which has for its primary end, sought by the will, the deprivation of particular sexual acts of their power to generate. From this position, Janssens argues that definitions of direct sterilization, although they clearly apply to the use of conception-preventing drugs, are too narrow.

Our analysis of Janssens' confusions with respect to "positive" and "intention" has shown, however, that rhythm does not necessarily fall under the condemnation of direct sterilization. All the acts which rhythm involves, including the policy decision to practice rhythm, can have a meaning other than conception-prevention. The "intention" of avoiding conception which rhythm certainly involves need not be the direct willing of anything against the procreative good.

In the second phase of this argument, Janssens offers a comparison from a physiological point of view between rhythm and the use of conception-preventing drugs. The two main points of this comparison are that certain progestational steroids are said to have their effect by delaying fertility and putting the ovaries at rest — thus preventing the development and waste of eggs — and that the use of these drugs enhances rather than inhibits subsequent fertility.

We do not wish to argue about the correctness of the physiological data. They are irrelevant. However, they can seem to be relevant for three reasons.

In the first place, the force of phenomenalism in our thinking may make it appear that a drug which does not set up any physical barrier and which does not do any physiological damage cannot be really contraceptive. It seems to be "natural" and good rather than "unnatural" and bad.

The naturalness of the use of such drugs itself must be questioned. The drugs so far marketed are not natural, hormonal substances; they are synthetic, hormonelike substances.[7] Moreover, how their long-term effects may differ from those of natural hormones is not yet known. Further, even if the drugs were themselves natural (in the physiological sense), their use would be an intervention of art.

But all these points really are beside the point, and it is most unfortunate — because completely confused — when the question of the morality of the use of conception-preventing drugs is argued on this basis. The drugs are not to be condemned because they are not natural substances nor because their application is artificial. On these grounds they more than likely would be approved, since medical art by "unnatural" means has worked great wonders in preserving life, health, and fertility.

The essential point about the use of the conception-preventing drugs is that however they work, their contraceptive use is an unambiguous deed designed to accomplish a definite effect. As such the act by which they are used happens to be immoral. The situation here is like the one which would occur if the physician of our example, who is tempted to use an anti-coagulant, were to point out that he only wishes to restore the blood of his patient to its physiologically normal condition. It happens that the normal condition is the one in which the patient will die quickly.

In this case, the "naturalness" of the effect of the treatment would in nowise alter the fact that the administration of the antidote would be murder. One commits murder when he uses an inconspicuous drug producing only a "natural" effect, if that effect is meant to be deadly, just as surely as if he had used a butcher knife.

Of course, the mess in the second case would make it obvious to everyone that murder was done, whereas the inconspicuousness of the first method hides its real meaning from unreflective minds. Naturally, the psychology of the two murderers would be different too. The wielder of the butcher knife very likely would be less fully responsible.

In the second place, Janssens' physiological data may seem relevant because many moralists have viewed the use of the conception-preventing drugs as a mode of temporary sterilization, and surgical sterilization is a mutilation — that is, a violation of the value of life and health. Clearly, the drugs in question, if they work as claimed, cause no mutilation.

However, some moralists, confused by the lack of phenomenal similarity between pharmacological and mechanical methods of contraception or influenced by the perverted-faculty principle, placed almost exclusive emphasis on the suppression of function itself, thus distracting attention from the contraceptive significance of a mode of behavior hardly likely to be considered seriously wrong on other grounds.[8]

There can be no doubt that surgical sterilization, performed for its contraceptive effect, is much more seriously wrong than simple contraception. It is more serious not only because it is permanent but also because it detracts both from the procreative good and from the bodily integrity of the person who is sterilized. A temporary and easily reversible suppression of function, on the other hand, hardly seems to warrant consideration as mutilation, whether or not there is a slight destruction of nonessential tissue.

Insofar as "sterilization" simply means the suppression of fertility, the use of the conception-preventing drugs is a temporary sterilization. Since the effect for the person himself is of no serious consequence, if there is any good reason for causing it other than one to be gained through the prevention of conception, I see no reason why such temporary sterilization should not be considered licit. However, if the prevention of conception is directly willed, as it must be if the use of the drugs is undertaken for their contraceptive effect, then the sterilization is direct — i.e., it is contraception. In such a case, everything we have concluded about contraception applies to the use of the conception-preventing drugs.

In the third place, Janssens' physiological data may seem relevant because they indicate that there are uses for progestational steroids other than contraception. Thus they have been used, as Janssens points out, to promote fertility, and they really do have a beneficial effect on certain previously infertile women.

Clearly, a drug used to promote fertility is not *simultaneously* used to inhibit it. One who used the drug to promote fertility, while knowing that fertility also would be suppressed for a certain period, certainly would will nothing against the procreative good. Some have concluded that since this use is licit, a conception-preventing use also is licit.[9]

But this conclusion is absurd. It assumes that if an act is to be intrinsically evil, it must be evil simply by the outward behavior itself. Our whole examination of indirect voluntariness showed how naïve this assumption is. Moreover, this argument assumes that the intention which determines the object of the act simply can be discounted in judging its morality. But again, our discussion of indirect voluntariness showed how mistaken this view is.

A moral act does not have determinate moral quality apart from intention. On the other hand, it does not have determinate moral quality by free meaning-giving alone. The fact that end-in-view sometimes settles the morality of an act, therefore, should not lead anyone to imagine that one need only examine the agent's "intentions."[10] However, intention and choice sufficiently grounded in the objective facts can make *ambiguous* behavior into a morally good act, while a different intention would make the same behavior into a morally bad act.

We conclude that Janssens has failed to offer any convincing argument to show that contraception by pill should be judged morally licit. Standing on solid arguments against contraception as such, we consider that the burden of proof is on him who approves any method of contraception.

NOTES TO CHAPTER VII

1. Janssens, "Morale conjugale . . . ," *Ephemerides theologicae lovanienses*, 39 (Oct.–Dec., 1963), 824: one should not use progestational steroids if periodic continence suffices, but if the latter is indicated but impracticable or ineffective, the drugs may be used "il nous semble" for a justifiable regulation of births.

2. *Ibid.*, 820–821.

3. Janssens begins — *ibid.*, 788 — by noting that moralists have condemned the use of sterilizing drugs as against the fifth commandment. Some moralists have, but the contraceptive use of these drugs should be condemned chiefly as against the sixth, rather than the fifth, commandment. They violate the procreative good very significantly, the life and health of the person using them less importantly, perhaps little at all.

4. *Ibid.*, 821.

5. Ford and Kelly, *Contemporary Moral Theology*, Vol. 2, *Marriage Questions* (Westminster, Md.: The Newman Press, 1963), 317–318, indicate that there is an extensive tradition condemning sterilizing drugs as well as other methods of contraception. Cajetan, *In S.t.*, 2–2, q. 154, a. 1, neatly defines the issue by saying it makes no difference whether "in toto actu utatur uxore extra vas naturale; sive in fine tantum, ut filii Iudae abutebantur Thamar; sive, seminando intra vas naturale, detur opera ut non sequatur conceptio, aut ex parte viri

aut ex parte feminae, quacumque id arte vel industria fiat, quoniam tunc ex intentione seminatio impeditur a naturali suo fine."

6. *Op. cit.*, 821–822. Ford and Kelly, *op. cit.*, 318–327, clarify the meaning of direct sterilization in a way which seems to me to preclude from a theological point of view Janssens' argument on this point.

7. Norman Applezweig, *Steroid Drugs* (New York, Toronto, London: McGraw-Hill Book Co., 1962), 174–202, provides a good technical introduction and an extensive bibliography. This treatment has provided the factual basis for several of our considerations in this chapter and in the appendix.

8. See notes 3 and 6 above.

9. O'Leary, "Some Thoughts about the Oral-Steroid Pill," *Jubilee*, 11 (March, 1964), 44–46.

10. *S.t.*, 1–2, q. 20, aa. 1–4; other passages cited, ch. VI, note 21, above.

VIII

THE SUBJECTIVE MORALITY OF CONTRACEPTION

WHY, some proponents of contraception will ask, do we find only toward the end of this long study a chapter about the subjective morality of contraception? Is not all morality subjective — or, better, a dialogue between subjective self and objective world? What questions have not been begged already when the objective morality of contraception is segregated so neatly from its subjective morality?

In one sense, indeed, morality is an interplay of subjective and objective factors. Not that it is a mixture of merely subjective meanings and merely natural facts in the way that situationists imagine. But morality is the process of self-determination, and the self comes to be, not apart from the world or against it, but only as the world enters the mind through knowledge and as the will enters the world through action. Hence in the integral unity of man's moral life we find the effects of both substantive, material values and reflexive, spiritual ones.

For example, the perfection of marital unity can be grasped only if we see marriage as a reality having both a transcendent good — normally procreation — and an immanent good, mutual love. Mutual love is meaningless unless it means real cooperation in achieving substantive values. Loveless reproduction, on the other hand, would be beneath human dignity.

Considered from this point of view, however, the important subjective realities are *objective conditions of morality*, and we have considered them throughout our discussion. Moreover, the special objective conditions which characterize the unique individual and his unique situation have been taken into account by our treatment of indirect voluntariness.

It is the special peculiarities of extraordinary occasions of human action which account for the fact that behavior which is the same as that involved in an intrinsically evil act sometimes turns out to be a different and better human act than it seems to be. The whole point of our previous argument was that after all reasonable allowances have been made for such subjective conditions, contraception remains immoral.

What is still to be treated in this chapter are certain ethically interesting aspects of the human action of a person who practices contraception. In the first place, we must consider factors which eliminate or lessen responsibility for the immorality that is done when contraception is practiced. Then too it will be instructive to consider the significance of contraceptive practice within the context of the development of moral personality.

Because these factors are not among those which reasonably should settle the rightness or wrongness of what we are doing, they cannot affect the objective immorality of contraception. However, since whatever affects freedom and the moral significance of action is interesting for ethics, we must examine the factors which limit — and may even exclude — immorality in those who engage in contraceptive intercourse.

It may be claimed that these factors which condition freedom and moral imputability also should be permitted to modify the inner meaning of the contraceptive act itself. But to allow this would be to fall into complete ethical relativism, which fails to discriminate between the proper roles of intelligence and freedom in human action.

The role of intelligence is to propose and that of freedom

is to choose. Strictly speaking, we simply cannot choose what *is to be* done; we can only judge that. But we do choose what *shall* or *shall not be* done, whether we will do what intelligence proposes or not. Freedom cannot give meaning except insofar as it gives actuality to meanings proposed by intelligence. To insist that freedom itself should be allowed to determine the meaning of action is merely to insist that those meanings which freedom chooses to carry out should for that very reason be judged sounder than the meanings intelligence has proposed as best grounded and most reasonable.

Subjectivism of this sort, though it might have a place in situationism, eliminates true morality. As we explained previously, such subjective relativism sets freedom against its own fundamental presupposition — the orientation of the will toward basic human goods which alone opens out the very realm of human possibilities in which freedom comes to exercise its sacred power of giving or withholding being.

Closely akin to this relativism, and thus suitably considered at this point, is the often expressed view that the whole question of contraception should be settled by individual conscience.[1] In a different sense this certainly would be true, because conscience is precisely the ability to make particular moral judgments, and no one can act in a human way without making such judgments.

The tasks of *recognizing* the moral significance of outward behavior and *determining* the limits for action indirectly willed never can be completed in any general consideration. Moreover, while bad acts cannot become good in virtue of subjective intentions or other circumstances, good acts can become bad through them, and only conscience can guard against these sources of evil in concrete action.[2]

In the present context, however, we must be wary of the appeal to conscience. If it amounts to a request for reconsideration entered after every relevant reason already has been considered, then it is nothing but a demand that reason be permitted to abandon its proper function so that under sufficient outside pressure it will be able to certify as intelligible a judgment for which it can discover no reasonable justification.

This demand, as we have seen, leads to situationism, and if the demand is complied with in even this single question — no matter how appealing the case for contraception may be — there is no reason why it should not be complied with in a whole series of similar questions.

We must take so harsh a view of the appeal from ethical judgment to conscience just because of the sort of issue with which we are dealing, an issue which concerns a kind of action which not only is subjectively appealing but also is intrinsically immoral.

Our judgment of the appeal to conscience would be quite different if we were concerned with an action defined as wrong in terms of some secondary and derivative value, such as property, which can be compelled to yield in difficult cases.[3]

But anyone who accepts our previous conclusions yet who still insists that contraception must be left finally to individual conscience, where it could turn out to be right despite the fact that it is wrong in itself, must answer whether euthanasia, abortion, torture, terror, and all the other cases where essential goods sometimes seem to demand that other essential goods be violated directly also should be left in the end to individual conscience.

If he should agree, he might mean, only what we also can accept, that the subjective factors we will discuss shortly have a very important role to play in determining one's ability to act as a human being in a fully responsible way, and so they modify in their diverse ways the moral status of the agent.

Or else he means — and this we never can accept — that following feeling and desire is a better way of making moral judgments than the use of rational intelligence, and that when this purportedly better way conflicts with the requirements of rational intelligence, intelligence rather than feeling and desire should yield.

The first of the subjective factors that we shall consider is error.[4] One is responsible only for what he wills and he can will only what he knows, or thinks he knows. There's the rub — it is quite possible to be mistaken. The hunter who kills his companion, mistaking him for a deer, has not committed murder, although he kills an innocent man by a human act and the killing objectively is a serious evil.

Of course, if one's lack of knowledge is his own fault, his error will not eliminate moral responsibility, although it may modify what he is responsible for. Thus, if the hunter has not been reasonably careful, he may be guilty of carelessness, and his guilt for this even can be serious, but carelessness is not the same as murder. We shall be interested mainly in failures of knowledge which are not the fault of those who practice contraception.

The obvious case is one in which someone is practicing contraception without realizing the actual effect of his own behavior. A woman who has asked a physician for advice about avoiding pregnancy may be given a prescription for anovulant drugs. The patient, perhaps having informed her physician that she does not wish to practice contraception, may use the pills without even realizing that they are contraceptive in their effects.

Even if a woman realizes that the use of the pills will prevent conception, she may not see that this form of contraception is wrong. The confusion even of experts in ethical reasoning about this question makes it clear that the average person easily could be confused. Thus, some who instinctively recognize that contraception violates an essential good and who intuitively know that the practice of mechanical contraception would be immoral feel no such repugnance toward the pharmacological method of contraception. They may not understand its moral significance despite their awareness of its physiological effects.

Much more interesting than mistakes of either of these kinds, however, is the state of mind in which the malice of contraception is more or less clearly understood but the limits of indirect voluntariness are not observed. Here we are not concerned with the error which may occur in a reflective, ethical analysis, but with the mistake which may happen in the practical thinking of a person who is considering for himself what is to be done.

In effect, such a person may think, contrary to our analysis, that intercourse and conception-prevention are equally well-grounded meanings of what he views as a single act — the act of contraceptive intercourse. He chooses the act insofar as it is intercourse, indirectly willing the prevention of conception because he wishes to avoid pregnancy.

This state of mind, which is much the same as that of the person who practices rhythm, seems to characterize many persons of real goodwill who nevertheless consider their practice of contraception morally licit.[5] It is of special interest, therefore, to see exactly how they come to make this mistake.

One way is to begin from the assumption that there is an absolute obligation to have intercourse if one's partner wishes it. A wife who believes this and who, for example, has serious medical reasons for avoiding pregnancy can reason that she is only fulfilling her obligations to her husband and protecting her own health as best she can.

If there really were no morally acceptable way to avoid intercourse and if there were a serious obligation to avoid pregnancy, it is plausible that conception-prevention might acquire another meaning than contraception — for example, the meaning of self-preservation, as this wife supposes. In this case, she thinks she may consent and cooperate and so she is not guilty, for she wills conception-prevention only indirectly. Nevertheless, what she is doing remains wrong, since her moral judgment is the product of an erroneous principle.

From this case it is an easy step to understand all those cases in which there are good indications of any sort for avoiding pregnancy combined with a putative obligation to have intercourse. If there are good indications for avoiding pregnancy, a couple could in good conscience decide that they should not have more children at least for the present. Having reached this judgment, they can come to think of it as an absolute assumption, which cannot be questioned or reconsidered.

This attitude toward the judgment that pregnancy should be avoided may indicate bad faith, but it need not. The judgment itself could have been a sound one. The tendency to treat such a sound judgment as an absolute condition of further practical thinking is very common. Great flexibility is needed to continue constantly reconsidering judgments previously made.

Thus, often a person deeply engaged in any line of practical reasoning will persistently run over the same unfruitful ground until a friend or counselor calls to his attention the fact that he has made certain assumptions which need to be reconsidered. Social workers often have to point out to their clients the most obvious practical possibilities.

Assuming absolutely that there must be no more pregnancies, the next step in this practical misreasoning is to conclude that every form of abstinence either is impossible or would have serious and unavoidable bad effects. We have argued previously that this assumption is not correct;[6] the bad effects even of prolonged abstinence can be counteracted through human effort. But the myth that orgasm is essential to mental health is widespread, and many accept it as a "scientific fact."

Also, many people, especially men, simply take it for granted that for them abstinence from orgasm for more than a few days is impossible. They have had an orgasm at least once every few days since puberty, and they can no more think of going without it than they can think of going without urinating. They have never had the experience of overcoming erotic tension, and they do not believe it really can be done.[7]

Once these assumptions have been made, there seems to be no reasonable alternative to contraceptive intercourse. The assumptions are made easily because the violation of the procreative good by contraception leaves no sensible evidence. A child is not conceived, but negations are not *real*. Besides, it can very well be true that the pregnancy in question *ought* to have been avoided.

Many other violations of essential human goods, such as the violations of life of which situationists approve, result in a phenomenal state of affairs which contains the effects of wrong action. Abortion, for instance, leaves its mark in flesh and blood. Even if these are disposed of smoothly, they remain *real* for imagination.

Reasoning on these assumptions, what alternatives seem to lie open before the married couple? There is intercourse in the best way possible — that is, with the use of a contraceptive. There is mutual masturbation; many people have had premarital experience of this sort, and it will seem to be a regression. There is solitary masturbation, which will seem immature to normal people. There is sex outside marriage, which certainly will be unacceptable to any couple who love each other.

Faced with these alternatives, the choice is not a clear one: to practice contraception or not to practice it. The choice is: to have intercourse in the best way possible or to do something offensive to their marital relationship.

If the assumptions were reconsidered, the whole matter would appear in a different light. For *even if the assumptions were true*, a consideration of all the alternatives would make it clear that the choice of contraceptive intercourse involves a distinct human act of choosing a means whose only meaning is conception-prevention. This act would appear distinct from the choice to have intercourse precisely because the two have been made inseparable only in virtue of previous actual or possible choices.

The couple thus conclude that contraceptive intercourse is a good. In their view, its primary meaning is that of an "act of love"; only incidentally is it also conception-preventing. Conception-prevention is not intended as an end, in the strict sense of "intended." Their intentions can be very much like those of a couple who practice rhythm. Nor is conception-prevention, precisely as such, chosen as a means. It is never chosen in a straightforward way but only accepted as a necessary concomitant of avoiding its alternatives. Since contraception is morally preferable to all the alternatives which are considered, it seems incapable of being seriously wrong.

The choice to practice contraception by a couple in this frame of mind is not directly against the procreative good. They consent to and cooperate in contraception without doing anything for which they are guilty, because they only indirectly will conception-prevention. They can be aware of the malice of contraception in itself and yet practice conception-prevention without being aware that they are doing what is wrong, for they do not consider their acts to have the only meaning which the facts really can support. Practical misreasoning has led to a mistaken judgment which allows the couple not to notice the objective malice of their action.

I am convinced that many sincere people — those of generally upright lives who see nothing wrong about contraception — are in this frame of mind. They are not ignorant of the intrinsic malice of contraception, *when it is directly willed*.[8] But they mistakenly think that they, and other good people, may practice contraception, because they do not see that their practical understanding of conception-preventing behavior is at odds with the facts.

For them, conception-prevention is only indirectly willed when contraceptive intercourse is chosen as a means to other genuine goods. Of course, such persons would never express themselves in our terms and their actual state of mind undoubtedly is less clear than our analysis, but our terms express in theoretical language a state of practical judgment which seems to be quite common.

Some such way of reasoning characterizes the views not only of ordinary people thinking about their own lives but also of those who are concerned about social problems and the trends of world population.[9] They point out the horrors which seem to them to be the only alternatives to contraception: on the one hand, overpopulation with a host of attendant evils; on the other hand, abortion, infanticide, and perhaps radical changes in the relationships between the sexes. If these are all the alternatives, contraception seems to be a less serious evil than the others.

We cannot say, of course, that population problems will be

solved by ethically acceptable methods. No important problem in human history has been met solely with methods of which we could approve. But the probabilities concerning what will happen and the ethical judgments concerning what should be done must not be muddled indiscriminately.[10] Ethics presupposes sociology, but sociology cannot replace ethics.

From the point of view of ethics, we can say that political and economic measures should be taken to meet social problems, and that those whose children would constitute excessive population should practice reasonable abstinence. In fact, however, we can be sure that action will be a mixture of good and bad.

There will be some improvement in social and economic policies, and there will be a few bettered opportunities for immigration. There will continue to be a great deal of contraception, abortion, and infanticide. There will be some later marriages, some practice of abstinence within marriage, some complete celibacy. There will continue to be misery, starvation, and war. These are all sage predictions, but that does not alter the fact that some of these actions will be right and that others will be wrong.

Undoubtedly, contraception is a lesser evil than many others. Still, it is intrinsically immoral. Whether, or to what extent, it may be moral to cooperate with contraceptive programs in order to avoid worse evils involves complex problems in the ethics of cooperation, which fall beyond our present concerns.

Some have asked how it is possible, if contraception really is intrinsically immoral, that so many persons having real goodwill should be unable to appreciate its immorality.[11] The objection seems particularly effective when one considers our way of demonstrating the immorality of contraception. We do not consider the knowledge that contraception is immoral to depend upon any subtle conclusions, of which the unlearned might be ignorant, but only to require consideration of what contraception is and of a basic and self-evident principle of practical reason.[12]

However, now that we have explained how an upright person

sincerely can reach a mistaken judgment about the morality of conception-prevention, this objection loses its force. Such people do not consider contraception right in itself and acceptable in all cases. They simply think, perhaps through no fault of their own, that indirect voluntariness applies in practice where it reasonably cannot be considered to apply. It is interesting that Van der Marck, who makes much of the opinions of ordinary people, has developed a position which errs at the theoretical level in the same way the ordinary person errs in his practical reasoning.

Catholics, of course, have authoritative guidance concerning morality. Can they sincerely make the kind of error we have described?[13] What does Catholic teaching and practice do, from an ethical point of view, which affects the situation?

To begin with, it indicates that abstinence is a real alternative which must be taken into consideration. Orgasm is not to be viewed as a necessity of life. It also urges that the judgment that pregnancy ought to be avoided should not be treated as an absolute, but that it should remain subject to reconsideration. In these ways the assumptions on which the practical error rests are undermined.

The Catholic requirement of self-examination, as part of the sacrament of penance, should heighten moral self-awareness, so that confusions in practical judgment are not so easily maintained. The advice of the confessor also can shape the process of moral reasoning so that the limitation of alternatives, required for the sincere error, is less likely to occur.

Most important, the Catholic Church has an authoritative teaching that contraception in all forms is wrong, and that its immorality does not admit of exceptions for any indications. This teaching, moreover, has been presented as a clarification of moral law, not subject to dispensation or alteration.[14]

Given all these facts, it hardly seems possible that Catholics can make the error in practical judgment we have been describing. It seems to me, however, that it is possible.

To begin with, the same process of practical reasoning can

be followed out leading to the same conclusion — that contraception really is not wrong. But a faithful and well-instructed Catholic will recall at this point that he has been taught differently. He may reconsider, and judge that for practical purposes he should do as he has been taught.

Still, his mind is perplexed, for it seems to him that the Church is requiring something for which he can see no reason. What he does in virtue of his practical judgment as a faithful Catholic diverges from what he would have done in virtue of the practical judgment he reached by his own efforts.

In addition to such cases, which I think are very common, there are now many Catholics whose inner voice tells them that contraception is right and whose listening ear no longer conveys a clear statement that it is wrong. The confusion about pills, increasing popular discussion of the theoretical issues, and some unfortunately ambiguous pastoral statements have led many to imagine that they are not acting wrongly if they practice contraception, especially by an inconspicuous method.

But even before the present confusion, it seems to me, limitations of communication made possible sincere mistakes in practical judgment. Some did not grasp the degree of authoritativeness of the Church's teaching on the matter; some did not realize how completely it excludes convenient "exceptions." Of course, these errors were perhaps to some extent faults in themselves, and in that case they did not wholly relieve from responsibility.

To bring home to someone's mind the intrinsic malice of contraception, it should be enough to point out the value of the procreative good and the fact that contraception is against it. As we shall explain shortly, if this consideration is not sufficient, the problem is one not of ignorance, but of malice.

However, to bring home to someone's mind *in a practical* way that his choice to practice contraception is immoral, more than his awareness of the intrinsic malice of contraception is required. He must recognize that his choice is a direct willing of conception-prevention. For him to see this, he must keep in mind that his choice is not either to have contraceptive intercourse or to have orgasm in some other way, but that it is either to prevent conception or not to prevent it in intercourse which itself either may be chosen or may be omitted as good reasons dictate.

To enlighten those who "see nothing wrong in contraception" it is generally useless to present a theoretical argument which shows why contraception is an immoral *species* of action. Instead, moral guidance intended to overcome practical ignorance must address itself to the actual sources of the mistaken concrete judgment — the false assumptions and the inadequate formulation of the moral issue.

It may seem that the Catholic is in an unfortunate position so far as contraception is concerned. Those who do not recognize any authoritative source of moral guidance can practice contraception with clear, though erroneous, consciences, but a Catholic is prohibited by his better formed conscience from employing this solution to the problem of controlling sexual activity in marriage.[15]

If only it were possible to consider together all the factors in the situation — the difficulties of abstinence, the values of intercourse, the good reasons for avoiding pregnancy, and the procreative good which may not be at stake from an operational point of view. If everything could be thrown onto a common scale, surely the balance would incline as feeling does to the view that contraception need not be so wrong. Why must we insist on considering matters so analytically, and making life so difficult?[16]

But our insistence on viewing this moral question in a certain way is not arbitrary. Contraception must be viewed primarily as conception–prevention, and hence it cannot be willed only indirectly, because this way of looking at it is the only accurate and reasonable one. The value of the procreative good must be upheld and the value of orgasm as an experience must be subordinated because this order happens to reflect their real relationship. An analytic process before practical judgment should be carried out because that is how our reason works.

Sometimes it is pleasanter to put reason aside and to follow feeling instead, but such irrationalism leads to action less fully human than does a more clearheaded and less passionate approach. Even a mere philosopher can observe that the Catholic Church has a peculiarly stubborn way of insisting on what is peculiarly human, natural reason and material values. Perhaps this is because she also believes that Christ Himself, though truly God, also truly is a rational animal like ourselves.

Moreover, there are advantages in having a correct practical judgment about the malice of contraception. A clear understanding of this matter prevents one from falling into possible errors in related practical judgments, errors which could lead one to consider wrong what really is allowable — e.g., the practice of rhythm — or errors which could lead one to consider allowable many actions which are more seriously wrong — e.g., abortion or the unrestricted practice of contraception even when there is no good reason for avoiding pregnancy.

Then too, since the practice of contraception remains objectively wrong regardless of how sincere one's mistaken practical judgment may be, lack of subjective responsibility does not prevent certain objective consequences of the practice. These consequences have been called "contraceptive civilization,"[17] and this phrase aptly indicates how extensive are the effects of contraception. But it must be remembered that the cultural consequences of the practice of contraception primarily are found in the moral personality itself. About this point we shall have something more to say shortly when we consider the effects of the practice of contraception on the development of the moral personality.

Besides failure of practical knowledge as a factor affecting the moral condition of one who practices contraception, we must consider the place of weakness as another such factor. "Weakness" simply designates all those motivational components which have escaped the control of freedom through no prior fault of our own and which tend to inhibit rational self-determination.[18] Both fear and desire can be designated as "weakness" understood in this way. It refers as well to the psychic tension of anxiety, hostility, and every other nonrational impulse which plays a role in motivation.[19]

Obviously, weakness is the chief cause of the initial decision to practice contraception made by those who see with clear practical judgment that it is wrong. Although there are good reasons other than procreation for engaging in sexual intercourse, those who recognize with practical awareness that contraception is against the procreative good do not begin to practice it in virtue of a reasonable desire to promote genuine mutual love.

Instead, the effective motivation ordinarily is to be found in a vicious circle of tension, frustration, hostility, and tension which is experienced by anyone who attempts to restrict sexual activity without avoiding erotic stimuli and making other uses of his energy. In other words, those who simply try to abstain without changing other motivations and practices feel painful erotic tension. To escape this tension, or some of its undesirable consequences, they often "give in" and practice contraception.[20]

To what extent does this weakness reduce a person's responsibility for practicing contraception?[21] To this question there can be no accurate answer that is true of every case. If the pressure is greater, the opportunity for free choice is less and responsibility is lessened correspondingly.

However, weakness does not mitigate responsibility if the inability to resist flows from a culpable failure to use whatever freedom of choice one has to do what one can to overcome irrational motivation. One cannot *permit* himself to be overcome by his passions when he has the means to undercut their force by employing strategy against them.[22]

Evidently weakness and the mistakes in practical knowledge previously considered are closely interrelated with one another. The conviction that erotic tension cannot be overcome greatly increases its relative power, while the presence of this tension itself seems to certify the assumption that orgasm, and so *some* mode of sexual activity, is unavoidable.

In many cases too, couples might resist if they had to contend only with inner tension. However, frustration leads to hostility which makes husband and wife quarrelsome with one another and bad-tempered with the children. Only after prolonged wrestling with these symptoms do some couples decide that contraception can be considered a lesser evil.[23]

Is it possible that the combined pressures we are calling "weakness" can be so great that no effective freedom of choice remains? To this question the answer is yes, but this lack of effective freedom may occur in two quite different ways.

On the one hand, it is possible that someone whose weakness is abnormally great may be unable from the beginning to think clearly and to decide responsibly with regard to certain matters.[24] This lack of effective freedom can occur in one limited area — that is, without any general psychopathology.

It may originate in an innate defect, or in a defect of habituation whose causality lies more or less completely outside the responsibility of the person who suffers from it. Thus a person raised in an environment where sexual tension always is released as soon as it accumulates and habituated to the regular experience of orgasm from puberty may be quite incapable on a particular occasion of choosing not to have orgasm.

Moreover, it is possible on particular occasions for anyone to become engaged innocently in a pattern of behavior beyond the point of no return and then through overwhelming weakness to do without real responsibility what he ordinarily would not do. This may happen to some who occasionally have contraceptive intercourse using last-minute methods such as *coitus interruptus*.

The further exploration of the possibilities of contraceptive behavior so compulsive that effective freedom is lost, and moral responsibility lost with it, would be interesting, but it is not essential to our present concerns. Rather, we must consider another and quite different way in which freedom is lost.

On the other hand, then, there are those who first choose to practice contraception, yielding to the promptings of weakness, but who later reach a state in which weakness is no longer an operative condition of motivation.[25] What had been demands of weakness come to be identified with the self; the goals of nonrational desire are integrated in the personality as overriding motives.

In a case of this kind, the contraceptive life has been adopted as part of one's ideal and it is endorsed so fully and freely by the will that for this very reason there no longer is any effective freedom to alter one's full commitment to this immorality.

The difference between the guilt of weakness and the guilt of full commitment, which also is called "certain malice,"[26] is an important one which should not be overlooked. The guilt of full commitment begins where temptation leaves off. Irrational motivation no longer causes a struggle because it has been made one's personal desire.

The guilt of weakness is much less serious.[27] There are several reasons for this. First of all, the guilt of weakness leaves open the possibility of reversal, because one's whole self is not engaged. Second, it does not transmit the distortion of its bias to all other segments of one's life, because it leaves one's better self intact. Third, it does not lead one to reject and to try to subjugate the violated good in all other contexts. One who falls through weakness can respect inconsistently the good he sometimes violates.

Contraception, unfortunately, is an immoral practice which begins in weakness but which cannot easily remain a merely intermittent fault. Effective contraception requires implements and cooperation; its use must be consistent even when one partner or the other feels no great pressure of weakness to have contraceptive intercourse. Thus the contraceptive couple, especially those who use artificial contraceptives rather than *coitus interruptus*, readily progress from weakness into the guilt of full commitment.

In our discussion of mistakes in practical knowledge we did not mention at all what is an important theoretical mistake, the notion that the procreative good is not a primary one and that it must yield to others in difficult cases. Instead we said that there is little practical difficulty in understanding the intrinsic malice of contraception directly willed. The error of situationism underlay many of the theoretical confusions we explored, but when we were considering practical mistakes we omitted it as a factor limiting freedom simply because it does not belong in that category.

As a practical judgment, the notion that procreation is not so important that it should not yield under pressure is a result rather than a cause of the willingness to violate the procreative good — e.g., by the practice of contraception. Such degradation of the procreative good is a clear sign that it is being violated with the guilt of full commitment, for when one reaches the point where an essential human good seems to be secondary he has distorted his own vision of what is valuable.[28]

Whether someone thinking at the level of theory might confuse the priorities among values without evidencing bad will is a quite different matter which I do not care to consider here.

If weakness can modify responsibility in indefinite degree, can it not eliminate guilt without eliminating freedom? Perhaps this is an avenue of escape for difficult cases, for weakness surely is great in these cases. May we not freely choose to practice contraception, if we are under great pressure, without incurring guilt?

The answer, unfortunately, is negative. Guilt is not merely psychological — a state of consciousness. Nor is it merely legal — an objective condition linked to damage and deserving retribution. Ethically considered, guilt is the engagement of the will in the realization of what is recognized to be irrational because opposed to the principles of practical reason and wrong because contrary to the basic human goods.[29]

Although weakness can modify guilt in endless degrees by limiting or increasing the depth and intensity of the will's engagement in evil, weakness cannot eliminate guilt until it eliminates effective freedom. This elimination occurs only when weakness is so great that the determination of nonrational motivation is in effective control and the exercise of rational choice is rendered unnecessary, since real alternatives no longer remain open for deliberate consideration.[30]

From this we can see more clearly why the guilt of full commitment is so much worse as guilt than the guilt of weakness. The former fully and permanently engages the will while the latter only partially and temporarily subverts its proper orientation.

Once this point is grasped, we can respond to the suggestion that contraception may be permissible for seriously troubled couples as a concession to their weakness.[31] The presupposition of this suggestion is that contraception still would be recognized to be wrong, or not to be an ideal, but that it should not be considered a seriously immoral practice for those who are handicapped by weakness in their struggle with the psychosexual aspects of moral development.

The source of this suggestion undoubtedly was sympathy for those whose sole difficulty in moral development seems to be inability to live a "happy" married life without contraception.

This suggestion not only is theoretically false but also is practically pernicious. It is theoretically false because it implies that temporary concessions to moral evil can be part of moral growth. It is practically pernicious because it implies that a morally acceptable solution to the problems in question is impossible.

This supposition in practice will make impossible what otherwise would have been possible though difficult. Moreover, anyone who follows this suggestion in practice simply yields to weakness in a way which leads to the practice of contraception with the guilt of full commitment, for the practice is not opposed by any segment of the self although it is still recognized as wrong.

Combined in this suggestion we see the effects of the two worst possible attitudes toward moral struggle — despair about the possibility of conquest over nonrational motivation and presumption about the possibility of deferred moral progress.[32]

When is the vice which is "temporarily conceded" to be set aside — at forty-five or fifty? By that time irreversible effects of the practice of contraception will have permeated the whole personality. Had resistance been maintained, even perhaps with temporary lapses, genuine moral progress would have become possible when the pressures of weakness were relieved by age.

But our assertion that this suggestion is unsound on theoretical grounds may be questioned. Is it not true that some concessions to weakness are required, that not everything can be demanded of the child or adolescent that can be expected of the morally mature person? Can we expect ordinary persons to live a life of continuous heroism? Have we the right to make impossible demands?

Let us be clear at the outset, we impose no demands whatsoever. If only there were a way through reality discoverable by reason to say that contraception is morally acceptable! But we find no such way and we cannot countenance pretending there is an escape from hard moral requirements where there is none. Only immorality and morality lie before us. There is no sanctuary from the demands of morality within the realm of freedom.

Next let us notice that the objection concerning heroism is ambiguous. In most cases the avoidance of contraception is a matter not of heroism but of a great deal of annoying inconvenience and painful struggles for self-control. Embarrassing as it is to admit that self-control is what we need to solve our problems — because this is an admission of the weakness of which we are ashamed — this remains the truth for most of us. For others, those whose situations really are difficult, something more than an ordinary effort is needed. The two groups must be considered distinctly.

The problem of contraception is so common simply because this is an area where the demands of reasonable judgment and of weakness directly conflict. Sexual sin can be overemphasized; there are worse forms of immorality. But this kind of immorality is important and common because it is an ordinary person's ordinary trouble.[33]

The number of us involved, therefore, is no reason for changing the rules unless one assumes that we should be able to make great achievements in the moral domain without difficulty. However, all the evidence is against the view that rational freedom can win control over weakness — irrational motivation — at any point without difficulty.

Let us be clear that this is the real challenge — deliberate choice must win control over irrational motivation. The problem is not merely to confront erotic tension with stubborn resistance to overt sexual activity. This path leads only to psychological difficulty and moral failure.

The problem is to use intelligence in finding the sources of erotic tension, and by working upon these sources to reduce it to manageable proportions. The sources may be many and not all equally accessible. But a sincere effort to solve this problem can lead to results.[34] And with results here, the way is opened for other even more significant advances by rationality and freedom into the territory held by irrational motivation.

The predicament of those whose cases really are difficult is another matter. To overcome the handicap of innate abnormalities or bad early training does call for extraordinary courage and perseverance. It would be wrong in these cases to say that only self-control is needed.

But with regard to heroism we must make a clear distinction. There is heroism in an action above the call of duty, an action of great value undertaken gratuitously. Such virtue is not expected of anyone. Then there is heroism in an action which is strictly obligatory but extraordinarily difficult. Such action is required of him on whom the obligation falls. Difficulty does not remove the obligation though it does mitigate the guilt of failure. In sexual morality, as in the rest of life, different persons receive very unequal burdens.

The suggestion that there must be concessions to weakness in the matter of contraception for those who are having difficult struggles is indefensible theoretically because it makes the error of viewing this immoral act as if it were not what it is: immoral intrinsically and directly opposed to a basic human good. Why does the direct opposition of contraception to a basic good make the suggestion of concession indefensible? Because the basic goods are not merely principles of practical intellectual orientation, of moral law. They also are starting points of moral development.[35]

To the essential human goods we have a natural inclination and affinity if we but allow ourselves to be drawn by them. Moral development is a process in which the possibilities of living more fully and more openly toward the goods are progressively realized, and the limitations which inhibit our full commitment to them are progressively overcome.

If, then, one sets his will against a basic human good, he loses the only starting point from which he could begin to open himself fully to its possibilities. In rejecting one value, also, a person must be committing himself excessively to some other value, and this overcommitment necessarily unbalances his whole orientation.

But if this is true, can there be any real concessions to development? Is not complete moral perfection immediately and unconditionally required of everyone? And since instant perfection is impossible, what difference does it make where the concessions to developmental necessities are made?

The answer, of course, is that moral perfection is the universally required goal. One can meet this demand at once without fully satisfying it simply by tending toward it. To tend toward and to seek it is to hold fast to the principles without which its achievement surely is impossible — the essential human goods. But, as we saw in Chapter IV, where we considered affirmative obligations, these goods make diverse demands of us. Not all of their demands are equally forceful, and we can delay meeting many of them.

Hence there are concessions to weakness where there are many possible goods, only one of which is strictly obligatory. In such a case, one may be forgiven if he does not choose the greater good as he would do if he were more fully committed to the value. One also may be forgiven if he delays fulfilling an obligation where this is possible without directly violating the good.

Thus a married couple, because of the imperfection of their moral development, may receive from the procreative good as a "concession" to their weakness the "permission" to have fewer children than otherwise would be good for them to have, to delay having those children longer than otherwise would be right, to omit altogether having children if there are serious difficulties although if they were more generous they would be willing to take risks for the sake of procreation.

But no matter how imperfect their moral development, a couple may not under any circumstances embrace contraception as if it were a concession to their weakness. The good cannot admit its own denial, and it is the good itself which allows the "concessions" we are considering. Like the generals of an army, the principles of moral development can condone sluggishness, but they cannot countenance treason.

Hence we must condemn the pernicious idea that contraception might be morally licit as a temporary practice. Anyone who holds a role of moral leadership and who makes such a proposal indeed must be a blind man leading the blind; we cannot believe that he is a malicious man perverting his office to encourage malice. For that is what the practical force of this notion is — that there may be an open engagement with the malice of contraception.[36]

We suggested above that the practice of contraception with the guilt of full commitment is particularly evil because of its effect on the development of the whole moral personality. To conclude our consideration of the subjective factors of the immorality of contraception, let us consider briefly some implications of full commitment either against the procreative good or in favor of it.[37] We must bear in mind that neither those who sincerely consider contraception morally allowable nor those who fall occasionally through weakness bear the guilt of full commitment to this vice.[38]

If one is fully committed against the procreative good, then he will be inclined to disregard the possibly evil consequences and side effects of the use of contraceptives. Although fully responsible to the extent that he is aware even of their possibility, he will regard these consequences as indirectly willed. Thus we see why some proponents of contraception seem little concerned by the possibility that one method really may induce abortion or that another method may have dangerous side effects.

If one is fully committed against the procreative good, then he need not necessarily be willing directly to violate human life itself, but he will easily "progress" from the one to the other. Contraceptive practice is only one step short of abortion and two steps short of infanticide. Statistics prove this point.[39] One who practices contraception wills not to have children and is not ready to accept them if they arrive, as they often do despite contraception.

If one is fully committed against the procreative good, then he must reject his role as a parent or modify it drastically, for the procreative good defines this role. This fact alone goes far toward explaining the widespread tendency of contemporary parents to abandon their proper authority and to assume non-parental relationships toward their children. Of course, not every parent who fails in this way is himself committed to contraception. But the redefinition of roles in a contraceptive society modifies the self-understanding even of parents who do not practice contraception.

If one is fully committed against the procreative good, then he must reject his role as a husband or wife or modify it drastically, for the procreative good defines these roles. What can replace the primary good of marriage? Whatever motivates contraceptive practice, whatever is chosen despite the sacrifice of the procreative good involved in the decision to practice contraception.

Will that good be genuine mutuality, real conjugal love? Hardly. It will be some subjective value to be had by the exploitation of the marital relationship. For some it will be simply the experience of sex. For others it will be security, status, and tension reduction. This point helps to explain the mentality of the organization man and why he is so willing to remain an undistinguishable member of the lonely crowd.

If one is fully committed against the procreative good, then he must distort his moral awareness and rational processes to avoid having his absurd condition constantly thrust into his focus of attention. Thus he must blind himself to the value or he must find some way to dominate it and put it at his service.

Many more similar implications can be pointed out. But these points should be sufficient to indicate that the practice of contraception is no solution to a moral problem. It is a mere placebo for an irritating moral symptom. While the placebo seems innocent, just as the contraceptive pills seem harmless, it turns out to be mortally destructive, just as they might yet turn out to be deadly.

If, on the other hand, one is properly committed to the good of procreation, other consequences follow.

On the basis of this commitment, one can understand the proper order of the essential human goods. One can see that psychosexual maturity belongs to good health, but he is not thrown into panic by the lack of it which weakness often reveals, for he realizes that of itself erotic tension is no more important than many other defects in health. Hence he does not believe that everything in life must be subordinated either to orgasm or to sexual development.

On the basis of a proper commitment, one can see that sexual functioning really is important in the scheme of life as a whole, because it belongs to the vocation of parenthood and married life. But he does not stare at it in fascination, making it meaningless by isolating it from the substantive values.

On the basis of a proper commitment, one can provide a proper example for his children. He does not find sex inexplicable because he sees what gives it meaning. He does not face the choice demanded of the contraceptive parent — to hide his practice and so to deny his children the guidance of his example in dealing with their own sexual problems or to admit his practice and so to give his children the guidance of an example of noncontrol which will lead them into the precocious sexual activity which is the center of America's adolescent culture, a culture which has been called very aptly a "teen-age tyranny."

On the ground of a proper commitment, one could find the remedy for concupiscence — remedy, not outlet.[40] Married sexual life lived with the proper commitment *is* the remedy for concupiscence. For sexual concupiscence is precisely one form of the weakness we have been considering, the familiar irrational motive which demands irrational fulfillment. The remedy is not the release of tension, for release of itself increases rather than diminishes subsequent tension. The remedy is discipline and a change of purpose. And the procreative good together with genuine mutual love rooted in it is a value sufficient to elicit the effort necessary to change.

Gradually the more self-indulgent use of sex yields to the more generous sharing which expresses real mutual love, the experience so much praised but so little realized by the practitioner of contraception. Concupiscence, man's normal psychic disorder, is cured by being gradually shaped and colored by intelligence and freedom, not operating in cold impersonality but working gently by the ministrations of love to love. The forces of irrational motivation can be overcome in the love talk of man and wife, through their wry appreciation of their own weakness, by their acceptance of one another in heart and soul and, on occasion, in organic union.

NOTES TO CHAPTER VIII

1. This has been the predominant Protestant view — see: St. John-Stevas, *Birth Control and Public Policy* (Santa Barbara, Calif.: The Fund for the Republic, Inc., 1960), 37 — and it is frequently found in the uncitable Catholic material. One finds it stated only in a tentative and qualified way in citable Catholic material — e.g., Dupré, "Toward a Re-examination . . . ," *Cross Currents*, 14 (Winter, 1964), 84–85, and the famous preface in Rock, *The Time Has Come* (New York: Alfred A. Knopf, 1963).

2. Lottin, *Morale fondomentale* (Tournai Belgium: Desclée et Cie, 1954), 142–150, 448–461, provides an introduction to the Thomistic doctrine. The chief sources are: *S.t.*, 1–2, q. 19, aa. 5–6; *De ver.*, q. 17. My article, "The Logic of Moral Judgment," *Proceedings of the American Catholic Philosophical Association*, 36 (1962), 67–76, is concerned with the difference between conscience in the narrow sense and prudence. Ford and Kelly, *Contemporary Moral Theology*, Vol. 1, *Questions in Fundamental Moral Theology* (Westminster, Md.: The Newman Press, 1958), 139–140, briefly indicate the correct role of conscience in contrast with situationist distortions. Most Rev. John J. Wright, "Reflections on Conscience and Authority," *The Critic*, April–May, 1964, provides (11–28) an excellent, contemporary introduction; he mentions (21) specifically contraception and situation-ethics.

3. *S.t.*, 1–2, q. 94, a. 4; see ch. VI, note 1, above.

4. *S.t.*, 1–2, q. 6, a. 8; q. 76; *De malo*, q. 3, aa. 6–8; *In 3 Eth.*, lect. 3.

5. I have in mind here conscientious Protestants; my suspicion that this is a common state of mind among religious, upright Protestants is based mainly on many conversations, secondarily on more or less official statements in the literature.

6. Ch. VI, note 22, above; see also: Lestapis, *Family Planning and Modern Problems* (New York: Herder & Herder, 1961), 195–214, who cites much additional material.

7. See ch. II, note 23, above.

8. This appears clearly, for example, in the resolution of the Lambeth Conference of 1930: "Where there is a clearly felt moral obligation to limit or avoid parenthood, the method must be decided on Christian principles. The primary and obvious method is complete abstinence from intercourse (as far as may be necessary) in a life of discipline and self-control lived in the power of the Holy Spirit. Nevertheless, in those cases where there is a clearly-felt moral obligation to limit or avoid parenthood, and where there is a morally sound reason for avoiding complete abstinence, the Conference agrees that other methods may be used, provided that this is done in the light of the same Christian principles" (cited by St. John-Stevas, *op. cit.*, 30). Those who drafted this statement evidently envisaged contraception as a last resort to be employed only in case of a conflict of moral obligations. Cf. Dupré, *op. cit.*, 84–85, for a remarkably similar point of view. John L. Thomas, S.J., "Contemporary Protestant Attitudes on Contraception," *Proceedings of the Annual Convention of the Catholic Theological Society of America*, 15 (June 20–23, 1960), 51–61, suggests that we need not consider Protestants who think thus to be in bad faith.

9. However, one also finds some outright antipathy toward procreation; see, e.g., William Vogt, *People: Challenge to Survival* (New York: William Sloane Associates, 1960), 83–127, a chapter entitled, "A Pathology of People." Vogt's book also contains some of the milder attitudes we are describing, and perhaps he personally does not hate procreation as much as his rhetoric suggests.

10. Lestapis, *op. cit.*, 219–316, has an excellent treatment of the population problem. In general (e.g., 228–229), he is clearly aware of the distinction between facts and norms, although there are passages in which he seems to lose sight of the distinction.

11. Dupré, *op. cit.*, 66; Van der Marck, "Vruchtbaarheidsregeling . . . ," *Tijdschrift voor theologie*, 3e, #4 (Jaargang, 1963), 394–396.

12. Aquinas explains the ways in which primary principles of natural law can be unknown: *S.t.*, 1–2, q. 94, a. 6; in this article, he refers back to: q. 77, a. 2, which therefore also should be read.

13. Ford and Kelly, op. cit., 9–11, discuss the errors of Protestants and consider the possibility of ignorance on the part of Catholics with regard to contraception.

14. Op. cit., 238–242, 256–314, provide the documentation for this statement.

15. It is a mistake to suppose that an erroneous conscience which allows greater liberty is an unqualified advantage; we may note that Aquinas holds — S.t., 1–2, q. 19, aa. 5–6 — that to violate one's conscience always is wrong, but that it is by no means true without qualification that to follow an erring conscience is good.

16. The attitude of this objection clearly underlies Dupré's argument (op. cit., 82–84 and passim) with its repetitious stress on the concrete and the totality against the abstract and the isolated.

17. Lestapis, op. cit., 69–94.

18. Karl Rahner, S.J., Theological Investigations, Vol. 1, God, Christ, Mary, and Grace (Baltimore: Helicon Press, 1961), 347–382, discusses the theological concept of concupiscentia, showing that it should not be understood as it usually has been. Our notion of weakness is close to his idea. However, because Rahner tends too much to value freedom as such, and mistakenly to oppose it against nature, he understands weakness to include the naturally good inclination which resists the bad use of freedom (370), apparently not excluding the natural volition to primary human goods (360). On the relationship between nature and freedom in Aquinas, see: Overbeke, "La loi naturelle et le droit naturel selon saint Thomas," Revue Thomiste, 57 (1957), 66 and passim; Klubertanz, "The Root of Freedom . . . ," Gregorianum, 42 (1961), 714–715.

19. The classical loci are: S.t., 1–2, q. 6, aa. 6–7; q. 24, a. 3; q. 73, a. 5; q. 77, aa. 1–8; De malo, q. 3, aa. 9–11; In 3 Eth., lect. 1–4; In 7 Eth., lect. 1–10. Aquinas makes important distinctions between different types of weakness — e.g., between fear and desire — which we are not taking into account; of course, the moral significance of all forms of weakness is not alike, but we do not have space to treat the subject more adequately.

20. Allers, The Psychology of Character (New York: Sheed & Ward, 1935), 311–318, throws considerable light on the significance of "giving in" to sexual sin; his remarks, mainly concerned with adolescents, apply to contraception as well.

21. Ford and Kelly, op. cit., Vol. 1, Questions in Fundamental Moral Theology, 174–247, provide a balanced introduction to this problem. Their treatment, although not expressly concerned with contraception, has three important implications for our problem. (1) We cannot consider that those who decide to practice contraception and who stick to this decision even when there is no immediate psychological pressure are sinning only lightly from weakness. (2) We can consider that some who practice contraception under immediate psychic pressure are not fully responsible, and can be sinning only venially. Weakness extends further than momentary impulse. (3) There is no general theoretical way, although there are practical criteria, for determining the degree of imputability in particular cases. Much more study needs to be done on this problem, both to determine what pressure married couples actually experience, and to clarify what the moral implications of "giving in" under various degrees of pressure are. John C. Ford, S.J., "Depth Psychology, Morality, and Alcoholism," Proceedings of the Annual Meeting of the Catholic Theological Society of America, 5 (June 26–28, 1950), 127–137, presents a

specific discussion of a similar problem; the entire article, including the assessment of psychology in relation to morality, can be applied *mutatis mutandis* to our present problem.

22. *S.t.*, 1–2, q. 77, a. 6.

23. L. Newell Moss, "Catholics and Family Limitation," *The Catholic Medical Quarterly*, 15 (October, 1962), 127–132, describes the problem in a more accurate and balanced way than does the current popular literature, such as the articles cited, ch. I, note 3, above.

24. Ford and Kelly, *op. cit.*, Vol. 1, 220–233; the articles cited by them are also to be noted. For such a person, it may be genuinely *impossible* not to sin *materially*. But this does not show the precept impossible of fulfillment, since in this case there is no guilt. Grace is sufficient that with it no one need sin *formally*. Morality only concerns *human acts* — i.e., those in which there is freedom and so the possibility of *formal* sin.

25. Aristotle, *Nicomachean Ethics*, 1145a15–1152a35; Aquinas, *In 7 Eth.*, lect. 1–10, is the classic treatise on the character-type we are now to discuss. This type of personality is integrated and mature, but vicious. Modern psychologists tend to deny the possibility of any such personality; this denial is equivalent to the denial of free choice, for the integrated and mature man simply can *choose* to be bad. How did Satan sin?

26. In addition to the passage cited in the previous note, see: *S.t.*, 1–2, q. 78; *De malo*, q. 3, aa. 12–15; *In 2 Sent.*, d. 43.

27. *In 2 Sent.*, d. 43, a. 4; *In 7 Eth.*, lect. 8; *De malo*, q. 3, a. 13; *S.t.*, 1–2, q. 78, a. 4.

28. *Ibid.*, also, very clearly, *S.t.*, 2–2, q. 156, a. 3, ad 1. It is no coincidence that first in the traditional list of the "daughters of lust" is blindness of mind — see: q. 153, a. 5. This blindness not only concerns the value itself. One who proceeds from sin of weakness to sin of malice also must blind himself practically by rationalizing — e.g., that the precept he has *decided* to set aside is impossible of fulfillment.

29. *S.t.*, 1–2, q. 21, a. 2.

30. *S.t.*, 1–2, q. 77, a. 7; a. 8, ad 3; *De malo*, q. 3, a. 10.

31. I purposely refrain from ascribing this suggestion to anyone, because although there have been several confused statements along these lines, it is always possible that their authors merely had in mind the legitimate point that the Christian can sympathize with and the Church can pardon all who, having sinned through weakness, repent and form a firm purpose of amendment. Realistically, also, we know that such a purpose of amendment is compatible with a history and character which permit one to predict (from a psychological and sociological point of view) that the same sin probably will be committed again.

32. I am applying here in a limited ethical sense what Aquinas says about the sins of despair and presumption which are against the theological virtue of hope: *S.t.*, 2–2, q. 20, a. 3; q. 21, a. 2. In the theological sense, presumption and despair both bear upon a wrong expectation in regard to *divine grace*.

33. Allers, *op. cit.*, 306–319; Oraison, *Man and Wife* (New York: The Macmillan Co., 1962), 90–102, go far toward explaining why sexual sin is common. Adam, *The Primacy of Love* (Westminster, Md.: The Newman Press, 1958), along with many contemporaries, dislikes the stress morals places on sex, since he insists correctly (107–136) that charity, not chastity, is the prime Christian virtue. However, chastity is necessary precisely to make way for charity, and if — as the whole development of modern psychology makes

clear — a developmental battle must be fought here, we must accept that, just as we must accept the fact that Vietnam and Berlin are persistent trouble spots in the Cold War, although disarmament and peaceful cooperation are the real goals.

34. Gibert, *Love in Marriage* (New York: Hawthorn, 1964), 108–131, presents a particularly realistic treatment. The point essentially is this, that the virtue of chastity must be developed, the disposition of self-restraint is not enough. The virtue brings one above constant temptation; the disposition does not. And one who suffers *constant* temptation sometimes falls. But this is no excuse if a real effort to develop the virtue is not made. See also: Moss, *loc. cit.* There are few good general treatments of asceticism; Ford, *op. cit.,* 138–139, makes some remarks and refers to: E. B. Maturin, *Self-Knowledge and Self-Discipline* (London and New York: Longmans, Green, and Co., 1905); Felix D. Duffey, C.S.C., *Psychiatry and Asceticism* (St. Louis: Herder, 1950).

35. *S.t.,* 1–2, q. 63, a. 1; cf. Overbeke, *op. cit.,* 66 and *passim.*

36. An open engagement with malice, since it is chosen and allowed to be integrated in one's personality — see: *S.t.,* 1–2, 78, aa. 2–3.

37. Lestapis, *op. cit.,* 69–94, 180–194, is particularly helpful here, although he does not indicate clearly that the effects in the moral personality are not the same if contraception is practiced from weakness, ignorance, or certain malice.

38. This is not to say that those who practice contraception through ignorance or weakness avoid all bad moral consequences. In particular, the psychological affects of incontinence and the loss of the psychological and moral benefits of chastity — treated by Oraison, Gibert, Suenens, and others — will be suffered to a greater or less extent even without the guilt of full commitment. Furthermore, there are infinite degrees of partial responsibility for one's own practical ignorance and moral weakness.

39. Lestapis, *op. cit.,* 56–57, 289–293.

40. Ford and Kelly, *op. cit.,* Vol. 2, *Marriage Questions,* 97–102, provide a basic introduction. The false meaning of "remedy for concupiscence" is based on a morality which assumes that only the restraint of external behavior is important; actually, marriage is a way of *virtue,* and chastity is an important good. If this aim is accomplished, restraint is no longer necessary, because irrational motivation does not build up tension.

Epilogue

REFLECTIONS OF A BELIEVER

The present world-wide furor over contraception clearly shows that the problems which tempt married people to begin this practice can no longer be ignored or passed over lightly. Something new is about to happen. So much agitation and confusion will not easily subside. The calm and complacency of the days when all Catholics agreed that contraception is evil but many couples practiced it for some years will not return again. Something *must* change.

The question is — what? What does the light on the horizon portend? Some seem to conceal lust under sentimental rationalization. Their maneuver promotes a disgusting confusion between a real and noble value — conjugal love — and a repulsive vice — self-centered eroticism. Others, less skilled in rhetoric, examine the fine print of manuals of moral theology and pharmacology hoping somewhere to find a loophole through which to slip the ever-widening applications of the new techniques of contraception.

Very many think that the Church will change. They say her doctrine on marital chastity is not infallible, and that she can and must yield under the combined pressures of the population explosion, modern theories of sexuality, and massive defections from her ranks. They foresee that the ideal of chastity, which never has been generally fulfilled, will now at last be set aside. They envision a peace-pact between the modern world and the Church, drawn up by the disciples of Freud and Kinsey on the one side and by noted Catholic gynecologists and moral theologians on the other.

I do not believe in this vision. It seems to me utterly unreal. The teaching of the New Testament, the clear words of Christ and St. Paul, cannot be sanely interpreted to sanction a "responsible parenthood" achieved by contraceptive techniques which implement a will unwilling to permit life to begin to be. The Catholic Church always has defended an ideal of marital chastity which demands that two values — the procreative good and the fostering of the marital union which is so essential to it — together and inseparably govern each sexual embrace. The Church cannot now surrender to Freud and Kinsey by setting aside her ideal of chastity, as the revisionists desire, without making herself absurd and invalidating her own claims to holiness.

Everyone is pointing out that chastity is not the highest virtue and that sins against it need not be considered so serious as sins against justice and charity. Of course that is true. Chastity is only a passageway to the Christian life. It is like the opening from the womb through which life must pass if it is to be born and to develop in the world. But if it fails to pass this point it is doomed to live and struggle and die here. If only imperfect chastity is achieved, then all one's life is a struggle with temptation, and all the works of the other virtues are inhibited and deformed. And first to suffer deformation is that mode of charity which perfects marriage — Christian conjugal love.

Hence I have a vision altogether different from those who expect the Church to change. I expect the practice of the Christian people to change. I foresee the coming of a new age of Christian asceticism — we should not hesitate to mention it —

when perfect chastity will be attained as an ordinary thing, not as an accomplishment of a few. I foresee the day when the Catholic child, encountering the crisis of puberty, will win an early and decisive victory, and will hardly experience temptations to sexual sin during later adolescence and adult life.

The problems which tempt married couples to practice contraception do not begin with marriage. These problems often are foreshadowed by a long flirtation with sin during late adolescence when company-keeping and courtship are marked by a great deal of pointless sexual stimulation. Even more commonly they are foreshadowed by the practice of masturbation which begins during early adolescence and which sometimes continues even until marriage.

We Catholics must begin to take our ideal of chastity so seriously that we set to work to do everything possible to improve this entire course of development. It is not enough to absolve the sins of children and young people over and over again merely because over and over again the necessary subjective dispositions seem to be present. The same modern knowledge which some would use to subvert Christian ideals of chastity also could be employed even now to help realize them. No child should be left alone to struggle by himself with incomprehensible tension, with anxiety, with guilt. Habits of self-denial and self-control of the impulses can and should be established before they are needed.

What might be done is too long a story even to be outlined here. The widely ignored programmatic second part of Cardinal Suenens' *Love and Control* suggests how to begin. Everyone mentions this book — in passing. The bold proposal to set out to realize the Christian ideal of chastity has not been taken seriously, because we do not genuinely *believe* it to be possible.

Our failure is a real failure of faith. Not only of faith in the teaching of the Church which points out what divine law forbids, but even more failure of faith in the teaching of Christ who promised sufficient grace and who told us that all things are possible with Him and through His Spirit. We do not genuinely believe, we never really have genuinely believed, that perfect chastity can be achieved by all.

But by the grace of God perfect virtue is possible, and that grace is given to all. Because we have not believed we have failed to see that what now must change is the complacently accepted sinfulness of so many of us. Instead, we are ready to suppose that the law of God might be reformed according to the requirements of "Christian experience."

Perfect Christian chastity is not sour prudishness, nor is it repression and frustration. For the unmarried, it is the avoidance of meaningless eroticism for the sake of the better use of energy, the higher aiming of desire. For the married, it is the wise employment and deep enjoyment of sex for the sake of its psychological benefits to love and its physiological effect in the wonder of the beginning of new life. Apart from its service of love and life, sex even in marriage must be limited by modesty and complete continence, in order that self-centered eroticism may not prevail over the genuine and important values of sexual love. Thus not only overt acts but also phantasy and attitudes must be measured according to a high standard of purity. Chastity is much less important than charity, and only a genuine charity which loves life and love for the love of God can make chastity easy and joyous. And that is how chastity, including complete continence in thought and deed whenever that is necessary, always should be for the Christian — easy and joyous.

Picture the new Church which will emerge with the coming of a new age of Christian chastity. Adolescents will be free to engage in genuine friendships, to unfold in mutual help and appreciation, for they will not be engaging in mutual sexual exploitation and contending with one another for "social" advantage. Young people will be able to devote themselves to their studies and to professional preparation without wasting hours in obsessive day-dreaming or in struggles against temptation. The adult, before assuming the responsibilities of his permanent vocation, while in the full force of his powers, will exercise his courage in some noble work or generous deed, and he will be able and willing to do this because he will not be besieged by erotic tension.

The mature Christian who marries will not be tempted to use sex to test his partner's love or to support his own ego. He will not be inclined to indulge in sex selfishly for he will seldom or never suffer the pain of frustration. Instead, the Christian couple will embrace with joy in the Lord, for their embrace will be a generous expression of love, a most perfect imitation of the love of Christ and the Church, and a willing cooperation with God in the creation of life.

Such married Christians also will be able to devote themselves to the works of justice and charity so needed in today's world, for their social and spiritual lives will not be distorted by anxiety and hostility arising from interminable struggles against un-disciplined erotic desire or by guilt arising from its lustful satisfaction. And for those who need not choose between marry-ing and burning, the possibility of a special vocation to the religious life or the clerical state will not seem so remote.

For many of us adults, life probably must remain something of a struggle between frustration and temptation. We are too old, our reflexes were conditioned and our personalities were formed long ago. Improvements in the technique of rhythm will help us, but rhythm will remain a crutch for our weakness and a cross for our married love, since no mere technique can solve what is really less a problem than a defect in psycho-moral development. But our children need not have the same difficulties.

For them, a highly perfected technique of rhythm could be much more than an effective method of avoiding pregnancy. If it were only that, their continence alone could be sufficient. But rhythm will be an instrument both of their completely self-controlled fulfillment of their procreative vocation and of their completely generous contribution to an ever-increasing communion in one flesh.

It may be hard to believe that a new era of Christian chastity is about to dawn. All the signs seem to indicate just the opposite, for never has the abuse of sexuality been so great in the world and never has defeatism approached so near to despair within the Church.

But just as in doctrine, so in moral life the teachings of Christ are realized only little by little over long ages. Think how long it has taken and with what struggles and difficulties — from some of which we still suffer — to begin to realize the Christian ideal of the dignity of the person, with its implications of individual freedom and rights. Yet today even those who belie their words with their deeds must affirm with the Christian community that each person must be free to dispose of himself according to his own conscience.

Christianity entered the world not to set it at rest but to set it aflame. Now all about us are non-Christians who preach revolution, and many of them, including the Marxists and agnostic proponents of secular liberalism, call for transformations which are but distorted fragments of the much more extensive and comprehensive revolution begun by Christ.

Now, in our day, one more aspect of Christ's revolution — the replacement of the old mankind by a new and transformed mankind and the restoration through Christ Himself of all things to the Father — is about to be realized. Soon — may it be very soon! — there shall be the dawn of a new era of Christian chastity.

Appendix

CONCEPTION-PREVENTING DRUGS

THERE is still some uncertainty concerning the precise effects of these products, and so we cannot be certain what all the effects of their contraceptive use will be nor what all of their other uses could be. The situation is further confused by speculation concerning imaginary drugs, possible drugs, and experimental drugs which are not yet available.[1] Also, there are disagreements among the experts concerning facts which are relevant from an ethical point of view.

In this situation, it seems to me best to avoid an overly extended treatment.[2] Consequently, I shall not deal with actual products but rather with a hypothetical family of drugs. Some of these approximate existing products; others are strictly imaginary. In every case it should be assumed that the drug has no property or effect other than those we attribute to it, and that its effect is temporary and easily reversible unless that is impossible in the nature of the case.

Let the first of our hypothetical drugs be XA. XA has the sole effect of preventing the fertilization of the ovum by the sperm. It may be used either by a man or by a woman, or by both — this point is immaterial. Also, XA may produce its effect either (1) by inhibiting the reproductive glands from

215

forming and releasing their cells, or (2) by killing or rendering nonfunctional such cells as or after they are produced, or (3) by setting up some other obstacle prior to fertilization to the normal functioning of the internal reproductive process.

Which of these modes of efficiency belongs to XA is immaterial, for on our general assumption that the effect of the drug is temporary and reversible, the slight mutilation caused in (2) and the physiological interference in normal processes caused in (3) are of no great significance in themselves.

Of course, if the interference or mutilation is so great as to impede significantly the functioning of the person as a whole or if the effect is lasting and not readily reversible, then we should have to consider whether anyone would have a justification for accepting such damage to his own life and health.

If XA is used by someone who wishes to engage in sexual intercourse and who wishes to ensure by means of XA that conception will not follow, then the use of XA is contraceptive, and this act is intrinsically immoral. In choosing this means of avoiding conception one precisely is choosing conception-prevention — it becomes an object of direct will. The fact that XA is not so obviously an artificial means of preventing conception as diaphragm and jelly is irrelevant, for the physiological naturalness or artificiality of the means of contraception has no bearing upon the immorality of the contraceptive act.

Let us suppose that a woman who does not wish to engage in sexual intercourse with anyone does wish to defend herself against violation by a rapist. Is this woman justified in using XA? Let us assume first that she has no better defense. The use of XA, after all, will not prevent an extensive violation of her person. Suitable resistance to this violence still should be offered. In no case may a woman use XA as a defense against "violence" while consenting and cooperating.

On these assumptions, it seems that the potential victim of rape could be justified in using XA. Self-defense alone must be the object of direct intent. If this is so, the act which prevents conception need not be contraceptive, since it will be the woman's best means of preventing the rapist's abusive violation of her right to choose her own partner in procreation.

The very unfruitfulness of the reproductive process as a natural reality may be directly intended insofar as this unfruitfulness is identically her self-defense. The same unfruitfulness should not be intended precisely insofar as it is a nonrealization of the procreative good. Notice that there is a real sense in which self-defense is not accomplished *through* the nonrealization of the procreative good. The two are *identical* in natural entity. In these extraordinary circumstances, conception-preventing behavior becomes genuinely ambiguous — the self-defensive meaning for it really is possible.

The fact that the very same act is both conception-preventing and self-defensive is by no means peculiar to the use of XA. The same thing is true if effective physical resistance to rape causes ejaculation outside the vagina, or if a diaphragm is worn, or if the semen is washed out after a violation has occurred.

In all these cases, the same physical act has two aspects, and it may be directly willed in one but not in the other. If this point is denied, the logical implication cannot be that the contraceptive use of XA might be moral. It rather is that all conception-preventing acts, even those undertaken in defense against violence, should be excluded as immoral.[8]

If XA can be used as a defense against violence, could a married woman who is regularly engaging in intercourse with her husband make such use of it? If the use is chosen as a sincere self-defense against the violence of a third party, at least a temporary use of XA is admissible by the principles of indirect voluntariness. The fact that the marital relations also are rendered infertile need not be directly willed, since the cause of this infertility is chosen to achieve a quite different and legitimate objective.

The fact that XA has some legitimate uses although its sole effect is conception-prevention does not mean that its use as a contraceptive is not intrinsically immoral. In the extraordinary cases, conception-prevention can be indirectly willed; in ordinary cases, the choice to use XA cannot be indirectly willed conception-prevention.

The reason, as we have explained at length above, is that when one has chosen to have intercourse, his conception-preventing behavior is not susceptible of an innocent meaning. Of course, those who would use XA normally would not *intend* conception-prevention as an end. The trouble is that they could not help *choosing* it as a means.

Someone may object, of course, that self-defense against rape and sterilization as a legal punishment cannot be interpreted, even according to the principles of indirect voluntariness, as anything other than directly willed conception-prevention. But we have considered these problems previously.

The only point which needs repetition here is that if, indeed, these extraordinary cases cannot be interpreted as we have proposed, then these conception-preventing acts too must be considered intrinsically immoral. Although this opinion seems to us improbable, it at least can be defended, while the idea that directly willed conception-prevention could be licit is indefensible.

Let us now suppose another drug, XB. Its sole effect is "safe" and early abortion — e.g., by preventing the implantation of the fertilized ovum. The use of this drug by anyone under any circumstances is intrinsically and very seriously immoral, for it is the killing of the innocent. The immoral act normally would be the direct willing of abortion chosen as a means to some intended good. The fact that regret might be experienced even while XB is used does not indicate that murder is not done. We often regret the evil we directly will in choosing means although we do not simultaneously regret the evil we do in intending improper ends.

The use of XB as a "contraceptive" is much more seriously immoral than is the use of XA. Needless to say, the use of XB is equally murder whether any abortion happens to occur or not, since one who uses XB is fully willing to commit murder.

The use of XB as self-defense is excluded because one is not free to interpret such killing of the innocent as self-defensive behavior. When conception has occurred, the time when defense was possible has passed.

The use of XB as a just punishment is impossible, because there can be no justice in such killing of the innocent. The seriousness of the immorality of using XB should lead every virtuous person to try to prevent its use. The principles of immoral cooperation must be applied stringently where XB is concerned, because its use always is murder.

Let us consider next a case in which someone has a product whose precise character is uncertain. It may be XA, it may be XB. Let us call it XAB, not because it combines the pharmacological characteristics of both, but because uncertainty makes its nature ambiguous for the moral agent.

The use of XAB as a contraceptive is much more seriously wrong than the use of XA. Even if the person who uses XAB for ordinary contraceptive purposes thinks that the probability of its being XB is slight, the choice to use it evidences a willingness to use XB — i.e., to commit murder.

What about the use of XAB in those extraordinary circumstances — defense against rape — where the use of XA is allowable? There would have to be no suitable alternative. Further, there must be a strong probability in the agent's mind that XAB really is XA, not XB. If these conditions were fulfilled, XAB might be used without anything wrong being directly willed, since there would be reasonable probability against its having a death-dealing effect and self-defense alone could be chosen by the agent.[4]

This point reveals an important truth. One who initially is willing to act immorally subsequently has much less leeway in judging the moral significance of objective probabilities than does one who is trying to do what is right to the best of his ability. If one is willing to do evil, being unsure precisely what evil he does, he is willing to do the worst of the evils which he thinks he might be doing.

Let us suppose another drug, XC. XC has no good effects whatsoever. On the other hand, it is suspected that XC could cause some damage to a child if it were used by his mother during gestation or lactation, and it is not altogether certain that it will not eventually cause some ill effects to the user. Obviously, no one ever would choose to use XC.

However, let us now suppose that the only available XA also has the C factor; let us call it XAC. The moral judgment of the contraceptive use of XAC should parallel that of XAB. However, if the probabilities represented by B and C are equally great the moral judgment of XAC will be less severe. The reason judgment on XAC need not be so severe as that on XAB is that the possible effects of XAC are not so bad as the possible effects of XAB.

Nevertheless, someone who is using XAC as a contraceptive assumes responsibility for possible ill effects. The fact that the choice to use XA is morally wrong means that a willingness to use XAC is much more seriously wrong, because even if the dangers designated by "C" are slight, one is not exempted from responsibility for them. When one does what is wrong, even bad effects only indirectly willed add to the moral evil because there is no justification for permitting them.

Let us imagine another drug, XD. XD is useful in treating pathological conditions common to persons who are celibate and to those who have intercourse. XD is so effective that it is the medically indicated and preferred treatment for patients who are not at all concerned with fertility or infertility. However, it happens also to have the effect of causing temporary sterility, somewhat like XA.

The use of XD certainly is allowable by the principle of double effect. The sterility which it induces may be indirectly willed *provided the usual conditions are fulfilled*.

Thus, if a different drug, XD-A is available, and if XD-A is exactly the same as XD except that it does not induce sterility, then XD-A must be preferred to XD for those who have intercourse unless there are really proportionate reasons to the con-

trary. A significant difference in side effects or even in price
might distinguish XD from XD-A sufficiently to render the use
of XD licit, always assuming that a true therapeutic effect really
is desired and that the temporary infertility is only indirectly
willed.

We might propose the following criterion. If a drug would
be used in a certain case by a single person who is abstinent,
a married person who has the proper intentions may use it in
a like case even though it has a contraceptive side effect.

These general principles apply whether XD is used to treat
physical or psychological diseases and whether the pathology
itself is related to the reproductive function or not. Thus, if
XD is the preferred treatment for hysteria when fertility is no
issue, it also may be used by a married woman who has regular
relations with her husband. (Such an XD is strictly imaginary.)
If XD is the preferred treatment for premenstrual tension or
menopause problems in the case of a single woman, the same
judgment follows.

However, it is quite another matter if XA is used for its good
psychological effect.[5] These effects could follow only because
XA prevents conception. Thus, while the intended end can be
unexceptionable, the chosen means certainly is immoral.

We might propose the following criterion. If the drug has
its good psychological effects whether its user knows that it
induces sterility or not, then it is used like XD. If the drug
has its good effects only if the user knows that it induces sterility, then it is used like XA.

Similar judgments must be made whenever XD is used without other good reasons in preference to XD-A. The sole point
of such a preference then would be that XD induces sterility
while XD-A does not. Hence it is false to think, as many have
imagined, that any therapeutic effect is sufficient to justify use
of a conception-preventing drug.

The principle of double effect has rules of application. Only
a sincere effort to apply the principle by these rules can exempt
one from moral responsibility for side effects. Hence if there

is no real need for treatment or if the indicated treatment need not induce sterility, to induce sterility with a therapeutic effect as an "excuse" simply is to practice covert contraception.

Let us imagine another drug, XE, which supports lactation more effectively than any alternative drug, but which also induces sterility, much like XA. (XE, it should be noted, is strictly imaginary.) If a woman wishes to nurse her baby and if she has difficulty in doing so, then she certainly would be justified in using XE and permitting temporary infertility. But if there exists an alternative, XE-A, which otherwise is preferable to XE and which does not induce sterility, then the nursing mother has no justification for using XE.

This conclusion will be challenged by those who think that the use of a drug like XA to reduce or suppress abnormal fertility might be justified. "Abnormal fertility" can refer to ovulation during the postpartum period which naturally is the time of lactation and which allegedly is normally infertile, or it can refer to ovulation during other periods of life, such as childhood and old age. It also might refer to unusually short cycles unaccompanied by any pathology, or to multiple ovulations within the same cycle. It even might refer to an unusually high sperm count in the male.[6]

Even though fertility in all these cases may be excessive in comparison with what is statistically normal, the use of XA to suppress it presupposes a direct willingness to prevent conception. The generosity of nature in these cases might be unwelcome, but by hypothesis it is not of itself a condition which deserves treatment as pathological, and so the principles of indirect voluntariness cannot apply, since no valuable objective will be attained other than that achieved through the prevention of conception.

But might one not say in such cases that the use of XA is chosen simply to correct the abnormal condition? One indeed might say so, and one even could be speaking sincerely. The difficulty is that the only abnormality in the conditions described — we have assumed no accompanying pathology — is an excessive capacity for achieving a good. Moral judgments should not be made simply by the consideration of what is natural or unnatural from the physiological point of view and of what is normal or abnormal statistically. The facts must be considered, but always in their bearing upon essential human goods.

An abnormality which interferes with the attainment of these goods may be dealt with by any means which does not include a directly willed violation of them. But an abnormality which is in no way at odds with these goods cannot be treated as if it were, even though an individual may wish he were not gifted in this peculiar fashion.

The sole possible interpretation of the conception-preventing behavior involved in the correction of abnormal fertility unaccompanied by pathology, then, is the suppression — perhaps only partial or temporary — of fertility. And since this suppression would be accomplished by a positive act which achieves nothing except by preventing conception, to choose to suppress such abnormal fertility is directly to will conception-prevention. Hence such a choice, objectively considered, always is contraception.

Let us imagine another drug, XF, whose sole effect is to establish a perfectly regular twenty-nine-day cycle with ovulation occurring on the fifteenth day.[7] (XF does not yet exist.) Note that "regular" here does not denote the merely apparent regularity that might be induced by the use of a drug like XA, which could cause menstrual-like periods when its use is temporarily suspended. Rather, "regular" means the dependable occurrence of the entire physiological sequence usually present in the cycle of a healthy and normal young-adult woman.

Let us assume that in a certain case the practice of periodic continence is justified. Given this assumption, would the use of XF to regularize the cycle in order to make the practice of periodic continence easier and more certain be justified?

We must notice that what is being eliminated by XF is unpredictability, and that such unpredictability in fact is not identical with fertility nor is it required for the procreative good or for any other basic human good. On the other hand, there can be a good reason for desiring the effect of XF.

But if the means are moral and the end is moral, nothing immoral is directly willed. Under these conditions, then, there is no doubt that XF could be used without anything immoral being done. Obviously, its use can be abused, since rhythm can be practiced with the same malice as contraception.

If contraception is thought to be wrong simply because it interferes with normal functioning, then the use of XF also will be condemned. But there is nothing inherently objectionable about such interference, provided it is not contrary to some human good. XF itself does not prevent conception. It induces dependability, not sterility. Hence its use can be good.

But will not XF sometimes have the effect of lessening fertility? For example, an irregularly ovulating woman — or, for that matter, any woman — who averaged more than one ovulation each twenty-nine days would ovulate less frequently when treated with XF. Hence her fertility would be lessened and XF would tend to prevent conception. Would its use be justifiable in such cases?

The question must be answered according to the principle of double effect. If the reduction of fertility is merely an unavoidable side effect of the dependability induced, then it may be willed indirectly if the usual conditions are fulfilled. If XF is used simply to reduce the number of occasions of potential fertility, however, the choice to use it is intrinsically wrong, because it is a form of partial contraception. The latter could occur in the case of a woman who already had very dependable cycles averaging less than twenty-nine days' duration, since her use of XF would not be open to the interpretation that it was a choice of dependability.

Let us imagine another drug, XG. XG induces dependability in previously irregular cycles, very much as XF does. However, to obtain its good effect, XG must be taken for a certain period — e.g., a year — during which fertility is totally excluded. If XG but not XF were available, could the use of XG be justified?

This problem also must be solved by using the principles of indirect voluntariness. If XG really does cause dependability, and if there are good reasons for wanting to predict the time of ovulation — which might be simply good reasons for practicing rhythm — then the use of XG could be justified *under the usual conditions.*[8]

The reason is that the temporary sterility XG causes could be willed only indirectly. Even by the principle of double effect this conclusion can be reached, since a year's sterility hardly would of itself cause the subsequent regular fertility; some unknown direct result of the use of the drug undoubtedly would lead to both effects.

Clearly the requirements of indirect voluntariness cannot be met in the use of XG if "XG" really is only another name for XA. In other words, if the true effect of the drug is that it suspends ovulation without subsequently improving regularity, then its use is strictly contraceptive, since no good purpose other than those to be gained by conception-prevention will remain for using it.

Moreover, the principles of proportionality must be met. A year's sterility hardly should be exchanged for a single month's predictability. Nor should a year's sterility be exchanged for a very small possibility of any real improvement in dependability. In assessing proportionality, we always must calculate as if procreation itself were an important human good, for that is precisely what it is, and it remains so whether we wish to avoid pregnancy or not.

Since XF and XG seem not to exist as yet, let us suppose one more drug, XH, which perhaps already exists. XH certainly does not induce abortion. Used with care it probably has no serious side effects. XH has this peculiar effect, that taken for some days any time after the fourteenth day of the cycle it will induce menstruation and the beginning of a new and possibly fertile cycle.

However, after the second day of its use, XH inhibits ovulation if it has not occurred already. Thus, for example, its use beginning on the fourteenth day of any cycle in which ovulation would occur later than the sixteenth day if XH were not taken will cause that particular cycle to be anovulatory as well as making it somewhat shorter than it would have been otherwise.

The question we must solve about XH is the following one. Let us suppose a wife with cycles which are undependable and which sometimes are very long. The couple also has solid indications for using rhythm. Under what conditions would this woman be justified in using XH to eliminate long cycles in order to introduce some predictability into her rhythm of fertility and sterility?

On the one hand, to terminate the long cycle seems to be to suppress fertility, since the use of XH renders impossible an ovulation which otherwise would have occurred eventually, and probably sooner without the use of XH than with it. On the other hand, extreme unpredictability in cycles can render the practice of rhythm almost impossible, and if its practice really is indicated, predictability in itself seems to be a good which may be sought. The use of XH, although it may lessen fertility, does have a real effect which is capable of being sought — i.e., it introduces some predictability.

The dependability caused by XH, moreover, is not only the certainty that ovulation will not occur beginning with the third day of its use. There also is the certainty that the long cycle will come to an end and that a new one, which by hypothesis can be normal and will be permitted this possibility, will be able to begin. Even regular use of XH leaves something real to predict — namely, that a true cycle with the possibility of ovulation will begin by a certain time. The use of XH, of course, does not exclude the need for abstinence if a couple wish to avoid pregnancy. Hence the practice of rhythm will remain possible.

It seems to follow that the use of XH can be justified. The characteristics it has which make it susceptible of an objectively different meaning than simple XA are its ability to limit a particular, interminable, irregular cycle and to initiate a perhaps more normal new one.[9] Of course, the use of XH must be for the sake of predictability, not for the accompanying suppression of ovulation as such. Moreover, there must be some reasonable proportionality, and no better alternative, because fertility really is being reduced when XH is used.

What would be the precise norms for the use of XH?

In the first place, it should not be used for more days than is required to assure the termination of the long cycle and the initiation of a new one which can be normal. If XH can achieve these effects in five days, it may not be used for eight or ten days.

The fact that XH might be a progestational steroid and that the progesterone-dominant part of the cycle normally lasts for a certain number of days does not of itself show that XH may be used, and so its use may not extend the time required to achieve its justifying effect. If the period of use of XH is extended beyond the minimum needed to achieve dependability, the additional "days of grace" amount simply to a period of contraception.

In the second place, since the only justification for using XH is that one is trying to achieve reasonable predictability where none exists, there can be no justification for using it if accessible methods to gain the desired information are not used.

In other words, one should not simply determine that beginning on a certain day of every cycle, XH will be used for the time required to assure its effect. One first should try to determine the time of ovulation and the period of infertility by less drastic means.

If the use of the basal-temperature method is practicable, for instance, a woman would have an obligation to use it, and to begin taking XH only if there is no clear sign that ovulation has occurred. If there is a clear sign that it has occurred, the evidence is that the particular period will not be unpredictably long. In such a case, the use of XH could not be justified.

This may seem strange, for if ovulation has occurred in the cycle, the use of XH will not be suppressing anything. However, its indiscriminate use in every cycle would show that one simply wished to cause an absolutely safe period — the time after the second day of XH use — rather than to induce reasonable dependability into the cycle.

In the third place, the start of the use of XH before the time in the cycle when ovulation normally should have been expected cannot be justified. The only justification for using XH is that one wants reasonable dependability. If ovulation is not allowed its natural time to occur, the sense of one's behavior will become contraception. But how long is it necessary to wait?

A determination must be made of what a normal cycle should be. In practice, probably, the only reasonable method for making this determination would be to apply general statistical norms. If this method were followed, *some allowance for normal variation from the average should be allowed.* For the sake of our example, let us assume that experts will agree that ovulation reasonably should be expected to occur by the seventeenth day of even a normally varying cycle.[10]

However, the less solid one's reasons for desiring dependability, the less the justification for using XH and permitting its fertility-reducing side effect. Hence, unless the indications for practicing rhythm are very strong, the day when the use of XH may be begun will be somewhat later than the minimum — for the sake of our example, let us say the nineteenth day.

According to these norms, someone who has good indications for practicing rhythm and whose cycles are irregular and undependably long, lacking any better method of introducing some predictability, might make use of XH to cut off long cycles and to introduce some dependability into the time of fertility and sterility. The following will illustrate this procedure.

1 2 3	4 5 6 7 8 9 10 11	12 13 14 15 16 17 18	19 20 21 22 23 24	25 26	27 28
A		B		C	D

A = the menstrual period at the opening of the cycle.

B = a period of watchful waiting. Abstinence must be maintained throughout if pregnancy-avoidance is strongly indicated. If there is evidence of ovulation which can be detected by reasonable diligence, XH should not be used in this cycle, because then there already is a dependable limit. But let us assume that there happens to be no such evidence this month.

C = the period during which XH is used. We assume it has been determined that ovulation reasonably should be expected before day 19. We also assume that C is as short as it can be consistent with the purpose of using XH — i.e., the cutting off of the irregularly long cycle and the initiation of a new and possibly normal one. Fertility is suppressed beginning on day 21; this cannot be chosen for its own sake nor permitted to continue longer than necessary. However, a couple might choose to have intercourse beginning on this certainly sterile day without willing anything wrong.

D = the end of this cycle with a menstrual flow induced by the previous withdrawal of XH. This flow also marks the beginning of a new cycle which may be normally fertile. Nothing will be done to prevent it from being so.

If existing drugs have the characteristics we have ascribed to our hypothetical XH, then it is clear that the practice of rhythm with great security already is possible for everyone. The practice of rhythm has been impossible for some because they have had no reliable indication of the time of ovulation and they have experienced great irregularity in the length of cycles. XH would remedy these difficulties.

However, XH by no means is the ideal solution represented by XF. Those who want real security will have to abstain as long as three weeks at a time, if our estimates and reasoning are correct, and then there will be only a few days of certain infertility. Such a regimen, while not impossible, is not easy. Still it can be easier than what has been necessary in some difficult cases.

Our considerations in this Appendix, although they have concerned only hypothetical drugs and hypothetical uses, not only should indicate the implications of our principles, but our arguments also should show how less hypothetical problems can be handled. I say "less hypothetical," because even the most solidly based and factually oriented ethical consideration of a complex problem remains a judgment on what is at stake if the presupposed information is both *correct* and *complete.* And in a field like this one, the facts surely will not remain complete for long.

No one should conclude from these discussions that contraception directly willed ever could be right. The distinction between behavior and action has to be carefully maintained. Not every new drug which tends to prevent conception and yet which also has legitimate uses need lead to another general debate about the ethics of contraception. It should be settled once and for all that the good uses of drugs do not include contraception, even though in extraordinary cases, such as self-defense, they may include the prevention of conception. Such drugs also clearly have applications for other good purposes, including perhaps the support of rhythm as we have suggested, with only an incidental conception-preventing effect.

Some are sure to object that the distinctions in this Appendix are too fine for the average man and even for some moralists. No doubt they are *now,* but we can learn. The ethics of the use of firearms also includes a great many extremely subtle distinctions, but this fact would not have been a good argument, even when it was first invented, for saying that gunpowder might be used licitly to kill the innocent.

Subtlety in ethical reasoning and moral judgment simply must be brought up to the higher levels required by man's more complex existence as human nature evolves.

NOTES TO APPENDIX

1. Norman Applezweig, *Steroid Drugs* (New York, Toronto, London: McGraw-Hill Book Co., 1962), though recent, does not discuss all the drugs now being considered. For example, Philips Roxane Pharmaceutical House is testing a drug, Duphaston, which is supposed to adjust the time of ovulation; Clomiphene, and other antiestrogen drugs, which are being suggested as a replacement for surgical management of Stein-Leventhal or polycystic ovary patients, also may make women ovulate at the proper time. Such efforts are likely eventually to lead to something like XF, discussed below, but they have not yet done so.

2. Ford and Kelly, *Contemporary Moral Theology*, Vol. 2, *Marriage Questions* (Westminster, Md.: The Newman Press, 1963), 338–377, provide an excellent introduction; much of our discussion will be based on it, and on the sources they cite.

3. See ch. VI, note 12, above.

4. *S.t.*, 1–2, q. 20, a. 5; q. 73, a. 8.

5. Janssens, "Morale conjugale . . . ," *Ephemerides theologicae lovanienses*, 39 (Oct.–Dec., 1963), 791–792 mentions such use favorably: Dupré, "Toward a Re-examination . . . ," *Cross Currents*, 14 (Winter, 1964), 74–75, quotes P. Anciaux as considering the use of such drugs acceptable as part of psychotherapy; Ford and Kelly, *op. cit.*, 344–345, correctly judge the use in question contraceptive, and cite Joseph Fuchs, S.J., for the same position.

6. Ford and Kelly, *op. cit.*, 360–374, discuss this question at length without definitely concluding; Janssens, *op. cit.*, 823–825, weaves into his now more general conclusion his earlier stand for this use; Van der Marck, "Vruchtbaarheidsregeling . . . ," *Tijdschrift voor theologie*, 3e, #4 (Jaargang, 1963), 393, mentions the notion that ovulation-suppression during the lactation period is justified as if this idea were an established position.

7. Ford and Kelly, *op. cit.*, 350–360, discuss this problem, and cite the literature. Discussions of regulation have been marked, it seems to me, by the confusion of several different problems, and by frequent failure to distinguish between direct and the indirect voluntariness. Several moralists also have invoked the premise, *Everyone has a right to be normal.* This proposition seems to me simply false. Everyone has a right to what promotes normality in line with essential human goods, but no one has a right to normality which involves acting against them. If it were found that genius causes unhappiness and moral difficulty, would one have a right to be normal by suppressing his excess intelligence, if that were possible?

8. It is my impression from reports and conversations that a great deal of contraception is at present being condoned, because progestational steroids are being used without sufficient consideration of the *conditions of application* of the principles of indirect voluntariness.

9. It might be argued that very long and very irregular cycles probably indicate some pathology; certainly, very long cycles can on occasion produce excessively heavy menses if an unopposed estrogen effect is allowed to build up an extra-thick endometrial lining. In cases where such arguments can be developed, the use of XH surely would be justifiable by the principle of double effect.

10. No significance whatsoever should be attached to our use for illustration of the seventeenth day. The question of the day by which a woman normally should ovulate is strictly for physiologists and statisticians to answer.

INDEX

Abortion, by drugs, 218 f

Abnormal fertility, defined, 222

Absolute principles, in situationist theories, 55 f

Absolute vs. relative values, 69, 85, 114 f; see also Values

Abstinence, as alternative to contraception, 23, 31 f; and errors in judgment concerning contraception, 185; and indirect voluntariness, 153 f

Abstract and concrete, morality in, 129 ff

"Abstractionism," 120 f

Act, moral, as distinct from behavior, defined, 145

Adam, August, on charity and chastity, 207; on gravity of sexual sin, 105

Adler, Mortimer J., and Farrell, Walter, O.P., on end of man, 75

Affirmative precepts, in conventional natural-law theory, 49; obligation intensifies as realization approaches, 88

Affirmative principle, contraception violates an, 99; modes of obligation, 82 ff

Allers, Rudolf, on explanation of generality of sexual sin, 207; on psychology of sexual sin, 206; on selfishness as developmental incident, 104

Analysis, as rational mode of practical judgment, 191 f

Anovulants, see Drugs, Conception-preventing

Anthropology, and practical principles, 64

Anticoagulant, in example similar to contraceptive, 88 ff

Applezweig, Norman, on steriod drugs, 178, 230

Argument(s) against contraception, compared, 99 ff; formulated, 90 f; indirect, 24 ff; methodological reason for considering inadequate, 19 f; outline of, 76; popular, 32

Aristotle, on ejaculation and female "semination," 43; on perfect demonstration, 106; on requirements for demonstration, 18; on vicious character, 207

Arnold, Magda B., and Gasson, John A., S.J., on desire for pleasure as such, 104

Art, and nature in conception-preventing drugs, 174 f

Artificiality, and rhythm, 166 f

Asceticism, studies on, 208

Augustine, St., on sin, 126

Behavior, as distinct from moral act, 145; and moral action, have not the same positive factors, 159

Bergler, Edmund, psychological function of abnormal sexuality, 44

Bidney, David, on evolution of culture, 127

"Biologism," 108, 114 f; response to dualist critique of, 40

Canon Law, on consummation of marriage, 45

Cassirer, Ernest, on nature of man, 127

Casuistry, and conventional natural-law theory, 48 f; and probabilism, 72 f

Catholic Church, and chastity, 209 ff; and contraception, 209 f; and morality of contraception, 189 ff

Catholic practice, and fertility, 17

Catholics, and "burden" of moral knowledge, 156; and error concerning morality of contraception, 189 ff; and situationist theory, 59 f

44; on sexual sins as against procreative good, 106; on sin, 126 f; as
source of ethical theory, 60; theory
of moral law, studies on, 74 f; on
totality, 169; on vicious character,
207; on weakness, 206
Thomas de Vio Cajetan, on female
masturbation, 43; on immorality of
all methods of contraception, 177 f
Thomas, John L., S.J., on Protestant
attitudes to contraception, 205; on
sociological factors in contraception,
17–18
Time, as barrier in rhythm, 164 f;
as positive, 157 ff
Totality, principle of, applies to generative function, 28; principle of, defined, 140 f; principle of, and general theory of indirect voluntariness,
147 ff; why principle is limited in
application to generative power,
100 f
Transplantation, principle of, and
theory of indirect voluntariness,
148 f; and Van der Marck's views,
144 ff
Truth, as determining obligations of
scholars, 88; as example of substantive, immaterial value, 82 f
Twofold effect, see Double effect

Usury, and change of human nature,
124

Values, absolute vs. relative, 69; 114 f,
127; basic, constitute moral norms,
107 ff; basic, not always relative,
85; basic, and principles of practical
reason, 63 f; basic, require consideration, 84; basic, require effective concern, 84; basic, require support if
in peril, 84 f; basic, violated by contrary action, 85 f; controlling, in
situationism, 55 f; derived, admit of
exception, 130; finite and infinite
good in natural end of man, 71 f;
essential human, as principles of
moral development, 200; material,
irreducibility of, 111; material, in
situationism, 53 f, 115, 133; moral,
according to Dondeyne, 73; and
person as recipient of goods, 78; re-

flexive, defined, 126; reflexive, most
affected by evolution of human
nature, 124 f; reflexive, and situationism, 108 ff; secondary, and conscience, 182; substantive, including
material, as moral ideals, 82 f; substantive, and moral norms, 109 f;
substantive and reflexive, contrasted,
67 f; substantive and reflexive, material and spiritual, related, 70; substantive and reflexive, in moral life,
179 f; substantive and reflexive, in
situationism, 121 f
Vann, Gerald, O.P., on Aquinas' ethical theory, 74
Vermeersch, Arthurus, S.J., on sexual
pleasure, 43
Vogt, William, on population, 205
Voluntarism, absent from Thomistic
theory, 61; and conventional natural-
law theory, 47 f; of conventional
natural-law theory, criticized, 51 f; of
situationism, 59
Voluntariness, direct, defined, 135; direct, does not delimit moral significance, 145 f; direct, of ordinary
conception-prevention, 149 ff; direct,
in sequence of human acts, 152 ff;
direct and indirect, 135 ff; direct and
indirect, studies on, 168 f; indirect,
approaches to a general theory,
146 ff; indirect, and argument against
contraception, 151 f; indirect, and
conception-preventing drugs, 173; indirect, conditions of application, 231;
indirect, defined, 135 f; indirect and
direct, 135 ff; indirect does not render evil good, 138 f; indirect, and
erroneous judgment of concrete
morality of contraception, 187; indirect, error about in practice, 183 ff;
indirect, inapplicable to ordinary
conception-prevention, 149 ff; indirect, no general theory of, 143; indirect, possible new mode of, 143;
indirect, in principle of common
good, 141; indirect, in principle of
totality, 141; indirect, and rhythm,
162 f; indirect, and sexual abstinence, 153 f; indirect, use of in
defense against rape, 217; indirect,
and Van der Marck's views, 143 ff